MW01634813

A Time to Tell

A Time to Tell

THE PUBLIC LIFE OF A
PRIVATE MAN

Reuben Cohen

KEY PORTER BOOKS

Canadian Cataloguing in Publication Data

Cohen, Reuben, 1921-

A time to tell : the public life of a private man

ISBN 0-55013-957-6

1. Cohen, Reuben, 1921-   . 2. Central Guaranty Trust Corporation – Biography.

3. Capitalists and financiers – Canada – Biography. I. Title.

HG4358.C63 1998   332.2′6′092   C97-932725-3

The publisher gratefully acknowledges the support of the Canada Council for the Arts and the Ontario Arts Council for its publishing program.

Key Porter Books Limited
70 The Esplanade
Toronto, Ontario
Canada M5E 1R2

www.keyporter.com

Design: Peter Maher
Electronic formatting: Heidi Palfrey

Printed and bound in Canada

98 99 00 01 5 4 3 2

To the memory of Louise,
who, for 37 years, lit up my world.

Contents

Acknowledgements

In the fall of 1995, my secretary of 35 years, who had built her new home on the banks of the Miramichi, wished to retire there. She advised me that she would stay to type out some of my life stories if I could be persuaded to write them. As a result I set myself a schedule of two hours a day, four days a week, and finished off in about four and a half months.

My handwriting scrawl was always almost virtually illegible, even to myself, and often when I could not decipher it I would call upon my secretary who, over the years, had miraculously become pretty adept at transcribing my scribbling.

Add to this the fact that as a frugal depression kid I write about three lines in each single line of foolscap; my writing is therefore so small that in many instances she had to use a magnifying glass to aid in the transcription. The whole exercise contributed to much discomfort and eye strain, and I am indebted to Norma Jones for her incalculable help in this regard, and promise a new pair of bifocals.

In the spring of 1996 I had in hand the finished product of 300 or so typed legal-size pages with no real purpose in mind except perhaps to have a few copies made to share with some friends. Around that time I was invited to a reception in Fredericton for the Prince of Wales. Standing in line next to me was Dalton Camp, whom I knew only by reputation. We exchanged pleasantries; he told me about his recent heart transplant, and I mentioned just finishing writing down some of the anecdotes and passages in my life. I said that I had a chapter on New Brunswick politics, and knowing of his expertise in this regard, I asked if he might want to read it and perhaps make suggestions where I might have gone astray. He agreed, and a few weeks later we met for lunch in Fredericton. After I pulled out the manuscript, removed the chapter on politics and handed it to him, he said, "Why don't you let me see the rest of it?" I replied that I didn't think he would find it interesting, particularly the early chapter on growing up in a minority ethnic community. "Let me see it anyway," he said, and I replied that I would do so on the condition that after reading it he would be honest with me and tell me if it should be discarded in the fireplace, or if it merited publication, and if he felt it did have such merit perhaps he could be persuaded to write a foreword. To this suggestion he did not reply. About ten days later he phoned me to say that he had read the manuscript, and it was just like eating peanuts, he couldn't put it down. He said he found the early chapter of the ethnic story particularly fascinating, as he was not aware that this solitude existed in the New Brunswick to which his forebears came as United Empire Loyalists after the American Revolution in 1776. Dalton also said that he would be happy to write a foreword to the book but with the provision that a paragraph referring to Richard Hatfield, for whom he and his family had a great affection, had to be eliminated. I replied that I would leave this decision up to the eventual publisher, to which his response was that the publishers would want it in, because that's what sells books.

The editor assigned by the publisher to provide the editing was Dalton's daughter, Connie Camp, and while we feuded over many aspects of her editing, I am grateful to her for the many long and arduous hours that she spent making numerous suggestions and improvements.

Since the publishers did not remove the Hatfield reference that Dalton Camp found offensive, I regret that this volume is published without his foreword, but I am forever indebted to him for providing me with the incentive and encouragement for its publication.

Preface

I have always been amused by the number of people who open their auto-biography with a preface stating that it was written only at the behest of a great number of people, who persuaded them that their life's story should not be left untold, for the sake of posterity. It must be quite distressing to them, as well as crushing to their egos, to see their hard work relegated, a year or even less after publication, to the bargain bins at the chain book-stores. This is somewhat similar to most political types, who always seem to say that they were convinced to run for public office by the requests of countless of their fellow citizens. It seems that ego, status or career enhance-ment are never a motivation; instead, an unselfish desire to serve their fellow man is always given as the paramount reason.

Fran Liebowitz once wrote: "Your life story would not make a good book, don't even try." On the other hand, there is an old Chinese proverb that says, when an old man dies, the world loses an encyclopedia. Thomas Jefferson wrote: "Every experience deeply felt in life needs to be passed along—whether it be through words or music, chiselled in stone, painted with a brush, or sewn with a needle—it is a way of reaching for immortality." There are some episodes in my life that were created by a combination of time, events and circumstances that, in every likelihood, can never be even remotely duplicated again. Many of my acquaintances have told me over the years that it would be a loss if some of the stories I have related to them from time to time were not put down in writing, so that another generation could read, and hopefully enjoy, anecdotes and interesting events from an era rapidly vanishing with the twentieth century itself. Some of the stories may have more significance for readers in my own local area, but they are generally told in a context that gives them a much wider, if not a universal, interest and appeal. Therefore, even though with much trepidation, I have written these pages with the hope that they may make, somewhere, a faint footnote in history.

CHAPTER 1

Memories of Old Moncton

In his autobiography, written in 1957, Bernard Baruch, the famous American financier and statesman, recounts that while on his mother's side he could trace his ancestry back to a family that came to America in the 1690s, this was not the case on his father's side—for his father rarely spoke of his forebears. When the matter came up he would say, "It was not so important where you came from as where you were going."

I have always envied people who know their ancestry. I remember a financial mover in the Toronto of the Eighties telling me that he chose WASP 14 for his licence plates because he felt the poor WASPs were hard done by lately, but he was not to be intimidated and wanted to boast that he could trace his ancestors back fourteen generations. I can't trace mine much beyond my parents.

My parents met and married in Philadelphia. My father eked out a living by peddling fruit from a cart on the streets. He once recounted that whole watermelon was one of his staple products in season. They sold for about twenty cents apiece, and his advertising slogan, yelled out to passing customers, was "Plug 'em before you buy 'em!" which allowed customers to cut small plugs from the melons to taste so that they could be satisfied the fruit was sweet and ripe.

My mother, Molly, was born in the Austro-Hungarian Empire, in a village that became part of Poland after the First World War. Her father was a cantor, and she often spoke of the mellifluous voice that kept him in demand. My mother and three of her sisters were brought to Philadelphia by an uncle named Harnock, who owned a thriving blouse factory. From my mother's stories I gathered that he sent for the sisters not because of family duty or affection, but because they could provide cheap labour for piece-work in a sweatshop, being paid a pittance that barely kept them afloat.

I don't know how long my parents resided in Philadelphia. Their first son was born there in 1906, and the family lived briefly in New Rochelle, New York. Eventually they moved to Montreal, where two more boys were born, one of whom died in infancy.

Early in the second decade of the century my father was naturalized as a Canadian citizen under the name Cohen, although this was not his family name. He never explained why he discarded his real name, just as he never discussed his reasons for leaving the United States. Cohen and its variations—Kohn and Cohn, for example—usually indicate a descendant of a priestly family going back to the time of Moses. Outsiders assumed our family was of priestly descent, but according to my father we were descended from the tribe of Levites. If I can't trace my forebears beyond one generation, perhaps I should take consolation from my father's claim to ancestry in the tribe ordained to serve in the holy temple in biblical times.

During the First World War my father got into the horse business. He travelled throughout the Maritime provinces selling draft horses, which he brought in by carloads from western Canada. He would set up in small farming communities, go to church on Sunday and leave a twenty-dollar bill in the collection plate to ensure the blessing of the local parish priest. At the end of the war my father felt it would be more convenient, or more opportune, to live in the area where he earned his livelihood, so he moved from Montreal to Moncton with his wife and two sons. It was there that I was born in 1921.

In those years scarcely more than twenty thousand people lived in Moncton, a middle-class railway town with no old families of inherited wealth. The aristocrats were the men who held key positions with the Canadian National Railway or the Eaton's retail and mail-order outlet.

The first Lithuanian immigrants had settled in the small farming village of Hillsborough, but as they prospered they moved to Moncton, about fifteen miles away. And as happened with every immigrant wave throughout North America in that era, one family brought over another until a small community was established.

The Jewish population of some fifteen families was concentrated, or ghettoized, at Lewis and Pearl streets, which was looked on as the Bowery section of Moncton. The people were mostly pedlars, small grocery owners or clothing retailers. Since everyone else in the Jewish community came from the same village in Lithuania, they were all related. My father, coming from Russia, was considered something of an outsider.

I was born in a cold-water flat above a pool room in a commercial block on Main Street. The pool room remained until a little more than a decade ago, when the old wooden building was torn down after a fire and the land became part of the new city hall. Dr. L.N. Bourque, a family doctor and one-time mayor of Moncton, officiated at my birth and continued as my childhood doctor, mainly because his office calls were fifty cents compared with the dollar charged by his competitors.

My mother's older sister Sarah had lost her husband, the love of her life, early in their marriage in Europe and was beyond consolation in lamenting his death. Sarah, who was childless, persuaded my mother to name me Reuben, after the husband she expected to grieve forever. That is how I got stuck with a name I have never particularly enjoyed, despite its biblical import. Oh, how I yearned in my boyhood days to be called Jack or Bill, and later Rock, Brent or some other macho name. Aunt Sarah, meanwhile, went on to marry four more husbands, and died a widow.

My father had opened a livery stable on Robinson Street, just below Main. In those days people rented horses and wagons much as they now rent cars from a rental agency. Although my father still traded in horses, the business became more limited with the end of the war and was soon extinguished by the popularity of Henry Ford and the automobile.

As the horse business died out, my father opened a small grocery store. At first he rented premises, but in 1927 he bought a building at 702 Main Street for $7,500, with the mortgage of $6,000 held by the Central Trust Company, the institution that would play such an important part in my adult life. It was above my father's store that we lived.

Yiddish was the language of the immigrant community, and like English it had different accents, idioms and pronunciations, depending on geographic origin. My parents' Yiddish was distinctly different from that of the Lithuanians, or Litvacks, and each would poke fun at the other's pronunciation. But the Jewish community of Moncton was a fairly cohesive group, forced to stick together because of the overwhelming outside population and abiding fears of the rigorous discrimination that so many had fled.

Religious services were conducted by so-called rabbis. They were learned men from the old country and probably had been students of yeshivas, but it is unlikely their training qualified them academically as rabbis or that any authority in central Europe established their qualifications for the rabbinical designation. These men not only conducted services but also served as ritual slaughterers of fowl and cattle, as cantors, teachers of children, and often as *mohels*, or ritual circumcision practitioners. In this latter area I shudder to think of the many young men in small communities who may have been shortchanged in life.

Our "rabbis" were easily obtained and came inexpensively, brought from Europe for little more than a hundred dollars for passage and the grand salary of fifty dollars a month. Many of them used small towns such as Moncton as stepping stones on which to learn a bit of English and some of the habits of the new world before moving on, usually to the large Jewish community of Montreal, which was only an overnight train and a ten-dollar fare away.

By and large, these teachers did their jobs most effectively. The children in small communities could many times equal or surpass their counterparts in large cities in reading and writing basic Hebrew and Yiddish and in partaking in the ritual of the prayer services. Along with their other heinous crimes, the Nazis wiped out virtually all those European communities that had been a source of Jewish teaching for small-town Canada and, probably, for other parts of the world.

During the high holidays, services were conducted in rented rooms on the second floor of the Toombs building on Main Street or in the Labour Temple Hall. In 1926 the basement of a synagogue was begun and, with fifty-cent contributions, the building was completed a few years later. Warmed only by a natural-gas space heater, it could be terribly cold during our severe New Brunswick winters.

We observed the holidays strictly, and on the high holidays of Rosh Hashanah and Yom Kippur all stores were closed. For Simchas Torah, the holiday that commemorates the giving of the Law, and a time for joy and celebration, the men went house to house, while the women vied with each other to provide them with special food and drink. All this came to an abrupt end one year when a participant who had imbibed too freely relieved himself in my mother's bed. My mother, a compulsive housekeeper, barred any further visiting, and the building of the synagogue eventually ended the need to observe the holiday with a home routine.

It was of course a strictly Orthodox synagogue, and has continued virtually so until this day. Before the main sanctuary of the synagogue was built, services were held in the basement and a curtain was put up to segregate the women from the men. Later, when the main sanctuary was completed, the women were banished to a balcony where they could be heard but not observed. During the memorial remembrance for the deceased, which was held on certain special holidays, the crying and wailing of the women, who were all of European background, was so loud as to virtually drown out the voice of the cantor, no matter how stentorian his tones. Those older people are all gone now and I marvel today at how quiet these memorial services are, with scarcely a murmur being heard, and as dignified as any church service. Somehow, I miss the old display of emotion.

Almost all homes kept kosher kitchens, with two sets of dishes—one for meat and one for dairy—and separate dishcloths for drying them. A couple of the congregants who were in the cattle business toured the countryside to buy animals and then sold them to the local butcher shops or to the local Swift Canadian plant, an important packing-house industry in Moncton at that time. In their search for cattle the dealers roamed as far as Prince Edward Island and the farming areas of Nova Scotia. One man acted as the kosher butcher, skilled in the art of removing veins from the front quarter of the beef, which would then be available for sale as kosher meat one day a week, usually in a primitive shop or garage.

The names of most Moncton businesses in those years were embedded in brass letters in the sidewalk outside their doors. Spelled out in brass outside my father's grocery was the name Smiths, for the tobacconist who owned the store previously. Inside, the gas stove was hopelessly inadequate in the depths of winter, and the front windows would get so frosted up that the merchandise on display was obscured to the passing eye; fans had to be put inside the windows to clear part of the glass. Moncton then boasted of being the city of natural gas, an inducement to industries needing a source of cheap fuel. Most homes were heated with natural-gas space heaters, although those with central heating used coal or wood.

From the store's ceiling of ornamental tin hung large glass globes attached to gas fixtures, which provided illumination. Electric lights were installed years later and the old fixtures, regrettably, were discarded. A scrubwoman, usually a Mrs. Fagan, cleaned the hardwood floors of the store from time to time, earning thirty or thirty-five cents for the several hours she spent on hands and knees, with a tattered rubber knee-pad, a scrub brush and frequent changes of her pail of water.

Perishable products in the grocery stores of the Twenties were kept in coolers, sometimes walk-in size, with a hatch-door on the top, through which the ice was delivered each week. It was a tough manual job lifting the large blocks of ice with iron tongs and depositing them in the ice-holding compartment. Electrical refrigeration was at least a decade away, and each household kept a block of ice in a wooden cabinet with a pan at the bottom, which had to be emptied regularly to prevent flooding.

The ice truck made its rounds daily, stopping wherever an ice sign had been placed in a window. Blocks of ice were ten or fifteen cents, depending on their size, and were cut from frozen ponds during the winter, stored in icehouses and covered with sawdust to retard melting. Attached to the side of the wagons and trucks was a metal tank filled with water, and as each block of ice was picked up with tongs, it was immersed in the tank to wash off the sawdust.

Ice cream presented similar refrigeration problems. It came in metal gallon containers, not the paper ones we see today, and they were placed in the wooden cabinet with ice and salt packed around the tins. The creamery made daily calls on retailers to replenish the salt and ice.

Ken Milner, a former policeman who ran a dairy farm on what is now Milner Road, delivered milk by horse and wagon to households in the city and supplied milk to my father's store for retailing. When making his milk rounds, he would often stop to have a wee nip with my father. He also provided Passover milk, using scoured milking pails and new milk bottles. The advent of pasteurization and commercial dairies put these small milkmen out of the retail business. The Milner farm is now the Brentwood subdivision, with hundreds of houses sitting on the pasture where cows once grazed.

Milk that was turning sour in our store was never wasted. My mother poured it into large pots, and when the whey formed, she put it into cloth containers. The water was then squeezed out and the remains placed in bags on a wooden press with a rock on top. The solidified mass later came out of the bags as cottage cheese. A favourite dish in our family was *mamiliga*—yellow cornmeal cooked like porridge and flattened like a pancake on a plate, buttered and topped with a thick layer of the homemade cottage cheese.

We had a barn and a henhouse in the backyard of our building, just about where the parking lot of the Hotel Beauséjour is now located. My father was thus able to continue his kinship with horses. He always kept a horse with wagons for delivering customers' orders, but he also owned two or three sulky horses, which he took to racetracks around the Maritimes and into Maine. The Moncton track, where the horses were trained, was just off St. George Street on land now or lately occupied by the Federal No. 5 Equipment Depot and the Department of National Defence.

Tom Holmes was one of the men who drove my father's harness-racing horses, and Tom and his wife Suzy were the first black people I ever met. To this day I retain a most pleasant memory of Suzy Holmes. When I was five or six, my father took me to the races at Old Home Week in Charlottetown, where we stayed at a boardinghouse near the track. Whatever I ate for supper one evening—I think it was baked beans swimming in pork fat—made me so violently ill that I was certain I would die. My father passed me over to Suzy's care while he partied with his cronies. Suzy's quarters in the stable next to the stalls had cots laid out for sleeping and some rough kitchen equipment. She placed several large bottles of ginger ale directly on the ice in the ice chest and stayed awake with me all night, cuddling me and coaxing me to drink the liquid. If I have lived to tell this tale seven decades later, I owe much to Suzy Holmes.

My father was much more adept at catering to a sick horse than to a sick child. If a favourite horse had a fever, my father stayed in the stall with him all night, cooling him down with buckets of water. If the horse was constipated, my father responded with his own manual enema: he rolled up his sleeve, covered his hand with axle grease, inserted it into the rectum and hauled out handfuls of obstructing matter. Modern veterinarians would likely frown on such primitive treatments, but they seemed to work. The memory of them, however, has left me with little trace of my father's enthusiasm for horses.

As my father's domain was the stable, my mother's was the henhouse. The care of our large flock of laying hens was entirely her responsibility. My job, as the youngest in the family, was to take all the meal scraps on a plate down to the henhouse and deposit them in the food trough. One day as I performed my duties, a hen on a high perch relieved herself, splattering excrement all over the plate. When I told the kids at school about the incident, I used the Yiddish word for plate, which is *teller.* As a child I did not differentiate much between Yiddish and English words, and I was upset when the other kids, instead of seeing the humour in my henhouse tale, expressed sympathy for the poor bank clerk.

The eggs and the hens were mostly for domestic use, but surpluses were sold in the store. We kept the eggs that were for sale—they were not graded or inspected—on the counter in a large basket, mixed with those brought in by farmers, who often bartered their eggs, butter, poultry, meat and produce for tea, tobacco and canned goods.

The chickens to be consumed at home required, of course, ritual slaughtering. My mother would pick a fat hen or two for the weekend table and put them in a burlap bag, which I then transported on my bicycle to the rabbi's house for the *schechita,* as it is called. This was only a few blocks away, and I would be given ten cents to pay the rabbi. When I returned, my mother would pluck the chickens and rotate them over an open flame (an outdoor fire in the summer and the gas flames in the winter) to burn off the pin feathers. The baked, unhatched eggs, as well as the liver, were fought over as a family delicacy.

Not only were chickens raised in the backyards of many Jewish households but also, on occasion, ducks and geese. Geese were required for the Passover week to provide the *schmaltz,* the rendered fat used in cooking. During the Second World War the mother of Helen Kirsh, a former classmate of mine, put a boxed goose on the train for her sister in Halifax and then called to make sure the sister knew to go to the station to pick up the *ganz,* the Yiddish word for goose. Halifax was a strategic seaport with heavily censored communications, and when the sister went to collect the cargo, she was immediately surrounded by the RCMP. They confiscated the box to look for the *guns.*

Our geese were confined and force fed so that they would provide the maximum amount of fat. After the rendered fat was poured off, my mother chopped up the small balls of reduced fat, called *gribiness,* added them to mashed potatoes and used the mixture as a filling for knishes. The crispiest of these balls were eaten beforehand as a special treat—delicacies for the palate but horrendous for the cholesterol count by today's standards. For most of the year chicken fat was used, serving the same purpose as non-kosher lard or shortening and much cheaper than Crisco or other acceptable vegetable oils.

My mother's preparation of dill pickles, sauerkraut and ceremonial grape wine was an annual ritual. Every fall, dill pickles, usually mixed with green tomatoes, were stored in large earthenware crocks. The sauerkraut was prepared in similar crocks, sprinkled with caraway seeds and left outside during winter, because freezing was supposed to improve the flavour.

The wine was distilled in a medium-sized barrel, brought out each fall and filled through a small hole with blue Ontario grapes and sugar. When the wine was ready, it was drained and bottled. The superior product, or first wine, was reserved for Passover seders and other important holidays or shared with special friends. After the first wine was drained, my mother filled the barrel with kettles of hot water and left it alone to produce the second wine, a somewhat inferior product without the bouquet and body of the first. The second wine was for lesser occasions and less important guests.

Salmon was another staple my mother preserved each year. She would take an Atlantic salmon weighing thirty or thirty-five pounds—usually from the Miramichi River and costing about two dollars—and dry it and slice it, so that it could be enjoyed throughout the fall and into winter.

Now and then my mother sold live chickens to the local Chinese restaurants, mainly on Sundays, when they ran short and regular suppliers were closed. A Chinese restaurateur would go to the henhouse, carefully select a chicken, pay my mother fifty cents and wring the bird's neck before returning to the restaurant. Sunday patrons, at least, got chicken dinners that were fresh.

Charlie Wing was the debonair owner of the Paris Café on Main Street, one of the better establishments of its kind in Moncton. He was reputed to be a college graduate, which would have been a rare achievement among the Chinese immigrants in our area at that time, most of whom were unschooled and worked in the laundry or restaurant business. Charlie was married to Rosie, a Polish woman whose first language my mother could speak fluently.

Rosie often sought out my mother for conversation in Polish, and my mother in turn visited the Paris Café, where Rosie entertained the evening patrons on a player piano. Rosie sometimes let me play the piano, although I was too small to reach the pedals from a sitting position and had to press them with my hands. The magic of this piano enthralled me, and to this day I feel considerable nostalgia whenever I encounter an antique player piano with its rolls of perforated music paper.

Charlie Wing committed suicide in a room at the old Brunswick Hotel (by swallowing poison, it was said), but Rosie lived on to become one of

Moncton's eccentric characters. When she broke a leg and was too stingy to have it properly set by a doctor, she let the leg heal by itself. The result was one leg four times the size of the other, which caused her to limp around town.

Rosie lived in a seedy part of Moncton, where she was reputed to operate as a moneylender and purveyor of liquor and other favours. After she was found murdered in her home one night, police discovered thousands of dollars hidden in walls, nooks and crannies throughout the premises. Although published advertisements sought heirs, none were ever found, and Rosie's property and money (well over $100,000) was forfeited to the Crown and went into the coffers of the Province of New Brunswick.

There was always a camaraderie with members of ethnic communities who were not Jewish. The shoemaker Rudolph Hanusiak and his wife, the former Mary Schella, were a Polish couple who visited back and forth with my parents. He was the gentlest of men, whose children later made important contributions to New Brunswick. Mary Hanusiak's mother gave me one of my earliest toys, a plastic ball half-filled with water, with small ducks floating on top and snowy white particles that would scatter throughout the ball when it was shaken. For years it was one of the few possessions I guarded jealously.

The toy land at Mr. Parker's Boston Five-and-Ten held for us children more magic than any Toys R Us could possibly dispense. Each proprietor in the Moncton of my childhood left the unique stamp of his personality on his shop, his merchandise, his customers and his community. They were not the faceless managers sent in to run the chain operations of today, with their rigid manuals of procedure and centrally determined and delivered merchandise.

Stores had their own aromas; we didn't need our eyes to know where we were. D.F. Hoar's Harness Shop smelled of leather; Isaac Selick's General Store of hay and feed; R.R. Colpitt's Stationery of papers and books; Peter Hougaard's Furniture Repair of paints and varnish. Every butcher shop smelled of the sawdust on the floor, and the most wonderful aroma came from the apples in grocery stores, which sold their Gravensteins, Northern Spies and Bishop Pippins from wooden barrels. Milk lunch crackers, vinegar and grapes packed in sawdust also came to stores by the barrel.

Molasses was cranked into a customer's one-gallon or two-gallon stone jug from giant puncheons, which arrived yearly from Barbados in boats that navigated the Petitcodiac River and unloaded at Reed's Wholesale wharf. The puncheons were delivered in heavy-duty slovens, each pulled by a pair

of draft horses. After a puncheon was rolled into the shop, several sets of hardy hands were needed to turn it on end. A man then climbed on top with an auger to bore a large hole and insert the crank. The spout of the crank always dripped after use, leaving a coating of molasses on the top of the barrel that required periodic washing in summer. The goo was a better flycatcher than the sticky flypapers that hung from store ceilings.

Images of life in those years sweep across my mind from time to time. Ottie Reid travelled the streets with a horse, wagon and bell, summoning customers to buy an ice-cream cone for a nickel. Street cleaners with brooms and shovels pushed tin barrels on two-wheel carts, laboriously cleaning the roads of the debris left by horses. The porter from the Brunswick Hotel used a two-wheel cart to meet every train at the railway station across the road, and transport the baggage.

On winter weekends, fur trappers and ranchers, with bundles of furs flung over their shoulders, crowded Main Street. The merchants rented storefront windows to the fur buyers from Montreal, and trappers and ranchers would go from store to store, selling where they obtained the best price. Horse-drawn sleigh rides were popular on Sunday afternoons, and even though we were covered with buffalo robes—the rage at the time—we came back so cold my mother had to turn on the gas oven to warm us up.

I can close my eyes and travel the length of Main Street, seeing dozens of proprietors in shops that are now long gone. The stores reflected the personalities of their owners and so, in many ways, did their merchandise: Fergusson's fabric store, Hattie Tweedie's bookstore, Melanson's and Clogg's jewellery stores, Peake's Ladies Fashions, J. McD. Cook's and Spencer's drugstores, Mendelson's and P.A. Belliveau's men's haberdasheries, D.A. Macbeth's Grocery. My father would often stop at Tommy Arris's hat blocking shop to chew the fat or have a shoe shine.

The only department store in Moncton was McSweeney's, but it was doomed when Eaton's arrived with its retail outlet. At McSweeney's, small metal boxes transported the cash from every department over what seemed like miles of track to the central office, returning shortly after with the receipt for payment and change. Most of the salespeople were men, well along in years, whose jobs at the store were lifetime careers.

My mother sometimes took me to Mr. Helm's Sunbeam Bakery and for five cents bought me a scrumptious, fresh cream puff, loaded with real, heavy cream. If we were walking to Bore Park, I might be favoured with an ice-cream cone from the Farmers' Co-op Dairy, where we could get a three-scoop cone of the rich and creamy real thing, again for five cents. At the park, my mother and I sat on the benches, fed the pigeons and watched the summer tourists who came to see the Tidal Bore ride up the Petitcodiac River. It was a spectacular sight then, with hundreds of sea gulls riding the crest of the wave. In later years the causeway built across the Petitcodiac reduced the Tidal Bore to a shadow of its once-great spectacle and ended all navigation on the river.

Near the park my mother would visit with one of her closest cronies, Annie Selick, who was left a widow at an early age (as my mother would be), with four children, the youngest born after the father's death. She ran a broken-down secondhand store, buying and selling household furniture and bric-a-brac, thereby managing to put all her kids through high school and on the path to good careers in life. If her inventory were available today, it would bring big prices as valuable antiques at any Sotheby's auction.

I also recall visiting in the late Twenties the new addition to the old hospital on King Street, which was opened with much fanfare and promise for medical service to the community. It is hard to believe that this little building, still standing, could have housed much of a medical facility.

On Sunday afternoons my father often took me to the train station, where we met the news agent on the Ocean Limited from Montreal, with whom my father arranged for deliveries of smoked meat, salami, Richstone's pumpernickel and tins of halvah. On the way we would stop at Pete Molson's Olympia Candy Kitchen, where my father would buy me a five-cent bag of maraschino cherry chocolates, oozing with liquid filling, not cream.

A few years ago, as I walked down Yonge Street in Toronto, I passed a shop with maraschino chocolates in the window, and out of nostalgia I stepped inside to buy some to take back home. When the clerk asked how many, I plunked down a five-dollar bill and, like a big shot, asked that a full five dollars' worth be put in a box for travelling. I was more than slightly embarrassed to find only three candies in the box.

My father must have been a bit of a playboy. He loved his toddy, his cronies, his horses. My mother was, by contrast, strict, serious and disciplined. Certainly they were not what one would call "matched," and my mother had no hesitation in confiding to us that her marriage was more indebted to duty and convenience than to affection.

Still, she was distraught the night my father disappeared and did not show up until the next morning. I only understood the import of this episode when I was shown a caption in *Hush*, the *Frank* magazine of the day, which asked: "Did Moncton's flying sheriff and his sidekick try to kidnap poor old David, or was he the willing guest at a roadside party? How did they happen to go off and leave the poor old boy stranded by the side of the road?"

Everyone in the family kept mum about the incident, although it suggests that my father chose his drinking buddies well. I can still see him finishing off a quart of gin and singing French songs with Father Babineau, the parish priest from Rogersville. Only much later did I learn that the words of the songs they sang, such as "monte en haut, Rosée," were all quite risqué. This particular song invited Rosie upstairs to "coucher."

My father's favourite beverage was Jan de Kuyper gin, which he would sprinkle with sugar, heat in a pan and drink undiluted to help ward off colds in the winter. Sometimes he dipped a piece of sponge cake into the gin and gave me the saturated cake to eat. Just as I never inherited my father's infatuation with horses, I have never acquired his taste for Jan de Kuyper gin, or for other liquors either.

Charlie McClintock, who worked at the CNR, was another of my father's drinking companions. He would gaze longingly at his glass as he began his favourite toast:

Look at the snow, the pure white snow
That falls from heaven to earth below;
Once Charlie was as pure as that white snow,
But that was one helluva long time ago.

Another buddy was Tom Nowlan. Tom owned a large farm across the river with a herd of Guernsey cows and an extensive piggery. He had the city contract to collect wet garbage, which he fed to the pigs. His horse-drawn wagons, emblazoned with a sign that said "Nowlan's Farm—Pure Guernsey milk," provided daily home milk delivery.

Many times I saw my father sneak into Tom's office, which was just to the west of my father's grocery store, but I doubt that they were slaking their parched throats with Guernsey milk. The Nowlan farm was only a front for Tom's more lucrative business: helping to quench the thirst of millions of New Englanders during the days of Prohibition in the United States.

One afternoon when I was about six, the two men had to drive to Richibucto, about fifty miles north of Moncton. My father took me along for the ride, which was a good two hours on dirt roads. In the backseat of Tom's car, I peeked into a small carton next to me, but quickly closed it again when I saw the stacks of currency inside. I began to suspect that my father's interest in spirits might not be limited to his personal consumption. Tom delivered the contents of the box to several men who had boats tied up at the wharf and then wished them bon voyage to St. Pierre and Miquelon.

Years later, Leo LeBlanc of Richibucto told me that he had been a captain of one such boat and ran the smuggling route from St. Pierre to Boston. As a seventeen-year-old he earned $15,000 for a successful week's work, but when the U.S. Coast Guard caught up with him, he was forced to vacation in the States for a while. Prohibition provided an exciting stimulus to the Atlantic Canadian economy even as it spawned a decade of lawlessness and racketeering in the United States. The repeal of Prohibition must have had a devastating impact on the region, similar in a minor way to the collapse of the Atlantic fishery in recent times.

A few years ago I finally visited St. Pierre and Miquelon, the islands that made much of the smuggling business possible. The islands are only a short trip from Sydney, Nova Scotia, and much nearer to that province's coastline than to the western end of Newfoundland. It's surprising how few Canadians, even Maritimers, take the opportunity to step back to the eighteenth century by visiting this vestige of France's once-great North American empire.

Both Tom Nowlan and K.C. Irving, one of Canada's most eminent entrepreneurs, came from Buctouche, about thirty-five miles north of Moncton. In the Twenties, when Irving was an agent for Imperial Oil, he decided he wanted to go into the oil business on his own. It was rumoured that Tom Nowlan lent Irving $50,000 to start his venture, taking as security half the shares of the newly formed Irving Oil Company. The venture was successful almost from the beginning, and K.C., wishing to expand, went to Tom for further financing. This was in Tom's heyday, and he could easily have provided any money necessary. But believing that the young K.C. was moving too quickly, Tom felt it was his duty as an experienced senior to lecture him accordingly. On being turned down, Irving hopped on a train to Montreal and procured bank financing. He returned to Buctouche, repaid Tom's $50,000 and reclaimed the shares. The rest is history.

Tom later retired to Buctouche, where he built a small hostelry called the Kent Lodge. I once stopped by to chat with him about the old days, and when I asked about the rumoured Irving story, Tom would neither confirm nor deny it. Of course it would be painful for any businessman to acknowledge such a lack of vision. It would also be ironic if Irving, for whom liquor was anathema, got his start with alcohol-tainted money.

Not all the characters who associated with my father were drinking partners. His friend Lester H. Higgins was the local plutocrat, having amassed a large fortune by the standards of the time. He owned four blocks of property in the commercial area of Main Street, and his retail shoe establishment at Main and Botsford streets was directly across from my father's store. He would order, almost weekly, full crates of grapefruit, which came in wooden containers much larger than today's cardboard fruit boxes. The uniformed chauffeur Higgins employed to drive his large touring car was the only one I've ever seen in Moncton. Higgins built a beautiful large home called Shadowlawn, on Botsford at the corner of Queen, and it quickly became the talk of the town. The house was torn down in recent years to make room for a New Brunswick Telephone Company parking lot, a desecration that proves the need for strong heritage bylaws.

Higgins was a corpulent man, with a girth the size of my father's, and the two of them liked to throw a large ball back and forth in the gym at Shadowlawn. I was taken along so that, if one man missed the ball, I could pick it up and throw it back into play. Stooping to pick up a ball from the floor would have been tough for either of these athletes.

Higgins was also a showman, who on occasion threw handfuls of pennies from his open office window into the street. Kids came running to gather this manna from heaven, helping Higgins to entice their parents into the shoe store.

On Saturday nights the Salvation Army band paraded along Main Street until it reached Higgins's store, where the band members would play and sing hymns as a crowd gathered. Someone from the band would then pass around a tambourine-shaped collection plate and visit every store on the street, sure of a dime at each call, twenty-five cents at Christmas.

One weekend the town was agog with the news that Higgins had disappeared. The police search proved unfruitful, and it was feared that he had been kidnapped. His wife had died a short time before, and it turned out that he had gone to visit her at the winter holding vault at the Shediac Road Catholic Cemetery. The vault door closed on him and he was locked in until a caretaker heard his cries on Monday morning.

Sam Jones, another of my father's cronies, lived on a farm west of Moncton, where some Sundays I enjoyed the swing that hung from a large tree and the drive through the woods to Jonathan Creek to water the horses. The farm now forms part of the residential area of Westmount and Mount Royal. Farther west were other farms—now all taken over by housing—including that of one-eyed Oscar Gibson, who was often seen hauling ashes and cinders from the CNR pile into the city. He sold the ashes at fifty cents a wagonload for use in driveways and basement floors.

Among the itinerant medicine men who visited in the summer was Arthur Hill, who travelled with two black minstrels and set up shop at the back of the City Market lands, just beyond our backyard. We kids went out every evening to watch the performance. The minstrels would sing and dance to attract a crowd, and then Hill would start his spiel, rolling his r's and bellowing in a commanding voice: "I am better known in Chatham, Ontario, where I was born and raised, as Dr. Arthur Hill. And if that is any criterion to my reputation, then all I ask of you is your kind attention. I am about to give you some scientific demonstrations concerning the stomach, the liver, the kidneys, the bowels and the nerves."

After the speech the minstrels would go down into the crowd to sell the "medicine" at one dollar a bottle. My father was attracted to Hill, probably because Hill was also a large man. We soon found him at our house, where my poor mother fed him and he and my father exchanged bottles. When they toasted each other, I doubt it was with Dr. Arthur Hill's elixir of life.

Louis Grossman, a Jewish grocer in Newcastle and another friend of my father's, gave me my first lesson in business ethics. For several summers, when my mother visited her sisters in New York, I was shipped to Newcastle, about one hundred miles north of Moncton, to stay with the Grossman family. These were pleasant holidays, with excursions in the Grossmans' new Chev, occasional fishing trips on the Miramichi River, and picnics and swimming at Bushville and Vye's Beach, both now polluted by effluent from pulp mills. We also enjoyed the children's movie matinées at the Strand and the Opera House, where the admission was five cents, half the price of a ticket in Moncton.

One day, when Louis left me in charge of his store for a few minutes, my only customer bought a pound of shortening. Not knowing the price, I guessed ten cents and charged accordingly. When I recounted the sale to Louis, he told me that I overcharged the man two cents. Louis removed two pennies from the till and instructed me to deliver them to the customer at his house. I questioned this, since it was not an undercharge for which I could be blamed, but rather an overcharge for which I should be commended. But Louis said the man might become aware of the overcharge and be lost as a customer. Returning the two cents with an immediate apology would ensure the customer's loyalty. It is a lesson I have never forgotten.

Although adept at harnessing and driving a horse, my father never mastered the car. In the late Twenties we made an exciting car trip to Saint John on Labour Day weekend to attend the exhibition. A driver, as usual, was hired for this journey of less than 100 miles, and it took almost a day over unpaved roads, with several stops to repair or replace flat tires. We arrived in the evening in a thick fog, a novel experience for me, and unable to secure rooms at the newly opened Admiral Beatty, we settled for the old Royal Hotel.

On July 1, 1927, Canada celebrated the Diamond Jubilee of Confederation, a gala event observed with more patriotic fervour in our town than the Centennial in 1967 or the 125th birthday in 1992. Houses were draped in flags and bunting in a keenly fought contest for the prize for the best display. Milledge Taylor's home at the corner of Main and Cameron streets, in what is now a commercial area, won an award, and for years a snapshot of the house was kept at my mother's.

To celebrate the Jubilee, all schoolchildren marched in a parade to the music of bands, and each child was given a commemorative medal. Because I was not to start school until the fall, I envied my older brother for his participation in the parade and the medal he brought home.

School that September opened up a world of wonder and excitement for me—a world of language, reading and learning that was foreign to the home of an immigrant family. Our family had no bookshelves and no books. The only newspaper that came to us was the *Jewish Daily Forward* from New York, which arrived by mail a day or two after publication. But this newspaper was a virtual family bible, with articles on almost all aspects of life and living, and a source of information on world events for Jewish immigrants. My mother kept her subscription for over half a century, almost until her death in the Sixties. The paper was written in Yiddish but carried a weekend photographic section with captions translated into English. This section I always read with eagerness, and I soon became adept at reading the Yiddish as well.

At the Hub Tobacco Shop, Joe Bourgeois, the genial proprietor, let us kids browse through the magazines without kicking us out for not buying anything. The weekend edition of the *Montreal Standard*, with its pages of coloured comics, was a favourite, though we seldom had the fifteen cents to buy it.

But when it came to reading and learning, my teachers were inspirations in my life. I remember the names of all my teachers, and most of the teachers themselves with affection and considerable gratitude. My grade-school teachers were all unmarried, since married women were not hired then, and they earned about six hundred dollars a year. Almost each one had a special impact. I was a sponge, ready to absorb whatever they put before me.

My Grade 1 teacher, Miss Hazel Taylor, lived well into my mature years, and anytime I met her on the street, even in my fifties and sixties, she renewed my childhood. I once told her that I could never be considered old as long as my Grade 1 teacher was alive and kicking.

My Grade 2 teacher, Miss Allen, was a bit of a tartar. A relative of hers, possibly her sister, was the mother of Goodridge Roberts, an illustrious Canadian artist. It was in her class that a boy named Shirley Forbes, the son of a local doctor, led the class marks one month, beating out the bright girls who were usually the leaders. After school, Shirley was a hero, and the other boys crowded around to pat him on the back. The next month my marks were the highest—by accident, not by design—but none of the kids acknowledged my achievement. This disturbed me, probably to such an extent that I determined then and there to show them by always being at the top of the scholastic heap, and in this by and large I succeeded, in every class and in virtually every subject, throughout my entire academic career.

My Grade 3 teacher, Vera Staples, began every day with the Lord's Prayer and a passage from the Bible, starting with the Old Testament and finishing with the last of the New Testament. It was my first real exposure to the New Testament, but learning Christian stories at an early age did not affect my faith; it gave me a better appreciation of my own religion and a respect for the religions of others. My home indoctrination was undamaged, but my perceptions and understanding were broadened.

Grade 4, taught by the gentle Viola McNairn, was marked by tragedy. Max Peake, a charmer of a kid, was accidentally shot and killed by a schoolmate with a BB gun. It was extremely disturbing for me to see Max laid out in his coffin, with his forehead slightly swollen and discoloured in the area where the bullet had entered. His parents, Neta and Bill Peake, were so devastated that they never disposed of Max's clothes or changed a thing in his room. Almost fifty years later Bill Peake came to my office to give me an envelope. Inside were three time-yellowed valentines, their backs inscribed in my childish handwriting: *To Max from Reuben.* I still have these in my desk drawer.

Miss McNairn's practice was to give students an extra percentage point on their grades for good behaviour. When I achieved 100 percent on all my tests one month, I was disappointed she did not make my average 101. Feeling that my conduct had not measured up, I determined to try harder.

One day in Grade 5 a group of us from the neighbourhood accompanied our teacher, Pauline Murray, on the walk home at noon. She told us she couldn't wait for lunch because she was having chicken, a special treat. "That's nothing special," replied Helen Kirsh. "We have chicken in our house almost every day." Miss Murray, not knowing that most Jewish families kept their own chickens, thought Helen was putting on airs and never forgave her.

Those were the years when Jewish children were driven to succeed by their struggling immigrant parents and their own determination. With integration into general society, this no longer seems to be the case, although a similar strong motivation can be seen in the children of later groups of immigrants. Miss Murray once said she would love to have a whole class of Jewish students, but without Helen Kirsh.

My Grade 6 teacher was Connie Lambert. Her father, Murray Lambert, a senior and respected lawyer in the community, would come to our store almost weekly to buy the weekend family roast. He always found time to chat and would often pass on some interesting anecdotes. I think his stories may have helped plant a seed in my mind that influenced my choice to become a lawyer in later life. One of his famous cases was defending the Bannister brothers in one of the most bizarre and sensational trials in Canadian history. The Bannister boys were eventually hanged, and I'm sure the whole drama took a damaging toll on Murray Lambert physically, emotionally and almost certainly financially.

Connie Lambert married Russell Bennett, a high-school teacher and later my Grade 10 teacher. Russell was a brother of W.A.C. Bennett, the Social Credit premier of British Columbia, and, of course, the uncle of Bill Bennett, a later premier. I always attended the funerals of my old teachers, out of respect and gratitude. At Russell's funeral, held in the chapel of Cadman's funeral parlour, I was seated immediately behind W.A.C. Connie was a stalwart in the local Conservative party circles, and probably one of the few to remain loyal to Dick Hatfield to the very end of the sinking ship. Connie passed away just a few short years ago, fiercely fighting for the Conservative party to the very end.

I still have the scrapbook of current events from 1933–34 that I produced for my Grade 7 teacher, Clara Miller. Among the news items I have preserved from six decades ago are a picture of Italo Balbo and his Italian armada, which landed and refuelled at Shediac on a flight to the Chicago World's Fair, and a picture of Albert Einstein on his arrival to teach at Princeton University after his flight from Nazi Germany.

My first male teacher, in Grade 8, was Chester Eagles, who taught us about the First World War, telling us stories of the trenches which made that period of Canadian history come alive. In the last months of the war, Chester said, youngsters were recruited into the depleted German army, and he saw many of these kids shot and dying, the cry of *mutter* on their lips. Canada's history had always seemed dry and uninteresting to me, with so much given over to tales of exploration and minor conflicts. Much more compelling were the scoundrels and intrigue of English history, the War of Independence in the United States, the revolution in France, the stirring patriotic music of the Americans and the French. For us, Chester Eagles made Ypres and Passchendaele vivid, and we appreciated for the first time the role that Canadians played on the world stage.

His teaching was quite different from that previously experienced. He once asked us why Napoleon's pictures always showed him with his hand in his tunic. We gave various answers, but Chester negated all responses and said it was because he was lousy and had to scratch himself. Unusual teaching, but thoroughly delightful.

Before school was out that year, all Grade 8 students had to write high-school entrance exams set by the provincial Department of Education.

Competition was keen among teachers across New Brunswick to see how many of their students could achieve the 85 percent needed to make the first division. The success of their students might be taken to indicate teaching prowess and might possibly be a reason for advancement. In more than a decade at the King George School in Moncton, Chester had never had any students who brought him much distinction. He took personally their ranking near the bottom of the competition, although it probably had more to do with where his students came from—the rough east end of town—than with his skills. Annie Lawson, Chester's nemesis at the Edith Cavell School and the city leader in the competition, taught students from more privileged homes.

That year I wrote the exams, led the city and was a star in the provincewide standings. Chester's stature as a teacher was redeemed, and until the end of his teaching career he tried to inspire all his classes by telling them my story. I suspect some of his later students came to resent me.

So competitive were these provincial exams that they were not written under the supervision of your house teacher, presumably for fear that he or she might try to help a student in order to improve their own standing. Thus, each Grade 8 teacher was sent to another school to supervise the class there. Our supervisor was a nun, Sister Sonier, who taught Grade 8 at the French school, then called the Academy. While the pupils wrote the exams, Sister Sonier passed the time by doing likewise. Sometime after the day's papers were handed in, she would ask us to compare our answers with her own. I was appalled at the number of inaccuracies in her answers, and shuddered at the quality of education that the Acadian kids of that era must be obtaining. Happily, that situation does not exist in the New Brunswick Acadian schools of today, especially since examinations can now be set and written in their own language, in which they are more comfortable.

It was from Chester Eagles that I first learned about income tax. He paid more tax, he told us, than the doctors and businesspeople downtown, because the government knew what he made and didn't know what they made. This was probably the end of my age of innocence.

Almost everyone got caught up in the stock market mania of the Twenties, when it seemed the magic wand to prosperity was just a broker away. It was said that even the pimply-faced kids who delivered parcels by bicycle in big American cities exchanged hot market tips.

My father was no exception. His stock salesman was Lew Stratton, who loaded him, *inter alia*, with glamorous Toronto Stock Exchange mining stocks, all on margin. Two that I recall were Siscoe and Sudbury Basin. When the market crashed and calls were made, my father, of course, was sold out.

For good reason, the decade that followed the 1929 crash was called the Dirty Thirties. It was as if all commercial and industrial activity came to an abrupt halt. Men lined up for hours early in the morning for jobs on what little construction there was—the General Motors building on Downing Street or the Rubin Building on Main Street. Those who were successful were handed picks and shovels and for fifty cents a day went to work on excavations. There were no backhoes, tractors or mechanical bulldozers, and heavy wheelbarrows filled to the brim with earth were pushed by hand up wooden ramps from the deep holes below. For shallow excavations, a horse dragged up the earth with a V-shaped wooden plow.

Winters during the Depression were severe, and many families were too poor to clothe their children adequately against the cold. Victor Flood, who lived on Albert Street, would arrive at school clad only in a light jacket, so frozen that our teacher made him lie down by the radiator to thaw. Everybody walked to school then, no matter how many miles; there were no school buses or accessible public transportation. In those days the streets and sidewalks were cleared by horse-drawn wooden plows, and we often walked on top of snowbanks more than four times our height.

With the Depression came price deflation. A bushel of potatoes or turnips sold for about thirty cents, a loaf of bread for eight, a pound of round steak for ten. A family could rent a comfortable home for fifteen or twenty dollars a month. I remember the day a platter of lobster on ice was placed on a box outside our store with a sign that said, "Two pounds for nineteen cents." As two older women each picked out a ten-cent lobster for dinner, one said to the other, "Don't you feel sorry for all those poor fishermen up on the shore—all they get to eat all winter is lobster and potatoes."

Municipal coffers were strained to the limit and often broken by welfare payments, which were made in the form of monthly food vouchers, the amount depending on the size of the family. A family of five would get a voucher of about fifteen dollars.

Grocery stores competed for the voucher business, since it was the only way they themselves could survive. Some voucher recipients favoured stores whose owners would close their eyes and allow a bit of forbidden tobacco in a grocery order. The vouchers were meant strictly for food, and any grocer caught breaking the rule would be cut off by the municipal authority. If he didn't break the rule, however, there was always another who would. The subterfuge of that time was comparable to the underground economy that avoids the GST today.

The widow in charge of the city's relief department, a Mrs. Gallagher, lived on Archibald Street and let us pick bouquets of lilacs from the bush in front of her house. I always suspected that her Christmas presents were more extensive than the meagre lot received by relief recipients or the grocers vying for their vouchers. All of Mrs. Gallagher's children had moved away, mostly to the United States, where one became Tyrone Power's manager in California, and another, Pat, who once worked for my father, ended up in Pennsylvania. Pat mentioned to me that he once ate at a seafood restaurant in New Orleans and overheard another patron say it was the second-best seafood dinner he had enjoyed in his life. The best was at a restaurant named Cy's, in a place called Moncton, New Brunswick.

The Depression created a significant rift between the French- and English-speaking segments of the community. Jobs were so scarce that Acadians threatened to withhold their patronage if stores did not employ French-speaking clerks. The English element countered with what was called the English-Speaking League, which boycotted French proprietorships and those English stores that bent to French pressure. New clubs and organizations sprang up, with memberships based on religious affiliation. For the first time the Royal Antediluvian Order of Buffalo came into the community. I know nothing of its precepts, and it has long since disappeared from Moncton, but I am still intrigued by the order's name on a building in Saint John.

In Moncton the Depression was a time of ugly undercurrents of racial animosity, which had not been noticeable in more prosperous times. There were three distinct communities, or what might be called ghettos: our small ethnic community on the wrong side of the tracks, which also included a handful of Lebanese, Syrians and other immigrants; the Acadians, who kept largely to themselves, both residentially and socially; and the more prosperous Anglo-Saxon majority, the prominent force in the community. Like other wealthy and élitist communities, as was once said, their ghetto had gates that were locked from the inside.

One jarring experience of discrimination stands out from my childhood.

It happened the day our gang of English and Acadian kids—Ernie Richard, Charlie MacCallum and others—was invited to play on an outdoor rink in the backyard of a doctor's house on Alma Street. The gang took me along as a matter of course. But we had been playing only a few minutes when the doctor's son, Peter, told my friends that I was not included in the invitation. I left the rink and, to their credit, so did the kids who had brought me along.

I can't remember much overt discrimination, growing up in the small town. In retrospect I am sometimes amazed by the generous goodwill we experienced, especially in view of the ugly rumblings emanating from Germany. In the general community, the most serious complaint was the denial of jobs at most of the larger employers, including the CNR and Eaton's. This might be blamed in part on the general economic malaise, but a young woman coming out of school with full stenographic training would feel bitter when her classmates won jobs at the better-paying national companies while she competed for much less desirable work.

Financial stress inevitably produces friction, domestically and certainly socially, but ours was a relaxed community whose strain was kept well below the surface. As a young child I was not even aware of the religious cleavage in the Christian community of Moncton. To me, it was us—our little ethnic community—and them—the whole of the larger population.

Walking home from school one day with another classmate, the differences among Christians were dramatically brought into focus. That warm afternoon I was with Blair Wilmot, whose father was an official at the CNR. As we passed St. Bernard's Catholic Church on Botsford Street, which was mostly an Irish church, the doors were wide open and the choir was practising. I found the music entrancing and stopped to listen. "Why do you stop and listen to the heathens?" Blair asked me.

Somewhat perplexed, I later told my father what had happened and asked what it all meant. He explained some of the superficial distinctions among the Christian denominations and advised me not to be perturbed: as long as they fight among themselves, he said, we can be the referees, and hopefully they will leave us alone.

It was common for immigrant families in those days to bring family members over from the old country. My father brought a sister, Pearl, who stayed with us only briefly before moving on to relatives in Philadelphia. A short time later my father brought over his sister Esther's husband, Keiver Yanispoulsky.

Keiver arrived on the condition that he work as a farmhand, which was a requirement of the immigration regulations. Arrangements were made for him to work on the Albert County farm owned by Lewis Smith, the provincial minister of agriculture and a true gentleman. But Keiver bypassed the farm work and was quickly on the road, peddling merchandise with an old truck and a dozen words of English. Lewis Smith must have been a cooperative sponsor.

Keiver put together a few dollars and soon brought his wife and four daughters—Bertha, Ida, Tina and Sonia—from Russia. For the first time we had relatives with whom we could share tales of living, schooling, hardships and growing up, and I remember with nostalgia the part they played in my young life.

When the years for qualification had passed, Keiver applied for citizenship, using the services of Leonard C. Jones, a lawyer recommended by my father. Jones suggested, as was the common practice, that my uncle's last name be changed and perhaps anglicized to make it easier for the new world to pronounce. Jones first suggested Yanis, but not really liking the sound of that, he went the whole way—Keiver's naturalization was completed under the name Jones. This gave me an aunt, uncle and four first cousins with that WASP name.

After six years in Moncton, Keiver Jones and his family moved to Montreal, and whenever a cousin became engaged, Esther sent us a copy of the engagement notice as it appeared in the Montreal press. The notice carried the groom's name, always a good Jewish name, followed by the bride's name, Jones, with Yanispoulsky in brackets lest the groom's side get the idea he was marrying outside the faith.

Mixed marriages were a no-no, a complete anathema to Jews and looked upon with a jaundiced eye by Gentiles. No crime seemed worse than dating a *shiksa*, a Christian girl, and the thought of a Jewish woman straying was beyond the realm of comprehension, let alone acceptance. Dating alone was horrific, but intermarriage was considered so horrendous that the offender would be cut off from all family connection, becoming a pariah and an outcast for whom a family would often sit *shiva*, the seven-day mourning period for the dead.

With such indoctrination, very few in our town dared to incur the wrath or grief of their parents, and the few mixed relationships that did exist were kept discreetly under cover. One marriage that exploded in the Thirties involved the Selick family, the most well-to-do and prominent family in the Jewish enclave and leaders in the community at large.

Isaac Selick, the patriarch, began as a pedlar, working out of the hamlet of Hillsborough, where he eventually started a general store. Remembering the convulsions of Eastern Europe, he shrewdly anticipated the outbreak of war in 1914 and stocked his warehouse with large supplies of sugar and other staples. As the war progressed and these items became scarce, Selick profited handsomely by selling them at the new market prices. At the end of the war he moved his enterprise to Moncton, built a beautiful home and quickly was acknowledged as the leader of the Jewish community. He spearheaded the building of the synagogue and the consecration of the cemetery, the road into which is called Selick Lane. When he died in 1936, the newspaper carried an editorial extolling his citizenship. It was the practice in those days to publish the probate value of the larger estates, and Selick's was published at $210,000, a fortune that would be the equivalent of several million dollars today.

Selick's son Jake, an extremely affable young man, became enamoured of a beautiful Halifax girl whose family name was Conn. Regrettably, her name was not Cohen, and the Selicks fought the union. When she and Jake were married, he was evicted from the family business and the family circle, and with the few resources he had managed to salvage he opened a small store in Shediac. Jake took to drinking and died a short time later, apparently broken-hearted, but the battle continued after his death. The young widow wanted her way in plans for the burial, but the family was determined to bury Jake in their plot in the Saint John Jewish cemetery. The family, with resources the widow lacked, won the day, either by going to court or threatening to.

So where did Jews in isolated communities such as ours find their mates? They turned, for the most part, to the small Jewish communities in the rest of the Maritime provinces. These communities were always linked by visits and social contacts, and someone was always promoting an eligible bachelor or bride. The more affluent men travelled farther in search of a life's companion, and many a bride in our community was from Montreal. Some of the less affluent, or less energetic, stayed at home and died bachelors, though generally not celibate, and spinsterhood was the lot of many a woman, especially if she was lacking in feminine graces.

Happily, we are a much more civilized society today, and mixed marriages constitute almost half the families in our community, without any trauma to either side. Only a few diehards remain. There is always debate over whether this liberalism will lead to the complete assimilation and disappearance of Jewish ethnic groups in North America. I am not that pessimistic. Many of those who convert are more observant, perhaps in a zeal to overcompensate, than their counterparts who are born Jewish. Such unions have a tendency to produce most handsome and bright children; and the mixing of races, whilst possibly impacting on religious affiliations, could be beneficial to our society as a whole in the long run.

On the Saturday morning of my bar mitzvah in 1934, my mother packed me off to the confirmation service with half a sponge cake and half a bottle of Scotch. By then my father was seriously ill and could not attend, and my worried mother was not present either. The dozen or so men making up the *minyan*, or quorum, made short work of the cake and Scotch at the end of the service, and I wended my way home. I was now able to call myself a man, qualified to be counted as one of the ten males required to conduct a service. I've attended many a bar mitzvah since my own. The elaborate ceremonies and parties that have been known to run two or three days in length have caused me to wonder whether I was a bit short-changed in my early life. In the end, though, I felt more relieved than envious.

I do not remember too much of my father, as he passed away when I was 14 and he was quite sick for three or four years before that. He was a heavy man, weighing well over 250 pounds, and the diet my mother fed him, with the European delicacies, must have contributed considerably to his girth. It was in the days before the awareness of calories or cholesterol, and probably a well-padded husband in the old country was a sign of distinction to a wife's culinary talents and spousal devotion. This weight certainly contributed to his dying at the early age of 48, with the cause of death on the doctor's certificate listed as cerebral thrombosis.

The plain pine casket was transported to the cemetery on the back of a half-ton truck because there was no money for a fancy hearse. Accompanying the casket was my father's longtime buddy Harry Ruch. Harry had partaken of too many snifters, not only to help drown his sorrow over losing a friend but also as a protection against the cold. When the truck reached its destination, Harry bent over the casket to express the usual Yiddish wish when someone goes off on a trip: *"Fohr gesunter heit."* ("Travel in good health.")

In the Orthodox tradition of eleven months of mourning, sons are obligated to recite Kaddish, the memorial prayer, three times a day, morning, afternoon, and evening, and this is done with a fully constituted prayer service that requires at least ten men. My brother and I diligently observed this duty and never missed a service, although it was difficult at times to round up ten men. Mornings were the greatest challenge. We had to leave the house at seven o'clock to complete the service in time for school at nine. Luckily, most of the parishioners lived near the synagogue, but on many days we pounded on doors, seeking that seemingly always elusive tenth man. We might even have contributed to an unfavourable impact on the community's birth rate when, on some occasions, we had to haul a man out of the matrimonial bed.

Since 1933, when my father's health began to decline rapidly, any earning capacity had been limited, and our family's financial position was desperate. Even a roll of toilet paper was a prohibited luxury; for this we had to use the papers in which citrus and other fruit came individually wrapped. The week my father died, the utilities were shut off for non-payment, and we were left without heat or light in the depths of a cold December.

But all was not lost. During the prosperous Twenties my father had taken out $20,000 in life insurance—four policies of $5,000 each—with the Northern Life Assurance Company. He had a hard time passing the medical exam, particularly the urine specimen test, because of his heavy weight. As times got tougher and my father's health worsened, my canny mother used the cash surrender value of one policy to keep the other three alive, and then a second to keep two alive. When he died, two policies totalling $10,000 were still in force. This was a veritable fortune in 1935, and it had an incalculable effect on the course of my life. It also left me with a keen appreciation of the value of life insurance.

The insurance money, however, did not come easily. Leonard Jones, the lawyer, visited the house to offer his condolences and his help with any details of a legal nature. My mother was grateful and asked him to complete the formalities for the insurance claim.

In the meantime, the other Jones, the relative in Montreal, wrote a blackmailing letter, saying he was hard-pressed financially and wanted half the insurance proceeds. If my mother didn't give him the money, he would advise the insurance company that it was he who had provided the urine sample for my father's application, in which case she would get nothing. As

Jones, the relative, put it in Yiddish, *"Oib du vest nicht gibben yankov, vest du gibben asafen."* ("If you don't give it to Jacob, you'll give it to Esau.")

Jones, the lawyer, obtained the money but would not release it until he was paid a thousand dollars for his services. My mother took me with her to his law office. Never had I seen her so irate, and when she was through lambasting him, Jones seemed happy and relieved to settle for two hundred dollars and his life. The current practice of the life insurance industry is to have the company agent or representative deliver policy proceeds directly to the beneficiary, bypassing the need for a legal intermediary.

The blackmailing Jones was handled in an equally judicious fashion, which ruptured our relationship with that side of the family almost until the decade of my mother's death. Those desperate times demanded desperate measures to survive.

In 1935 people across the country were champing at the bit to turf out governments that had been in power since the beginning of the Depression. This made the provincial election that year especially memorable. The Conservative government under Premier Leonard P.D. Tilley had begun paving the highway between Moncton and Saint John, and the rumour spread that the Liberals would stop the project and the few precious jobs that went with it.

Allison Dysart, a small-town lawyer with a warm personality, led the Liberal forces. In those days, before coverage by television or even radio, campaigns were much closer to the grassroots and much more exuberant; by contrast, today's campaigning, largely conducted through TV debates, seems quite sterile. Parades with bands ushered the leaders through the streets, while supporters sang and shouted. One such parade had the crowd singing "How do you do, Allison Dysart, how do you do." Leaflets with the words of the songs were distributed to people standing on the sidewalks so that they could join in. I remember the crowds lustily singing another Liberal song to the tune of "Old MacDonald Had a Farm":

> Premier Tilley had a province, ee-i-ee-i-o
> And on that province he had a debt, ee-i-ee-i-o
> With a gas tax here, and a licence there,
> Taxes, taxes everywhere
> If the people will pay one more, why care, ee-i-ee-i-o.

Every night a large white sheet was hung from a three-storey building on Main Street to serve as a projection screen, and from a window directly opposite a projection lantern beamed slides showing the devastating figures of debt and mismanagement. Meetings were held in town halls throughout the constituency, and supporters gave their leaders' words raucous approval. The Liberals won the 1935 election handily and stayed in power for the next seventeen years.

As a child I could not help being infected with the political virus, and politics at all three levels—municipal, provincial and federal—have held a fascination for me almost from the crib.

Municipal elections were then held annually, with voting taking place on New Year's Day. The contests at both the mayoralty and ward levels were hotly contested, and crowds would gather on the sidewalk outside the *Transcript* newspaper office to wait for the results. The figures were written out by hand on long sheets of yellow paper and posted in the front windows facing Main Street. When it was over, people rushed to city hall, where the candidates, both victorious and defeated, were expected to give speeches. From the age of about six I did not miss one of these gatherings.

It was usually the most prominent citizens in business or the professions who ran for the mayor's job, giving the city a succession of capable and dedicated incumbents. There was scarcely a breath of impropriety or scandal— a circumstance that seems to have continued to this day—and municipal councils often served as training grounds for provincial and federal politics.

Hanford Blakeny, an articulate man who operated a gravel and sand business as well as dealing in coal and ice, was the mayor of Moncton for several years in the Thirties. During his tenure the slippery winter sidewalks were sanded as never before or since. One of his scows, named the *Sherman B* after his father, plied the Petitcodiac River, hauling the sand and gravel from lower down in Albert County.

Blakeny had always been a staunch Conservative, but in the provincial election of 1935 he smelled the climate of change and ran for the Liberals. He served as minister of education but never achieved his ambition to be premier. It was widely held that if he had not turned Liberal, he could easily have become the leader of the Conservative party, and in the 1939 election, which was a close contest even with a rather obscure Conservative leader, Blakeny's leadership would have provided the edge to lead the Conservatives to victory and Blakeny to the premier's office.

One of the most persistent campaigners was William Emmet McMonagle, a bright lawyer who for years had a rough time trying to break into the more remunerative areas of practice dominated by a few old-time and largely WASP families. To bolster his legal career, Mac, as he was called, tried his hand at politics, running for mayor at least six times before making it. A less stout heart would have abandoned any political aspirations long before. Mac's Roman Catholicism probably would not have been a political advantage in the Moncton climate of that time, but with perseverance he became a popular mayor for several terms.

His office was on the second floor of the Maritime Press Building, which was next to my father's grocery. Mac would come down to the store almost daily for his package of Turret cigarettes, and his secretary, the former Ermina Sears, came in just as often for an ice cream or a chocolate bar. As a kid I frequently waited on them.

Mac also wrote copy for my father's weekly newspaper advertisements, starting each with "Cohen says" . . . "If Methuselah were alive today, what an awful hole he would make in the old age pension fund," said one ad, which may turn out to be prophetic even without a Methuselah. The ads were an eagerly anticipated topic of conversation in the town, and as recompense Mac stopped paying for his cigarettes, a unilateral move on his part.

McMonagle's fortunes changed for the better after he successfully defended a prominent salvage operator who faced serious charges of dealing in brass and other materials stolen from the CNR. Soon after the acquittal Mac was driving a new car and other improvements in his lifestyle became apparent. For affectation he sometimes wore a monocle. He was also a gifted orator, always precise in his speech and sometimes flowery. When he was mayor and the first police cruiser was introduced, Mac asked an officer who was to be promoted to the car patrol, "Ern, do you know how to operate a vehicle?" The policeman was flustered for a moment, but came back for clarification. "Do you mean, do I know how to drive a car?"

McMonagle ran as a Conservative in a federal election in the early years of the war. His campaign advertising made little or no reference to the Conservative party, with all the emphasis being placed on "Vote for Mac," with the hope that his by-now-achieved popularity in civic politics could spill over into the larger field. However, the lingering spectre of R.B. Bennett and the "Conservative" Depression was too hard an obstacle to overcome. Combined with this was the usual natural reluctance of electors to reject an administration in a time of national emergency. McMonagle was obliged to stay home.

Dr. O.B. Price was a local dentist who became the member of Parliament in the 1930 Conservative government of R.B. Bennett. His great political achievement was securing for his constituency the new post office at the corner of Main and Highfield streets. This Dominion Public Building was a striking piece of architecture and gave a significant lift to the Depression-weary community. O.B., as he was always called, was a very convivial gentleman, and during his many visits with my father the conviviality was usually enhanced. O.B. was defeated in the 1935 election when the Liberals swept into office and R.B. Bennett, defeated as prime minister, assuaged his disappointment by moving to England and becoming a titled gentleman, Viscount Bennett of Hopewell—Hopewell being the tiny settlement in Albert county where he was born, about thirty miles from Moncton.

Although my father died when I was 14, my mother lived into my own mature years, and therefore she had a far greater impact on me.

She had a pet Yiddish expression for almost all of life's incidents, and scarcely a day passes even now when something does not bring one of them to mind. People often asked me, for example, why I stayed in the small city of Moncton instead of moving to Toronto or Montreal, especially at the pinnacle of my business career. My mother once heard the same question from her sisters, who lived in Philadelphia and New York.

"*Vizoi kanst du leben dortan auf ein dorf?*" the sisters asked. ("How can you live there in a remote hamlet?")

"*Uz a vorm burgt sich arein en chrain, meint er uz kein besser kan nicht zein,*" my mother answered, with her typical quizzical smile. ("If a worm burrows into a horseradish root, he thinks there is nothing any better." This means that he could have burrowed into a pear, peach, apple or any such sweet fruit, but having gotten into the bitter horseradish he was content, because he didn't know the difference.)

Yiddish is an expressive language, which can sum up dramatically in a simple phrase or sentence what might take a whole paragraph to put across in another language. And just as Yiddish started out as a patois German, the English environment soon spawned a patois Yiddish.

Louis Attis was the patriarch of one of Moncton's founding Jewish families, whose offspring are still prominent in the community. The family became comfortable financially, largely by buying up old houses, which were patched up and rented out. Vita Leah, the matriarch, was a tough, down-to-earth old bird. My mother once asked her why the Attis family didn't buy a car, a purchase even the less affluent families were making. Vita Leah quickly made it clear she wasn't going to let car dealers and gasoline stations drain her resources. *"A hoiz melk ich, a car melkt yener,"* she told my mother. ("A house I milk, a car someone else milks.")

My mother lost her hearing early in life and learned to speak her limited English by lip reading. She was a motivated and determined woman, with boundless ambition and tireless energy. With the advantages of a Western education she would have made a valuable contribution to the social fabric, although I suppose the same could be said of countless other immigrants.

I inherited some of my mother's drive, as did, to a somewhat lesser degree, my older brother. At the age of about ten he was already tending to a small satellite convenience store on Botsford Street, and would cash up and walk home at night to deliver the day's receipts. I tried selling the *Transcript*, the afternoon newspaper, on Main Street after school. The paper sold for three cents and we turned in two cents for every paper sold, keeping a penny for ourselves. With tough competition from the other kids selling papers, I decided to try a more rewarding enterprise.

I persuaded Harvey Steeves, who ran a livery stable on Wesley Street, to rent me a horse and wagon on credit. Then I persuaded Bob Healy, the manager of the Willett Fruit Company, to give me credit on bananas, which were fifty cents a stalk. We would go into the ripening room where the bananas were hanging, and Healy would choose one, generally overripe, stalk, and I would choose the next, generally more merchantable, until the wagon, with a bed of hay, was filled.

After recruiting some paperboys to join me with a stack of paper bags, we drove to the suburban areas of Humphrey Mills, Sunny Brae and Lewisville, knocking on doors and peddling the bananas at ten cents a dozen. It seems that every house we called at had a huge dog that came bounding out, barking and jumping and sometimes nipping at our heels. Whoever said barking dogs don't bite must have had different experiences than mine, for by the end of the summer we all had a few frayed clothes and the odd nick from a dog's teeth. I learned to have a healthy respect for barking dogs, and my enthusiasm for dogs in later life was only a very little bit more than for horses. At the end of the day we cashed up, paid Healy, paid for the horse rental and divided the balance, based on individual sales. It was no gold mine, but it beat selling papers, for which ten cents was the payoff on an extremely good day.

When I called for bananas at the Willett Fruit Company one day, I found Bob Healey in an altercation with an employee named George Melanson, who was complaining about the burden of heavy work, long hours and meagre pay. On that day, long before local union activity, I heard Healy say to George, "We don't tolerate any of that Red element in this warehouse." This was my first appreciation of the Western capitalist's fear of Communism, although from conversations at home, especially with relatives from Russia, I was already familiar with the Cossacks and with Lenin and Trotsky. I knew how people were tricked into exchanging gold for the new currency; they were duped into believing gold coins would no longer have value, despite their intrinsic metal value. I could even sing "God Save the Czar," which I learned in Russian on my father's knee, long before I knew the words to "God Save the King."

By 1933 I had accumulated a few dollars and opened an account at the Bank of Montreal, one of the five banks in town at the time. The others were the Commerce, Royal, Nova Scotia and Provincial. I still have my first passbook, showing interest credited half-yearly at 2 percent. The front of the passbook lists the officers and directors, a virtual Who's Who of the Canadian business élite of the day, including Sir Frederick Williams-Taylor, a Moncton native, as vice-president. The same page boasts of the bank's capital of $36 million and total assets of $750 million, the accumulation of more than a hundred years. Today, the bank's assets probably grow by more than $750 million each month.

Some of my savings from the banana business went to violin lessons. The teacher was a Professor Joseph Surette, who advertised that he was a pupil of Leopold Aeur. In 1934, I bought my own violin, and I still have the receipt: $13.14 for the violin, case, shoulder pad, music stand, rosin and sheet music. Lacking a musical ear, I never distinguished myself as a violinist, but did learn to play a passable Beethoven "Minuet in G" and some of the popular songs of the time, such as "The Isle of Capri." The next year I played in the high-school orchestra—until my father's death. For the eleven months of mourning I was not allowed to listen to music, and I never picked up my treasured violin again.

Surette did not stay long in our community. Shortly after I stopped lessons, he was charged with a homosexual offence under the Criminal Code, allegedly involving a hobo he picked up off a CNR freight train at the station. This was my introduction to homosexuality, which was not a topic of open conversation at that time. The professor left the country before being tried.

Sex was never spoken of freely in those days. Rarely did the word occur in print, let alone in the classroom. Children of seven or eight today probably know more about sex than we did when we were twice their age. Irving Schelew and Myer Mendelson attended *chedar*, or Hebrew classes, with me. When we were about twelve, Irving went to Sydney to visit his relatives, including his Uncle Len, who was only a few years older. On his return Irving told us the facts of life imparted to him by his Uncle Len. Myer shook his head, saying he didn't believe it, that it couldn't be right. This made Irving angry, and he asked what proof Myer had to contradict him. "I have irrefutable proof," Myer said. "The rebbe wouldn't do that."

Myer was born in Lithuania but came to Moncton with his parents as an infant, and he was my closest buddy and confidant during our school years. Though frail after being stricken early in life with tuberculosis, Myer persevered to graduate in medicine and go on to teach psychiatry at the University of Pennsylvania. His textbook on depression is now in use throughout the academic medical world. When Myer died on Christmas Day in 1994, I was honoured to participate with two of his colleagues in delivering the eulogy at his memorial service in Philadelphia.

Myer was always hungry for knowledge. Moncton had a good public library for a small town, with a children's section set apart from the adult section. By the time he was twelve Myer had read every one of the books in the junior section, so the librarian, Bertie Moore, broke the rules to give him adult privileges. It was one of the happiest moments of his young life, as well as mine. In trotting along with him to the adult section, I too entered a new world of books. Myer also wrote short stories, which the rest of us devoured, and plays, in which we performed.

For all its hardships, the Depression was not without its pleasures. For the ten-cent admission to the matinée we kids could get lost in the Wild West and the world of Tom Mix, Ken Maynard and Hoot Gibson. Radio, after breaking from the frustration of crystal sets into the miracle of tubes, entertained us as well.

The first local programming was from a Canadian National Railway station with the call letters CNRA, which broadcast a popular children's hour with the "kiddies' Uncle Steve." Jack Benny was another favourite, and later Kate Smith, the "Songbird of the South"; Burns and Allen; and Fibber Magee and Molly. Later still, the dramas of the incomparable John Drainie kept us enthralled. We listened avidly to comedy programs, especially "The Chase and Sanborn Coffee Hour," starring Eddie Cantor, which came on every Sunday night. At the end of each show Eddie sang his closing song, which always brought us back to reality and the week ahead:

> I love to spend this hour with you
> As friend to friend I'm sorry it's through
> Let's make a date for next Sunday night
> I'm here to state it will be my delight
> To sing again, and bring again, the things you want me to
> I love to spend this hour with you.

Hockey was another happy diversion. By 1934, Moncton had assembled an outstanding hockey machine that won the Allen Cup as the top amateur team in Canada. That summer the team lost its home ice when the Stadium Building was burned to the ground in what was rumoured at the time to be arson as a make-work project. The town was so hockey mad, the rumour went, that the municipality would just have to find the money to rebuild and provide jobs in a bleak employment landscape. The assumption that the city would rebuild was correct. The Moncton Hawks played the 1935 season in a new stadium, winning the Cup again and returning to be greeted by thousands of jubilant fans at the railway station.

Until Miss Fairweather taught us English in Grade 9 in 1935, all of my teachers had been middle-aged. Miss Fairweather was the first who was young and attractive, and at fourteen I had my first crush. I would often sit enraptured in her class. Soon after teaching me, she married, though the kinship must have been mutual for she kept in touch with me, intermittently, throughout the years.

The new Moncton High School had opened in September of that year, and I had to pinch myself to believe it was not a mirage. It was a magnificent building, architecturally and functionally. Its elegant auditorium had an opulence and grandeur not before seen in our town, but worthy of a large, cosmopolitan city.

The general contractor was Ambrose Wheeler, then a builder of most of the major construction in the area. Before the school opened, we sneaked in for a preview, following my brother, the ringleader, who had told us not to worry—he knew Ambrose Wheeler. When we were caught and evicted by a guard, we complained to my brother.

"You said we could go in because you knew Ambrose Wheeler," I said.

"Sure I know him, but he doesn't know me," was the reply.

At the opening ceremony Fred Edgett, the school board chairman who was also the head of Reid Grocery Wholesalers, spoke of how he had been criticized for having the city incur so much debt in such depressed times. His answer to the critics was that the construction provided desperately needed work and came at a time when labour and material costs were at a historical low. How right he was. The cost of the original building was about $450,000. A few years later, the first minor addition cost more than $650,000. Today his contribution is largely forgotten, but I have often thought that a monument should be located somewhere in the school to perpetuate his most valuable contribution.

At first my enjoyment of high school was diminished by my father's deteriorating health and the eleven months we mourned his death. During this time we abstained from entertainment of any kind, including movies and even music on the radio. But the excitement of meeting students from all parts of the city and beyond was a helpful catharsis. And all my teachers were now university graduates, unlike my teachers in grade school, who came out of what we called Normal School.

One of the first teachers to walk into our high-school room was a Miss Hachey, an Acadian lady. She stood in front of her desk, hands folded over a book clasped to her chest, without uttering a word. She then placed the book on the desk and went through a series of motions—picking up the book, opening it, looking at a page, closing the book and throwing it back on the table—and simultaneously described each motion, as follows: *"Je prends le livre; j'ouvre le livre; je tourne la page; je regarde l'image; je ferme le livre; je mets le livre sur la table. Répétez après moi!"* This being our introduction to French, we stumbled along with her. This was her method of instruction throughout the whole term, and by the end of the year she had us all jabbering away in French, reading the French classics, writing short stories and thoroughly enjoying it all. This was all undone by the teachers of French in Grades 10 and 11, who, being English-speaking, concentrated on grammar rather than conversation.

In Grade 11, Muriel Steeves instilled in us an appreciation of the wealth of English literature and the genius of its writers and poets. She was a born teacher, with a smile and low-key approach that soon won over even the most reluctant of students. The same year, the students came up with a nickname for Bernice MacNaughton, the French and geometry teacher: "Chis" MacNaughton, short for "chisel face." She was a high-strung woman whose lover, it was said, had been killed in the First World War. She used to tell us to drive hard to succeed, as she herself had done, but her high-pitched pep talks left me in turmoil, and she is one of the few teachers I do not remember with any great fondness, although she came to be recognized as one of our premier teachers with a school now named after her.

I preferred the softer style of Ethel Murphy, my Grade 11 teacher of history and Latin, who always wore a long shawl around her shoulders and was such a fixture in local education that she was nicknamed Queenie. Latin was anything but a dead language in her classes. She got us to translate Virgil's *Aeneid* into English and the English into Latin, and I still recite *"Arma virumque cano"* with gusto.

Greek was not on the curriculum, but after class Miss Murphy met those of us who were interested in the language, and because of her I thought I would like to become a classical scholar. The financial requirements of years at Oxford or Cambridge was too daunting an obstacle, and I later abandoned the idea for a more practical career.

In testing us in Greek and Roman history, Miss Murphy would often make ties to contemporary life. "What Canadian city might be said by the ancient Greeks to have an Acropolis?" she asked us once. The few of us who answered said Montreal, because we had heard of Mount Royal. Miss Murphy accepted our answer but was disappointed that no one mentioned Halifax and its Citadel Hill. I had never heard of Citadel Hill. In fact, although I was already sixteen years old, I had never been out of New Brunswick. Most kids of my generation did not have much opportunity for travel.

In the Thirties one of the kids at our school was Northrop Frye.

Although he was a few years older, I remember him well from those days. He always rode a bicycle, with his long blond hair blowing in the wind. Other students looked upon Frye as different, if not eccentric.

About fifteen years ago, long after he had become one of Canada's pre-eminent literary critics, I ran into Frye pushing a cart in Ziggy's, the Toronto grocery store near St. Clair Avenue and Yonge Street. I immediately recognized the shock of hair, which by then was a shade of white, and introduced myself. I asked when he had last been down to Moncton and the old homestead on Pine Street. He had been down to bury his mother, he said, and if he never saw the place again it would be too soon.

Moncton was proud of Frye and celebrated him as one of its most illustrious sons. I attributed his apparent distaste for the city to the financial hardship his family suffered during the Depression. But several years after our meeting I read John Ayre's 1989 biography of Frye, in which his Moncton teachers are described as "a rabble of screaming and strapping spinsters." Frye's memory of the quality of Moncton schools was so damning that I felt compelled to write him in protest over what he called his educational "penal servitude." In my letter I pointed out that we had many teachers in common, that by and large they were excellent and that most of them had a profound effect on my life. Surely Frye's biographer had misinterpreted his comments? Frye replied to me in a one-sentence letter: "I stand by what my biographer wrote."

At the time I thought the reason for Frye's boredom in school was that his talented mother tutored him so well that he was always too advanced to gain much value from a classroom. For a child of immigrants, on the other hand, school was an introduction to a novel and exciting world. I was prepared to accept this distinction in our lives until a few years later, when the Université de Moncton persuaded Frye to give a lecture.

The city made quite a fuss over the visit, and the local newspaper carried front-page pictures of Frye at his old residence and at his mother's grave. His lecture was superb, and no one in the large gathering was disappointed. I offered to drive Frye to the airport for his flight back to Toronto, but first I took him to lunch at Cy's. Again I raised the matter of our Moncton teachers and the harsh treatment they and the city itself got in the chapter of his biography called "Moncton Exile."

"What about Muriel Steeves in English?" I asked.

"She was an excellent teacher," Frye said.

And Miss Murphy in history and Latin?

"Outstanding."

Frye was equally effusive about the other teachers we had shared.

"Why then did you let your biographer say all those nasty things about all the Moncton teachers?" I asked.

"We lived for a short time in Sussex before coming to Moncton, and I must have confused the Moncton teachers with the ones in Sussex."

By then Frye's health was visibly failing. He didn't eat more than two ounces of the lobster set before him, and it was painful for me, and to my frugality, to see those dollar bills pitched into the garbage can. On the drive to the airport I asked him about his reception in Moncton.

"They were two of the best days of my life," he said. Within two months he was dead.

In 1938, I graduated *summa cum laude*, the leader in a class of about 150 students. With this achievement came the Governor General's Medal and newspaper headlines, all of which I have kept. Before we graduated, universities stopped requiring students with a grade average of 85 percent or better to write provincial matriculation exams. But there was an Aleta Mae Miller Prize of fifty dollars for the student who led the provincial matriculation exams, and to qualify for the prize I had to write the exams. I wonder how many today would endure a week of examinations for fifty dollars. In 1938, however, this was a formidable prize.

Students from our small Jewish community were the academic leaders of the high school for three years in a row. In recent years many of the leaders have come from more recently arrived immigrant families: Indian, East Asian and other ethnic groups. Jewish pupils have been significantly absent at the top, another illustration of the role that adversity and hardship play in the will to succeed.

The summer of my graduation, recruiters from Acadia University in Wolfville, Nova Scotia, visited me twice to try to persuade me to choose their school, offering me a $200 scholarship the first year. I had not applied to Acadia and was flattered by the attention. Dalhousie University in Halifax, when I applied, offered only $150. But my goal was a Beaverbrook Scholarship at the University of New Brunswick in Fredericton, which was $500 a year for each of the four undergraduate years.

In one of the saddest crises of my young life, I did not get the Beaverbrook Scholarship, although the leaders of the Moncton, Saint John and Fredericton high schools had always been chosen automatically. The winner from Moncton was Murray Stephenson, a good student and somewhere near the top ten in our class. He went on to study medicine at McGill University and for a few years was Lord Beaverbrook's private physician.

My bitterness at being passed over by the Beaverbrook scholarship committee was only assuaged when the university granted me an honorary degree in 1988. On that occasion I told the story of my earlier disappointment and said it was pleasing to know we now lived in a more civilized society, in which a selection committee considered the merit of a student, without bias or prejudice.

When I was rejected for the Beaverbrook, I had a hard choice to make between Acadia and Dalhousie. My heart wanted Acadia, so impressed was I with their emissary and the extra fifty dollars in scholarship money. But my mind voted for Dalhousie, which offered the advantages of a larger city and the opportunity of an affiliated degree. The first year of law school at Dalhousie would be considered as a year of arts, so that I could graduate in six years instead of the usual seven, with degrees in both arts and law. The saving from that one year was the deciding factor.

Although the choice was my own, my mother preferred Dalhousie for motives that she soon put into motion. The local rabbi's wife had a young sister in Halifax, who was married to Rev. Abraham Greenspan. They were both in their twenties, and he was the teacher, *mohel, shochet* and jack-of-all-trades in the Jewish community of Halifax, although I believe he later attained the status of rabbi. My mother arranged to have me stay with the Greenspans. She was now assured that her little boy would be in good hands in Halifax, protected from the dangers and temptations of the big city and provided with kosher meals.

Dalhousie Days

In September, I boarded my first train ever, with a heavy heart, an eight-dollar return ticket and a wardrobe trunk packed with clothes to last me, without the expense of laundering, until Christmas. This was the first time I would be away from home all alone.

The train took almost six hours to cover the 180 miles from Moncton to Halifax, stopping at every small station along the way. When I reached Halifax in the rain, I carried my trunk to a streetcar, which for ten cents took me to Agricola Street, the working-class neighbourhood in the north end where the Greenspans lived.

My first look at my room left me dismayed. It had space enough for a small cot, and a wooden table and chair, although if the chair was pulled out from under the table, it blocked access to the bed. There was no room at all for my trunk, which I had to manoeuvre into a corner in the hallway. I doubt that my pillow was very dry when I woke up the next morning.

If my mother sent me to the Greenspans' home to protect my innocence, it is fortunate she never learned how the reverend rounded out my education. Preparatory to morning prayers on the first day, I wound the phylacteries around my arm and placed one on my forehead, as I had done every day since my bar mitzvah at age 13. Abraham Greenspan came by the door, looked aghast, and asked, *"Potz, was tust du?"* ("Prick, what are you doing?" *Potz* is usually used in a much less pejorative sense than its literal translation, and is applied, at times endearingly, to someone doing something foolish.)

This was my introduction to what was to be a broadening and worldly experience. The first Saturday night after Sabbath, Greenspan took me with him to visit some of his parishioners who operated shops on Gottingen Street. His first call was at Zwerlings, a shoe store.

"How are you?" Greenspan asked Mrs. Zwerling in Yiddish.

"Not too good, rabbi," she replied.

"What is the matter, Mrs. Zwerling?"

"I have lots of headaches, rabbi. I've been to all kinds of doctors, but they can't find a cure for me."

"You know, Mrs. Zwerling, I have a cure for you."

"Yes, yes, yes, rabbi, tell me already your cure."

"If you come to sleep with me, you won't have any more headaches."

Mrs. Zwerling thought this was a great joke. Greenspan was a prankster, whose sense of humour was appreciated by his parishioners and his friends. They knew that he never spoke out of malice, and that he used a light-hearted approach to help relieve people's burdens and tensions.

Sophie Greenspan was kind and helpful and one of the world's worst cooks. After a steady diet of her stringy, overcooked veal chops, I never ate veal or veal chops again. She was also flat-chested, unlike the couple's maid, Annie, who was amply endowed. Greenspan was impressed by the maid's attributes in this regard, but not believing that a woman could be so naturally buxom, he charged me in a jocular fashion with the task of finding out if her *sagdas*, or breasts, were for real. I failed in this responsibility, although I suspect Greenspan was probably more disappointed than I.

Greenspan was among the last of the ritually trained men to leave Poland before the fast-approaching Holocaust, and he had a dedicated and serious side. He sometimes took me down to the docks to meet the ships carrying German refugees, who were not permitted entry into Canada. Passengers were allowed to leave their ship, but only for guarded, wire-caged rooms, where they were confined while the ship took on fuel and supplies. They then set sail in search of a country that might accept refugees.

Greenspan would stay with the refugees until the early morning, offering encouragement and hope, taking addresses for letters he was asked to write, doing whatever he could to try to relieve their anxiety and fears. On one of these visits I met a German lawyer, impeccably dressed and distinguished in manner and speech. The man recited the many countries where he and the other passengers had been denied refuge, and he expressed hope that Venezuela might ultimately prove a haven. I have often wondered if this was the infamous "ship of fools" that, after being forbidden entry around the world, had to return its passengers to Germany and annihilation.

Greenspan was only 29 when I met him, and with his exceptionally good mind he was frustrated he did not have the opportunity to achieve what his talents warranted; he would have made a brilliant surgeon. I have often reflected on the hundreds of thousands like him who perished in Poland and the contributions they could have made to the world. Greenspan ended his career at the Baycrest Centre for Seniors in Toronto, where I am sure he brought comfort to many an older citizen. I had always been a serious kid, but he taught me to temper the responsibilities of life with a lighter side, and for this I am indebted to him always.

The Dalhousie campus was a good two miles from the upper end of Agricola Street, and I walked it at least twice a day. Although Dalhousie was the largest university in the Maritimes, its total enrolment was only about nine hundred, including the professional schools of law, medicine and dentistry. The president was Dr. Carleton Stanley, a tall, imposing man, who invited each first-year student to tea at his home. At my visit, seeing that I was from Moncton, he commented that we had a better public library system there than the one in Halifax, where the Catholic Church's influence vetoed many an important book that it found objectionable. As a young kid of my background, I was somewhat startled, to say the least.

My tuition the first year was $187, and with the entrance scholarship of $150, I had to come up with $37. I have no idea what salary a full-time professor rated in those years, but it had to be minuscule by today's standards. Dalhousie's professors, however, were mostly top-rate academics in their fields. I studied philosophy under Dr. H.L. Stewart, who was well known at the time as a regular public-affairs commentator on national radio.

Professor R.A. McKay, who taught political science, had been a member of the Rowell–Sirois royal commission, set up by the federal government of the day to make recommendations on the division of federal and provincial powers under the British North America Act. The report, which we were obliged to study, came in three huge volumes bound in red covers. Even then, the conflict between Ottawa and the provinces was a burning issue, but it was relegated to the back burner by the outbreak of war in 1939. The commission's volumes were left to gather dust and were to be overtaken decades later by more severe strains on the body politic, with renewed battles over the division of powers. McKay's son, Andy, was later the president of Dalhousie, after serving as dean of law, and now sits on the Federal Court of Canada.

Professor Burns Martin taught English 1, and it was to him that I confided my concerns and fears after meeting the refugees and learning of their desperation. Martin told me I was too young to carry the burdens of the world on my shoulders, but this did not console me. He organized a class in Gaelic, and a small group of us who were interested met after classes, bought Gaelic grammars and had a great time trying to master the language. A Reverend Nicholson, a Cape Bretoner, fluent in the language, would come to help us with pronunciation, and we had great times in this class, which, of course, was a non-credit labour of love. I felt a special affinity for the language, with its guttural "ch" similar to the Hebrew.

Professor Nickerson taught chemistry, in what was the largest lecture room on the campus. Called the "chem theatre," it had a large scroll on the front wall with Mendeleef's table of the elements. It served too as the classroom where C.L. Bennet, a New Zealander, who was also registrar, taught English 2 in his own fashion. It was in this class, with a required weekly essay, that I was trained to write in a cogent and precise manner.

George Wilson was the dean of arts and science and a figure that looms large in my mind's eye. He had the physique of a wrestler but the disposition of an avuncular saint, a sensitivity and humanity that seemed incongruous with his physical proportions. He taught history with a benign smile and a twinkle in his eyes that made his classes a treat. He was also a pacifist who had stood firm in his refusal to bear arms. Occasionally he would invite me to his home on Morris Street to listen to a new classical record he'd just acquired.

When Wilson retired, he moved back to his native Ontario. Shortly before his death he wrote about his life in *All for Nothing*, one of the saddest books I have ever read. In it Wilson described his strict Presbyterian background, his struggle to conquer the physical urges that reduced man to the animalistic world, his life's complete futility and lack of purpose. I found it depressing that a man who had influenced so many young lives, and in many remarkable ways, could have ended a most useful life in such abject pessimism. Had I been privileged to speak with him in those last sad years of his life, I would have reminded him of the words that Henry Adams wrote in his book *The Education of Henry Adams*: "A teacher affects eternity: he can never tell where his influence stops."

Economics, taught by Professor Russell Maxwell, was my introduction to Adam Smith and *The Wealth of Nations*, and it spurred me on to take two courses in advanced economics, including one from Stewart Bates, who later headed the Central Mortgage and Housing Corporation. I also took two years of Latin, always one of my favourite subjects, from R.E.D. Cattley, who had just come from the University of New Brunswick. We read the odes and epodes of Catullus and learned that dirty old men existed even in the Roman poets of that day.

A few weeks after I started university, I spent an evening with Bill Gefter, a commercial traveller from Moncton who was staying at the old Queen Hotel in downtown Halifax. On my way back to Agricola Street at about eleven o'clock, I cut through the red-light district on Brunswick Street, where a hard-looking brunette was sticking her head out a ground-floor window.

"You vant to have good time—no?" she said in broken English as I walked by. I ran as fast as I could, yelling "No," but I have often wondered what might have happened if she had taken a course in positive thinking and asked, "You vant to have good time—yes?"

That same night twenty-eight people died and dozens of others were horribly injured when the Queen Hotel burned to the ground. Bill Gefter survived but was blackened from head to toe. He was never the same again and died a few years later.

In Moncton, I had coasted along in school and with only a little effort was always at the head of the class. At the end of my first semester at Dalhousie, I was surprised to find I was not the leader in any of my courses and realized with a jolt that I was now up against the bright students from all over the region. With more diligent application, I reversed the situation in the next semester. I learned early to respect and never to underestimate the competition.

For my second year at university I was determined not to stay with the Greenspans. The thought of that long walk was discouraging, but the prospect of another year of those veal chops was a complete deterrent. A few of the boys belonging to the Jewish fraternity, Tau Epsilon Phi, rented a house on Dresden Row, a short walk from campus. I joined this parade and stayed for several months.

The war had just started, and things were tightening up in Halifax. The fraternity house had no cook, and in the beginning most of us ate at a nearby boardinghouse run by a Mrs. Meikle. The food was atrocious—a slice of meat loaf or Spam for lunch—and since I was trying to observe the dietary laws, I usually left everything on my plate. Bread and butter, and the odd care package from home, sustained me. When they had a few extra shekels, some of the fellows would eat at a restaurant. A favourite eating spot was the Cameo on Spring Garden Road, a good and popular restaurant run by a Greek.

One student became friendly with Myrtle, the head waitress at the Cameo, who soon came to be a frequent visitor at the frat house, often being entertained in her boyfriend's bedroom. This liaison was a bonanza for all the boys in the house, who would order the top items on the Cameo menu— steaks, lobster, the finest of desserts—and get a bill for only fifteen or twenty cents. Still tied to my kosher principles, I could not enjoy these advantages to the full and was limited to fish with scales and egg dishes. This arrangement went on for weeks but was too good to last. The Greek proprietor finally caught on, fired Myrtle and kicked the boys out of the restaurant.

I did not dare patronize the Cameo for the rest of my school years. But about thirty-five years later, as a middle-aged and successful professional, I flew into Halifax late one night for a meeting and, needing dinner, summoned up enough courage to try the Cameo. With shoulders back, I bravely entered the restaurant, ordered a meal and ate, all the time looking over my shoulder, expecting to see the old owner rushing at me with a knife.

While the Cameo feasting was at its height, the boys looked for other fields to conquer. They occasionally used the services of a Chinese laundry around the corner. The young woman who tended the counter lacked the physical attributes of Myrtle, but it was felt that if someone could be persuaded to court her, we could have it made in laundry services as well. Not being able to find a volunteer, it was decided to draw lots. The lot fell to a student from Saint John, who unflinchingly did his duty. Never were the boys of the frat house kept so clean, at least until the boy from Saint John abandoned his responsibility. I was still saving up my laundry to be done at home and was not involved.

When the frat house was not filled, rooms were rented to navy personnel, who by the end of 1939 had been moved to Halifax by the thousands from all parts of Canada. A young man from Belleville, Ontario, who was assigned to ships' stores, often returned to the house with steaks and other delicacies, all rare treats in rationed, wartime Halifax. The goodies were intermittent, however, since the man was often away at sea for weeks. Once, after a prolonged absence, he banged on the door and woke us all up in the middle of the night. He was a pitiful sight, having been rescued from the waters of the hostile Atlantic after his ship was torpedoed.

One of the problems that came quickly to the fore at the frat house was the use of the bathroom facilities in the morning. There were ten or twelve of us, and a single, tiny bathroom. At first there was utter chaos in the mornings, with many a frustrated student standing impatiently in line and worrying about getting to classes on time. Something had to be done and fast, forcing our little society to organize along democratic principles. A schedule was agreed upon, assigning a fifteen-minute time slot to each roomer. A disciplinary committee was appointed to deal with infractions and hand out punishment. Fines were levied, based upon the time overstayed. So, even in such an elementary group association, it was quickly evident that the rule of law was needed to govern human conduct and to promote a civilized society. How much more so would this be the case in society at large.

When the housekeeping at the frat house became intolerable to my fastidious and queasy temperament, I looked around for an alternative and settled on Mrs. Shofer, a Jewish woman who had operated a large boardinghouse in Halifax for years and was well known for her kosher cuisine. The house at 34 Morris Street had been the residence of choice for many Jewish students from all over the Maritimes, particularly those from Cape Breton, but I had always resisted because of financial constraints. In my desperation for clean towels and sheets, and for a full meal I could eat while still maintaining my religious scruples, I threw financial caution to the wind and decided to move in. To bring the cost down I arranged to share a room at Mrs. Shofer's with two other students.

Mrs. Shofer was a sweet woman, with a heart so big it required her large body to encompass it. The house, now the Haliburton House Hotel, was almost at the waterfront end of Morris Street, which runs all the way to the university. The plumbing was antiquated, but such deficiencies didn't matter; they were compensated for many times by the overflowing bounty of the dinner table. Every Monday morning Abraham Greenspan arrived to ritually slaughter fifty chickens in the basement, which were plucked by the houseboy, named Ray. Chicken in various appetizing forms was served almost every day, and always with copious bowls of vegetables and a variety of desserts, fruit and pastries.

Mrs. Shofer was the hardest, most tireless working person I had ever encountered—up in the dark hours of the morning and still at it late at night, always with a genuine, maternal smile and a concern for all her "boys." A generation of college kids passed through her portals, and she followed their careers as they went on to law, medicine, dentistry, business and government, delighting in their achievements in a manner akin to a mother's pride.

With money accumulated by her sweat and toil, Mrs. Shofer and her husband bought small rental properties and over the years began to enjoy a comfortable investment income. She eventually gave up her hard labour and moved to a private residence on Tower Road. In the meantime I had become something of a favourite, perhaps because I could talk to her in Yiddish. When Mrs. Shofer became upset over troubles with the Income Tax Department, a new experience in her life, I suggested she get in touch with Charles Gavsie, one of her star boarders of years gone by. But Mrs. Shofer told me she had already talked to Gavsie, a Cape Bretoner who was then the deputy minister of finance. *"Uz der government darf auch machan a leben,"* she said. ("He told me that the government also has to make a living.")

Mrs. Shofer would slip me special delicacies that the other boarders would not see, including strawberries when they were out of season and expensive. She insisted I live with her for the rest of my college years, and when she came to my graduation, she was probably bursting with more pride than my own mother. Later I suggested my young wife get some of Mrs. Shofer's recipes, particularly for cabbage rolls. I was somewhat deflated when my wife returned after a visit to Halifax with the news that the base for the fabulous sauce for Mrs. Shofer's cabbage rolls was Heinz tomato ketchup.

The Shofer residence was affectionately named Shofer Hall by the college crowd. It was almost an adjunct to the university, which at that time had no men's residence, although a fine women's residence, Shirreff Hall, was built through the efforts of one of its distinguished graduates, R.B. Bennett. Other boarders, not only college students, were accommodated from time to time, among them two rabbis. Rabbi Kessler, a North American-born military chaplain, was a tall, broad-shouldered man and most handsome in his officer's uniform. With his perfect English diction Kessler was quite a contrast to the physically lesser specimens, the Europeans with broken English, who had comprised my experience, and I was quite impressed with him as a representative of the rabbinate.

Rabbi Phil Berger, from Toronto, was only about twenty-five and recently ordained. He was hired by the local synagogue, and being little older than the rest of us, he joined in many of our activities. One of these was the odd game of blackjack in our rooms. Whether he had the Lord on his side or was highly practised in the art, Berger invariably relieved us of our meagre spending allowances, so that even the rare treat of a trip to the movies became a casualty. In the end, however, he must have been more adept at blackjack than in his rabbinical talents, for his incumbency was short-lived, forcing him to move on.

During my undergraduate years I earned a few welcome dollars by writing essays for both the O.E. Smith and Halifax Overseas prizes. These were awarded annually in the amounts of fifty and one hundred dollars for essays on topical matters of the day. A student who won theses prizes once was not eligible to enter again, so after my initial success I was reduced to submitting my work under the names of fellow students, with whom I had to share the proceeds. But even these depreciated amounts helped substantially to improve the quality of my student life, and proved the truth of the old adage that half a loaf is better than none.

The Dalhousie Law School was stuck in a corner of the antiquated Forrest Building, which also housed medicine and dentistry, and was not too far removed from the morgue, where the bodies were kept for anatomy classes. It had three classrooms, one for each year of instruction. The tables and benches, even under many coats of black paint, were so riddled with the initials of generations past that it was almost impossible to write on them without a stiff underpad. This hallowed law school, the first in Canada and steeped in tradition, had a faculty consisting of a dean and two full-time professors, who taught most of the basic courses. Downtown lawyers and a few judges volunteered for the rest.

The dean, Vince MacDonald, soon went off to be an aide to Angus L. Macdonald, who was serving in Ottawa as a part of the naval war effort. For two years we had only two full-time instructors. But there were only ten in our class—most young men were in the services—and that number included two women, Lorraine Johnston of Vancouver and Mary Kinley of Lunenburg, Nova Scotia. The eight men were all physical rejects from the army or academically deferred. I was in the former category.

When I got my call-up notice, I did not seek academic deferral but presented myself for the required medical examination before three doctors. All my youth I suffered with recurring nasal polyps that had to be snipped out with wire snares three or four times a year. When I was examined for military service, not only were the polyps inflamed, but a condition called extreme tachycardia also showed up. I was rejected for service as a Category E, the lowest physical rating. The nasal polyps have been an affliction to this day, but the tachycardia was never a serious problem, except when life insurance examinations sought to rate my premiums because of it.

The Canadian Officers Training Corps, or COTC, was an alternative to military service and was a rugged regimen under an extremely tough sergeant-major named Hogan. During strenuous marches the boys stepped stalwartly, singing:

> Our sergeant-major has an awful dose of clap
> Our sergeant-major has an awful dose of clap
> Our sergeant-major has an awful dose of clap
> Yes he has, like a pig's asshole.

Only God could help anyone caught singing the tune when Hogan was within earshot, but I still sometimes find myself humming it to aid a brisk walk.

During physical training I experienced great difficulty with many of the exercises, which most of the other fellows seemed to accomplish with ease. Most trying for me was vaulting over the leather horse. I invariably held up the line, either stopping dead on reaching the horse or, on the rare occasion when I was able to propel myself into the air, falling down on the horse, with a painful jolt to certain vital male parts. The gym instructor was a Scandinavian with a thick accent, and he would try to encourage me by yelling, "Come on Coon, come on Coon." My Latin professor, Major Cattley, who also taught military practice and theory, said that I excelled on the written tests, but he doubted I could ever make much of a physical soldier.

Despite my lack of prowess in most sports, I did have an interest in boxing, as incongruous as this may seem. I even joined the university boxing team, only to be knocked out cold in the first round of my first bout. That ended my boxing career. While today I have no interest in watching a hockey, football or baseball game, I will try to watch a good boxing match. A top boxer is like a well-oiled machine and requires a skill bordering on the realm of science. He also has to rely completely on his own talent and judgment; no teammates are there to help or blame.

John Willis and George Curtis were our two professors. John, who became acting dean, was a small, wiry Englishman with only a bachelor of arts in law from Oxford University. But he was the most eminent legal teacher ever to bless our shores, a testimonial endorsed by every lawyer in Canada who was privileged to study under him. He quickly became my mentor. In our first year John taught the history of English law, and as a background for the study of the common law his course was an essential and fundamental grounding. He taught his class with such enthusiasm for his subject that he literally bobbed up and down in his chair. His excitement was contagious.

John could make the dullest of legal tenets vital and challenging. He spoke of what he called the myth of Magna Carta, which was always taken to be the great charter of English liberties, when in reality it was only the favoured few of the gentry who were able to wrest privileges from King Richard at Runnymede in 1215. It would be more than six hundred years before slavery was abolished by the British parliament. But John likened this to Christianity; if the myth of the virgin birth were to be disproved, its impact on the Christian faith would be in no way diminished. Myth could sometimes be more potent in history than fact, a somewhat startling, liberal concept for someone of my background.

John Willis was the author of many learned treatises in the law, and his opinion was sought after by members of the bench and bar. He would become infuriated when the reputation and legend of the school were equated with the large number of graduates who dominated the top political offices of the country, rather than with the eminent lawyers and judges that the school spawned. After he retired, he wrote a definitive history of the Dalhousie Law School. His influence on me I can never fully acknowledge.

So widespread is the school's political reputation that Pierre Trudeau, when he was prime minister and received an honorary degree, made a cute comment in his convocation address. It was remarkable, Trudeau said, that he had achieved what he had in political life without being a graduate of Dalhousie Law School. John would say that the purpose of a great law school was not to turn out political stars but to provide lawyers who practised in communities such as Musquodoboit, Nova Scotia, and who never earned more than $1,500 a year but could draw a damn good five-dollar deed.

Prior to his death in the summer of 1997, John lived in a rest home in Nova Scotia and was so frail that he refused to see people. I did not hear from him directly for decades, although word reached me indirectly that he was disappointed my career had taken a direction away from the academic legal path he had hoped for me. I did hear from him at the time of my appointment as chancellor at Dalhousie University in 1990. On the afternoon of the announcement I walked to my office to check the personal mail, and among the letters of congratulations was one written by hand, which I immediately recognized, even after half a century, as the handwriting of John Willis. In the solitude of my office I read the letter and sat motionless for a good five minutes, overcome by emotion and flashes of nostalgia for a simpler, happier time. The short note said:

Dear Reuben—I see by the Dalhousie alumni magazine that you are to be the new chancellor. I am glad, both for you and the university. As one of your teachers at the law school around 1940, I remember how fond I was of you and your "values." I know you have made a great success of your life and become a financial wizard, but to me you will always be the quiet "scholarly" boy I knew and admired in those long ago days. John Willis.

George Curtis, the only other full-time lecturer, left Dalhousie soon after my graduation to be the founding dean of the University of British Columbia Law School. Having to start from scratch, he wrote me for my course notebooks, which I was happy to send, although I felt sorry for those law students in the first years of that new school who may have been weaned on my notes.

The UBC law school recently celebrated the fiftieth year of its founding, and George, now of course in retirement, was suitably acknowledged and feted on the occasion. When I visited, as chancellor, a Vancouver alumni meeting, George and I met after fifty years, and for me it was an emotional embrace, as I am sure it was for him.

The downtown Halifax lawyers who came in to fill the teaching gaps did an admirable job. A member of the judiciary, Judge Doull, taught evidence. Gordon Cowan, who later became a chief justice of the Nova Scotia Supreme Court, taught contracts, and was an excellent lecturer, always extremely well prepared. Art Patillo taught the law of agency, and after a distinguished legal career served as head of the Ontario Securities Commission. During his tenure I had a small matter to bring before the Commission, so I made an appointment to see Art in Toronto. Not having met since his teaching days, we had a pleasant time reminiscing, after which I asked for a date for a hearing.

"You've had it," he said.

Somewhat flustered for the moment, I did not fully appreciate the import of his words.

"I accept unequivocally the undertaking of a Dalhousie Law School graduate, and all the more so if he has been one of my former pupils."

In 1943 the law school was privileged to have a visit from R.B. Bennett, who was by then Viscount Bennett of Hopewell. In the old Forrest Building, Bennett appeared wistful as he examined the tabletop in which, as a student decades earlier, he had carved his initials, still visible under the layers of black paint. At four o'clock, students from all three years of the law school assembled in a classroom and Bennett addressed us for a full two hours, speaking uninterrupted to a spellbound audience.

Bennett was a huge man, well over six feet, and impressive in stature as well as in speech. He told us how he had tried to initiate much of the social legislation that was later to transform the country into a gentler society. This included unemployment insurance legislation, which was held by the courts to be *ultra vires*, or beyond the powers of the federal government without the consent of the provinces. The 1935 Statutes of Canada, about the thickest of all federal annual volumes, bore testimony, Bennett felt, to the many legislative changes he tried to obtain. He was hurt at being branded in Canada as having personal responsibility for a worldwide depression. His rejection in the election of 1935 caused him such anguish that he moved to England. Bennett provided two of the most enthralling hours of my entire university years.

R.M. Fielding taught criminal law. He was a Crown prosecutor and also the son of a former federal cabinet minister. An aging bachelor, one day he announced that his next lecture would be dealing with rape, and suggested that two ladies in the class avoid the lecture as they might find the topic embarrassing—though I'm sure the old bachelor was more concerned about his own embarrassment than that of the two ladies, who accommodated him by duly absenting themselves.

Austin Parsons, the son of a Newfoundland lawyer, was an exceptionally hard-working student and probably the best legal mind in the class. I was able to beat Austie from time to time, because I was better at anticipating the questions on the examinations than he was. He was very proper and straightlaced, almost a Milquetoast in temperament. When Austie missed a lecture one day to attend a blood donor clinic, he borrowed the notes taken by Mary Kinley, the neatest note-taker in the class. I sat opposite him in the library as he wrote them out, and when he finished I saw his neck and face turn red. Concerned because of his blood donation earlier in the day, I asked him if he felt all right. Austie then showed me the last page of Mary's notebook, on which she had written, "Love is the shortest distance between twin beds—it's a quick jump over, but a long, hard drag back."

"And I thought Miss Kinley was such a nice girl," he said.

Mary and I laughed over this at the time and recalled it with affection on the rare occasions when we met later in life.

In law school Austie often spoke of getting a large neon sign for his law office—"Privy Council cases given special attention"—and of the title he would take when honoured by the King for his legal contribution: "Baron Parson of Twillingate." He went back to Newfoundland, but his dreams were unfulfilled; he spent most of his career as a legislative draftsman in the Newfoundland civil service, and passed away at an early age. In any event, it was only a few years after our graduation that civil appeals to the Privy Council in England were abolished, leaving the Supreme Court of Canada as the final arbiter for legal argument.

Bill Lawrence, a classmate from the Annapolis Valley, injured his back in an automobile accident and completed law school in a wheelchair, and the boys had to carry him up and down the steps of the Forrest Building. Our graduation banquet in 1944 was held at the Lord Nelson Hotel, and some of the students, including Bill, started celebrating early and were well oiled by the time of the dinner. When a plate of roast beef, gravy and vegetables was set in front of Bill, he uncapped a bottle of ketchup and, pounding the bottom to get it running, emptied half the bottle on his plate. Then he passed out, his face falling flat into the plate, where it remained for most of the dinner.

The chief justice, Sir Joseph Chisholm, was a patrician-looking gentleman, who was just beginning to respond to the toast to the bench when Bill came to. Bill raised his head groggily from the plate, and with ketchup, gravy and vegetables running down his face and his white shirt, he bellowed, "Is that old bastard going to talk all night?"

Perhaps this was not the most auspicious way to start a legal career, but I am told that Bill went on to have a very successful practice. Years of practice on the bench would have immunized the Chief Justice against being provoked by human frailties, and he scarcely raised an eyebrow over the interruption. Chisholm would have been one of the last sitting members of the judiciary with a knighthood, since titles for Canadian citizens were abolished in the early Thirties.

One night in my final year, another fellow student, R.T. Vaughan, asked me to join him downtown for dinner at the Carleton Hotel dining room. Arkie, as he was nicknamed, ordered the roast beef dinner for seventy-five cents. I was still adhering to the dietary laws, so I ordered my traditional fruit plate. But when Arkie's sizzling dinner arrived, it looked so appetizing and its smell was so tempting that in a moment of weakness I sent back my untouched fruit and ordered the roast beef.

Never has roast beef tasted so good, nor seventy-five cents provided such value. I waited for the thunderbolt to come down from heaven to strike me dead, and when this did not happen, I was soon well on my way to heathendom. Arkie went on to spend most of his career as counsel with Air Canada; but I am indebted to him for my fall from grace at the age of 20.

CHAPTER 3

An Office on Main Street

When I arrived in Fredericton the night before the New Brunswick bar examinations, I could not find a hotel room and tried to sleep, in my street clothes, on a sofa in the lobby of the old Queen Hotel. In the morning I washed up in the public lavatory as best I could, and duly presented myself for the first morning exam.

It was not an ideal preparation for these oral and written exams, but I completed them successfully and was admitted to the bar in December 1944. My notarial certificate is printed on parchment, with the name of Edward VIII as the reigning monarch crossed out and George VI written in by hand. Eight years after Edward's abdication for the woman he loved, the government of New Brunswick was still using up old certificates. I wonder if governments would be so frugal today.

I had graduated from Dalhousie that spring, taking the top prizes in many of my courses. Now it was time to find a place to practise. The Moncton legal office of Roscoe Allen, where I had articled, had been dissolved after Roscoe's serious liquor problem led to his disbarment. After applying at a couple of other offices without success, at the suggestion of John Willis I tried the federal Income Tax Department, which agreed to hire me in the prosecution branch at the princely sum of $3,200 a year. The job, however, required admission to the Ontario bar, whose $1,500 entrance fee was beyond my reach, as the Department offered no financial assistance.

Having wasted more than half a year, I determined to brave it on my own in Moncton, although many people advised me this was financially foolhardy. Premises were hard to find, and I lost another six months waiting for an office in a Main Street building that was being renovated. With the barest of furniture and equipment, stationery, a telephone and a sign, I moved into the small two-room office before the building was finished. In January 1946, I opened for business.

The first week was bitterly cold, and the special curved windows for the Belgium Glove and Hosiery Shop that was to occupy the ground floor had not yet been installed. Since I was directly above this window area, then wide open to the elements, thick frost came through the hardwood floors of my office, turning them into a virtual sheet of ice. I had sprung for the luxury of a beautiful three-hundred-dollar carpet under my desk, which froze solidly to the floor. With the heating system inadequate for the weather and the office unfit for human habitation, I ran down to Eaton's to buy an electric reflector heater for seven dollars.

For almost three weeks before the weather moderated, I sat huddled over the heater, waiting for the telephone to ring or for someone to come to the door. When the phone finally did ring and I picked it up with racing heart, it was a life insurance salesman, Jordan Smith, wanting to talk about insurance planning. Though discouraged, I did eventually see him. I could afford no premiums at the time, but Smith became a friend, and Maritime Life, which he represented, came to play a special part in my career.

During these weeks of quiet dejection I suffered many misgivings and much despair over my choice of law as a livelihood, and at times I regretted that I did not take the advice of the young practising lawyers in Halifax who tried to dissuade me from a legal career. Medicine, they had told me, afforded a much better opportunity. I conjured up visions of summers during the Depression, when I would watch lawyers standing on the sidewalk outside their offices, their shirtsleeves rolled up in the heat. There they would wait for a client to come by to have a deed drawn for a dollar, hoping the same client had not been intercepted by a justice of the peace offering the service for fifty cents. An awful lot of thoughts and memories go through an idle and troubled mind.

I always promised myself I would preserve under glass the first dollar I earned in law. In my fourth week, a client consulted me on a domestic matter. My charge was five dollars, and I still have that first five-dollar bill. It's dated January 2, 1937, and bears a picture of a youthful George VI and the signatures of G.F. Towers, governor of the Bank of Canada, and D. Gordon, the deputy governor. For whatever reason, the client never came back to me for the divorce, and to my chagrin I later saw it going through another law firm. But I hold the man no malice and think of him only fondly.

A few months later a startling event occurred when I arranged an appointment for what was to be my first incorporation and asked Avard Marven, a young chartered accountant with Lee and Martin, to be present. The client, an older man, walked into my office with two young members of his family, and as I rose to introduce him to Avard, the client dropped dead in front of my desk. It made for a distressing afternoon as we called the undertaker and had the body removed.

Avard was just starting out as well, and we hoped this was not a portent of events to come. Thankfully for us both, it wasn't.

A young lawyer could not have started practice at a more propitious time. With the war just ended, the economy was ready to burst out. The returning military personnel needed homes, and construction boomed in all areas—residential, commercial and industrial. When I was admitted to the bar, I was number thirty-two on the roster of Moncton lawyers. Today there are more than 200, and although they serve a much larger population, they enjoy a smaller volume of legal business, certainly on a per capita basis.

I quickly built up an active practice in almost every branch of law, working long and hard hours, but very satisfying ones. An early client was Byron Dobson, a young farmer and lumberman, who had a vision of developing his father's old farm, across the Petitcodiac River in Albert County, into a housing subdivision. I drafted the first newspaper advertisement to initiate the sale of three-bedroom houses at $6,800, or $7,200 with fireplaces. The ad spoke of cool suburban summers with all the amenities of city living. The area, then mostly rural, is now a thriving community of about twenty thousand. Byron was a man of impeccable integrity and generosity, and the town of Riverview would do itself proud to erect a monument in honour of its founder.

Two young men incorporated a real estate arm to handle the sales of Riverview houses: Claude Taylor, a former schoolteacher, and Blair Steeves, a barber. While agreeing on business, they differed on politics, the one being a Conservative and the other a Liberal. Byron also caught the political bug but adhered to the CCF, the forerunner of the New Democratic Party.

During a provincial campaign in the late Forties, each man—Byron and Claude as candidates and Steeves as a Liberal party worker—came to me for help drafting his campaign orations for radio, which I confess I accomplished with more than a moderate degree of versatility. Byron never made it, since it was hopeless to run on a socialist ticket in his Albert County constituency. Claude lost that round but won in the next election and became minister of education in the Conservative government of Hugh John Flemming.

After coping initially with temporary stenographic help and feeling the need for a full-time secretary whom I could train, I called Don Cooke at Success Business College and asked him to send me his best graduate. Norma Pippey was in her teens when she came to my office, but with a good Newfoundland background she had to be reliable. In those early years, whenever I needed a certain document, Norma looked on as I searched the books for the required information. This valuable training was rarely available to a young secretary, and Norma eventually learned to gather the information with the adeptness of many a lawyer and much more than some. Countless young lawyers sought her assistance over the years, particularly in matters of conveyancing, and she always gave it graciously. In time Norma was billing hundreds of thousands of dollars a year without my having to glance at her work. Nearly any weekend or holiday, morning or afternoon, that I happened to drop into the office, I would find her diligently working away at her desk. When, after forty-two years, she reluctantly accepted retirement, I worried for a time about her ability to adapt to a life of leisure, but her good old Newfoundland genes soon proved I need not have been concerned.

An early visitor to my office was an Englishman named Winston Aitcheson, a law book salesman with Butterworth and Company who told intriguing stories of the lawyers he met during sales trips throughout the British Commonwealth. Even the young Mahatma Gandhi, when he was practising in South Africa, bought Butterworth law books, on credit, from Aitcheson. I was offered a complete library of Butterworth publications, including the full set of essential Halsbury's *Laws of England*—thousands of dollars' worth of books—with a lifetime to pay, in monthly instalments over fifty years. This was an opportunity I could not turn down, and I soon enjoyed a respectable working library.

The curtains for my first office were made by the wife of a crusty character named Merle Densmore, a janitor at the Bank of Montreal. The Densmores lived in cramped quarters above the banking floor, and after every snowfall Merle was up shovelling before sunrise, so that the entrance to the bank was immaculately clean before opening hours.

Densmore also served as the bank messenger, delivering, among other items, bank drafts to business offices. Demand for payment by draft was a popular form of mercantile practice then, but it seems to have fallen into almost complete disuse today. Once when Densmore delivered a draft to my office, he confided that in all their years of marriage he and his wife had never been to a movie. Knowing how carefully they counted their pennies, I invited them to be my guests at a movie. Densmore appeared excited about the prospect, but he called the next day to decline. Curious, I pried the reason from him. He did not wish to appear ungrateful, he finally said, but he and his wife decided they could not accept my invitation for fear they might like the movie so much they would want to go back.

Greg Bridges, a senior lawyer in the community, worked just across the street from me, and I often ran to him for legal advice or documentary assistance. Greg had been a soldier in the First World War, never rising above the rank of private, and later was elected mayor of Moncton. When General Dwight D. Eisenhower, then commander in chief of all Allied forces in the Second World War, passed through the Moncton railway station, Greg, as mayor, officially greeted him at the platform. Political office had certainly enhanced the stature of a lowly private.

Greg's brother Frank, a lawyer from Campbellton, New Brunswick, was the federal minister of fisheries in Mackenzie King's Cabinet but died in office when only in his mid-forties. King called John McNair, the Liberal premier of New Brunswick at the time, for advice about a replacement for Frank. "Why don't you try to get Greg?" McNair suggested, whereupon King called Milton F. Gregg, a First World War hero and a recipient of the Victoria Cross, then serving as president of the University of New Brunswick. And that, according to Greg Bridges, was how he mistakenly got passed over for political office and Milton Gregg became a federal cabinet minister.

Greg eventually became chief justice of the New Brunswick Court of Appeal. His appointment to the bench soon after Milton Gregg joined the Cabinet was not, I believe, an attempt to make amends for the confusion in names but a recognition of Greg's integrity and dedication to the law. On the day of his appointment he invited me to dinner but apologized profusely on learning that his wife, Jessie, was serving roast ham. I assured him that there was no problem; I had long since fallen from grace.

Tuttle T. Goodwin, an old-time lawyer, was clerk of the New Brunswick Supreme Court, but he became ill and asked me to fill in. For more than a year I served as acting clerk, which brought me into contact with many of the litigation lawyers throughout the province. A drawback of taking your law course at a school outside your home province is that, once back home, you do not have ready contact with the lawyers and judges who were at school with you or participated in your instruction.

Tuttle T., as he was generally called, sold his Queen Hotel, a second-rate hostelry in Moncton, to Gordie Carr, who ran a similar small hotel in Sydney. Gordie, a young man from Hamilton, Ontario, was extremely personable, with a taste for high living, fancy cars and custom-made suits from Cy Mann in Toronto. When Gordie drank, which was often, he was an absolute terror. He got into scrape after scrape, and I defended him under countless sections of the Criminal Code. With his cherubic face and nimble defences, he always got off.

One night Gordie ran into some people alongside a stalled car and nearly killed them. He was charged with dangerous driving and leaving the scene of an accident. His defence was that he was coming from Sydney with more than twenty thousand dollars in cash from a property sale, and that when he encountered the stalled car, he was afraid he was being held up. The judge bought the story. With each episode I sent Gordie a bigger bill, hoping to discourage him and his habits, but it didn't work. The cheque for payment was always in the next mail, a scrape always around the next corner. Gordie was only 36 when he died. Had he lived and stayed in the area, I would surely have become the top criminal lawyer in the country.

One of my interesting early victories involved Rev. Henri Lanctin, a Huguenot who had come from France to work with the Grande Ligne Mission in Quebec, an organization that tried to convert French-speaking Catholics to Protestantism. In due course Henri was sent down to New Brunswick to open a branch of the mission in Moncton. Finding lots of support, particularly in the strong Baptist community, he broke away from the Grande Ligne Mission to form an independent church to proselytize Acadians. He called the church La Bonne Nouvelle (The Good News), and it became part of the Maritime Baptist Convention.

Among Henri's strongest supporters was Victoria A. Mullans, who died and left a substantial bequest in her will to "the Grande Ligne Mission, at the city of Moncton branch." At the time the will was made, this branch existed, but at the time of Mullans's death its work had been taken over by Henri's new church. An application was made to the Chancery Court, which was then a separate entity, for an interpretation of the will.

Acting for the Grande Ligne Mission was Thomas Babbitt Parlee, who claimed that the money should go to the Mission and argued that the "city of Moncton branch" was simply the place it was designated to be paid. George T. Mitton, representing the First Baptist Church, the residuary legatee, argued that the gift failed for uncertainty and therefore should fall into the residue and go to the First Baptist Church. Acting for Henri, I argued the application of the *cy-près* doctrine.

This old English doctrine, devolved from French law, holds that when a will contains a charitable bequest which, because of changed circumstances, cannot be fulfilled at the time of the testator's death, the court shall apply the bequest in a manner "as near as possible" to the general intentions of the deceased. The presiding judge allowed me to bring in witnesses to testify to Mullans's interest in the work of Henri Lanctin—parol evidence that offended all the rules I had been rigorously taught in law school. The judge found in Lanctin's favour, but I held my breath until the appeal period expired. An appeal court, I felt, could well have disallowed a good deal of the evidence and found for the Mission.

New cars had just come back onto the market in 1946, civilian car production having been completely curtailed during the war. Thanks to Henri Lanctin, I bought my first new car, a beautiful Ford coupe, for nine hundred dollars.

A rather unusual application of the *cy-près* doctrine occurred in Nova Scotia a few years later, according to my old friend Henry Hicks. Rebecca Cohn, an immigrant Jewish woman, lived on Brunswick Street in Halifax in the most modest of circumstances and living standards. However, she accumulated a respectable estate, and at the time of her death her will was probated in the half-million-dollar range. She wanted her money used to found a home for orphan Jewish girls in her native town in Poland. At the time the will was made, this community existed, but by the time Cohn died, the Nazi ravages had wiped out the Jewish population.

Since circumstances had frustrated Cohn's original intention, the money could be applied, under the *cy-près* doctrine, to the nearest thing possible, perhaps to found a home for homeless refugee girls in Israel. But Hicks, the president of Dalhousie University at the time, persuaded the executors, who were Cohn's nephews, to have the money applied as the nucleus of the financing for a new cultural centre on campus. The court so ordered, and the Rebecca Cohn Auditorium went on to become the centre of much of the cultural life in Halifax.

Cohn's name is now associated in perpetuity with the world of music, art and drama, a world that was probably quite foreign to her. I told this little-known story of the Cohn Auditorium to Peter Waite, the retired historian writing the history of Dalhousie. Even he had not heard of it.

Babbitt Parlee, the lawyer who acted for the Grande Ligne Mission, soon became a close friend and confidant. He was extremely bright and a superb orator, with eccentricities sometimes associated with genius.

His father's dismissal from a government job when the New Brunswick Liberals won the 1935 election had turned Babbitt into a rabid Tory. He was a contender for the leadership of the provincial Conservative party, but he lost to the more senior and experienced Hugh John Flemming, who then led the party to power in 1952.

Babbitt was elected in Moncton, and as one of the brightest young lights in the rejuvenation of the Conservative party he assumed he would get a senior cabinet post. In the days when Moncton was represented by two legislature members, the cabinet seat for the area was given to Joe Bourgeois, Babbitt's Acadian constituency mate. Bourgeois was an affable fellow but a neophyte, with only a small fraction of Babbitt's ability. Hugh John argued that the Bourgeois appointment was a necessary recognition of the Acadian fact in the Moncton area. But Babbitt suspected that the Premier, worried about his position as leader, did not want to give a onetime rival too much prominence.

Babbitt decided he would not be present to be sworn in as a member of the legislature, a protest that would throw the new administration into turmoil even before it took office. Knowing I was a close friend of Babbitt's, and with the swearing-in ceremony scheduled for that evening, Hugh John called me in desperation. I rushed up to Fredericton, where I found Babbitt in his room at the Lord Beaverbrook Hotel, taking a bath, and Hugh John ensconced in the presidential suite. Running back and forth a dozen times between Babbitt's room and Hugh John's suite, I tried to negotiate a compromise. Throughout, Babbitt remained in the bathtub soaking.

At the eleventh hour we came up with a solution that employed an old precedent. The position of president of the executive council, which had not been filled for years, permitted the holder to preside over meetings of the Cabinet and enjoy cabinet remuneration, but it carried no portfolio responsibility. With that title, and the assurance of a portfolio soon down the road, Babbitt agreed to be sworn in. The ceremony was carried out on schedule, and shortly afterwards, a new portfolio was created, that of municipal affairs, with Babbitt its first incumbent.

Babbitt's exuberance and sometimes childlike excitement were contagious and provided a lift to those of us who knew this side of him. His mother had two sisters, but Babbitt was the only child among them and as such was fawned upon by all three women. Some locals, however, resented him and what they considered his affectations, especially during his university days, when he was known to walk down Main Street carrying a cane.

Babbitt, another Dalhousie Law School graduate, ran a one-man office above a jewellery and china shop. He was a voracious reader and spent every dollar he could muster on books, which would arrive dozens at a time from booksellers all over the country. His reading tastes were eclectic. He had an extensive library on the battles of the American Civil War and, at the other extreme, volumes on the art of belly dancing. He was also intrigued with circuses and bought any book obtainable on circus history.

When the Bill Lynch Side Shows paid their annual visit to Moncton one year, Babbitt was seen night after night watching the featured performance of a belly dancer. Confronted with this information by me, Fred Forbes and Ned Murphy, two other legal colleagues, Babbitt had his explanation ready. The provincial attorney general, Bill West, was out of town, and Babbitt was named acting attorney general during his absence. As such, he felt a duty to check the show nightly to ensure that no offences to public morals occurred.

Babbitt insisted the three of us accompany him to a performance, which we did, looking around furtively during the show to see if we might be recognized and embarrassed. For me, watching the rapture on Babbitt's face was more interesting than the contortions of the female torso, even though the latter, in Babbitt's expert opinion, were not to be underrated. It was after we left the circus tent that Ned, Fred and I hatched a plot involving Babbitt and a woman called the Duchess.

During the final years of the war a character known as the Duke had arrived from Montreal, apparently seeking sanctuary from some big-city rivals whose wrath he had incurred. For months he only ventured out in Moncton in the company of two, reportedly armed, bodyguards. The Duke brought with him his lady friend, who was often referred to unkindly as his moll and was soon known as the Duchess. The Duke bought a property called the Boreview Cabins, on the Salisbury Road just outside the Moncton city limits, and it was there that he ensconced the Duchess.

Her real name was Evelyn Moran, and her claim to fame was that she had been the cigarette girl at the Tic Toc nightclub in Montreal. The Duchess was petite, attractive and always well dressed. Soon after the war the Duke moved off to greener pastures in Halifax, but he did not abandon his Duchess to the wolves. He gave her the Boreview property and the business, which she continued to operate with the help of some of her women associates from Montreal, somewhat to the annoyance of her Baptist neighbours.

Ned, Fred and I were convinced that Babbitt, for all his sophistication, was still a virgin. In a plot to assuage what we assumed to be his frustration, we each chipped in ten dollars and drove Babbitt to the Boreview coffee shop, leaving him to get a cup of coffee and slipping the cash purse to the Duchess.

We heard no more about the incident until we received reports that Babbitt, who never learned to drive a car, had been seen many mornings walking along the Salisbury Road to his downtown office, two miles away. Only then did we begin to worry about the possible fallout from our innocent plot. Babbitt's straightlaced old aunts were horrified and asked me to help get their boy out of the clutches of "that nefarious woman." But Babbitt was smitten, and to the utter consternation of his proper family, he and Evelyn were married. She became a devoted wife, dedicating her life to Babbitt's well-being, providing excellent talents as a chauffeur and homemaker, and making him happier than he ever dreamed.

One year, the Duke of Edinburgh and Princess Elizabeth, before she became Queen, visited the city and were paraded through the streets in open convertibles. Babbitt, as the then mayor, got in one car with the princess and Evelyn got in a second car with the duke. As the cars proceeded slowly, the duke nodded and waved to the cheering crowds on his side, and Evelyn waved to those on her side. It was said by many at the time that the Duchess had truly arrived.

I always felt that, had Babbitt Parlee lived, he would have become prime minister, such were his talents and political acuity. But it was not to be. As a minister of the Crown he was asked to speak in Fredericton one evening to an association of New Brunswick land surveyors. The meeting was at the Lord Beaverbrook Hotel, and Babbitt planned to stay there overnight and return to Moncton the next morning.

A Moncton contractor had flown himself to Fredericton with another man that day, and they planned to fly back that night. When Babbitt was invited to come along, he apparently hesitated over the invitation because of a winter storm already underway. But the contractor, who had just received his pilot's licence and had only a few hours of solo flying experience, was a persuasive salesman. And Babbitt, having never driven a car, would hold in some awe anyone talented enough to fly a plane. Still, he was heard to remark as he left the hotel lobby, "I'm doing this against my better judgment."

The small, single-engine plane, with almost no controls for night flying and none to meet the fierce weather that evening, disappeared over a heavily wooded area. Search parties combed the woods for days, and when hope was fading, Babbitt's friend Duncan Wong, who ran the Palace Grill Restaurant, volunteered trays of sandwiches and loads of coffee to keep the search going. In the spring, months after the effort was abandoned, someone in the woods stumbled on the wreckage and the three bodies, badly mauled by animals.

Babbitt had once said he would never consider himself dead unless he was buried from Tuttles, the Moncton undertaking parlour that had been a family tradition for one hundred years. His wish was granted when he was barely forty. His name, however, lives on in New Brunswick.

A client once conveyed to Babbitt, in payment for fees, a waterfront lot in Barachois on the Northumberland Strait, somewhat removed from the main cottage areas around Shediac. Babbitt began building a cottage on the land, using labour and old materials whenever they could be scrounged or bartered. He even tried to have a well dug by hand. He was so proud of the project that he insisted Fred, Ned and I come see it. We drove down one summer evening to view the sad mess, and afterwards, as a lark, had a sign painted on a large board: "Parlee Beach—finest in the East." All summer the sign remained stuck in the ground by the roads leading to the beach in front of Babbitt's cottage. Little did we realize how prophetic our joke was.

In the Seventies, the government of Richard Hatfield took over the major Shediac Beach area, seven miles from Barachois, and created what is perhaps the prime tourist attraction of New Brunswick. As testament to the memory of Babbitt, the area was called Parlee Beach. The name now appears in all provincial tourist pamphlets, and the beach is visited by thousands every summer. Very few, however, know anything about the man in whose memory it was named.

It was Babbitt Parlee who suggested I buy a few shares in local institutions as a possible door-opener to obtain legal work. When I saved up enough money, I made my first purchase: ten shares of the Central Trust Company of Canada, headquartered in Moncton, at $125 a share.

These shares were split many times over the ensuing years, but I did not obtain any great advantage from the purchase. Too many local lawyers were gathered at this trough, and any crumbs that fell in my direction were meagre. The trough itself was pretty shallow, with little room for another snout. Central Trust at that time had less than $50 million in assets and annual profits of possibly $25,000. I saw more scope in trying to court larger institutions in the region, and having been at school in Halifax for six years, I found it only natural to look in that direction.

Jordan Smith, Maritime Life's local branch manager and the first person to ring my office phone, agreed to set up an appointment with Bernard Lockwood, the general manager of the company in Halifax. Lockwood, a Yorkshireman, was brought in to run Maritime Life in the Twenties, and his Yorkshire thrift was largely responsible for keeping it afloat through the Depression.

The head office was above a Chinese restaurant at the corner of Sackville and Barrington streets. When I arrived in late morning for my appointment, the smell of Chinese cooking permeated Lockwood's office. As we talked, a young woman from the outer office came in and handed Lockwood the stub of a pencil. He opened a drawer in his desk, took out another stub, compared the two and gave the woman a new pencil from his drawer. Noting my puzzled look after she left, Lockwood explained that he controlled the office supplies to make sure nothing was wasted. Employees were only entitled to a new pencil if their old one was smaller than the stub in his desk.

Lockwood and I were still talking when a distinguished-looking older man came into the room. He rummaged through the papers on Lockwood's desk and the books in the bookcase behind, taking each volume out, holding it by the stem, shaking it and replacing it. After he left, I timidly asked Lockwood what this exercise was about. The gentleman, I was told, was a Dr. Murphy, who was appointed by the board of directors as the company's medical referee. As such, the doctor was paid two dollars for approving, rejecting or making some other determination about the medical information that was required in every application for life insurance. But because Lockwood felt most of the applications were routine and did not need a professional opinion, he himself reviewed the medical forms and saved the company the two-dollar fee. The applications were kept from Dr. Murphy, although he obviously still made an effort to find them. It was then that I first learned that compared with a Yorkshireman, a Scotsman was a reckless profligate.

I developed a healthy business relationship with Lockwood, and the legal work for the company in New Brunswick quickly became an important part of my practice. Eventually, in 1947, I asked him when I might buy some shares in Maritime Life, whose stock was unlisted.

The stock was originally issued at $25 a share and was subject to a call of $75. There were only ten thousand shares outstanding, and a substantial amount of the stock had been sold to people in Bermuda and parts of the West Indies by a company representative who had gone to the islands in the Twenties in search of investors. It must have been difficult then, within the Maritimes alone, to raise even this amount of capital to found a life insurance company.

When people wanted to sell their Maritime Life shares, they contacted head office in Halifax, and Lockwood would contact me sometimes, letting me know that the stock was being offered at $40 or $50 or $60 and advising me that the asking price was too steep. But not having the advantage of his Yorkshire background, I always disregarded the advice and took up the stock, accumulating in the next twenty years a holding of more than 45 percent.

The Mutual Life Assurance Company of Canada, with its head office in Waterloo, Ontario, was another contact I investigated for legal work. While it was well represented in the Maritimes with a sales-branch network, it had no investment office in the area. Here again my footwork was done through the local life branch manager, Graham Steeves. Company officers came from Waterloo to inspect the territory and agreed to proceed with an investment office in Moncton, which would enable me to control the legal end.

Don Laird, who was to be the branch manager, told me later that the company officers had decided on Moncton before they travelled to Saint John, their last point of call. But in Saint John the group was entertained at dinner by a senior lawyer in the city, whose attractive and engaging wife had once been, I believe, a Miss Canada. The next morning Laird was astounded to be told that the new office would be located in Saint John instead of Moncton.

It was then that I learned the power of a woman. I was 27 when this incident occurred, and it taught me, forcibly, that it was time to take a wife.

CHAPTER 4

Family Life

My first romance, which began a few years after I started practising law, was with an attractive, beautifully spoken young woman for whom I developed a genuine fondness. For several years we had a relationship of mutual trust, respect and affection, and we would have long since made a formal commitment but for our religious differences.

Although she would have done anything to accommodate my problem, conversion was still not an acceptable option in the Jewish community, and I dreaded the repercussions such a course would have on my mother. The old indoctrinations and convictions were too strong to overcome, and the eventual breakup with this woman was devastating for me.

In the summer of 1950, however, came the happening that changed the course of my life.

A friend who operated a local supermarket was involved in an accident that killed his wife and son and laid him up in hospital for a year. His brother in Florida came to Moncton to look after the business, moving with his wife and children into a cottage at Point du Chêne in the Shediac beach area. The wife's mother, who lived in Los Angeles, was sent a ticket to come visit, and she was accompanied on the journey to New Brunswick by a younger daughter, Louise.

One day the brother of my recuperating friend was in my office to have papers witnessed and asked if I might take his young sister-in-law out some evening to show her the area. This I agreed to do, and several days later I called the cottage, spoke to Louise and arranged to call on her that evening at seven thirty. But Don Laird, the Mutual Life man, was in town from Saint

John, and when we got tied up and didn't arrive at the cottage until after nine thirty, I was told Louise had retired. Don and I stayed talking to the family until about midnight, and only much later did I learn that Louise had been annoyed by my lack of consideration and refused to meet me. She spent the evening fuming in a small anteroom, not being able to get to her bedroom without passing through the living room, where we were being entertained. If that boor called again, Louise told the family, she would not see him.

This was an inauspicious beginning to a courtship, but a few days later I ran into Louise at the supermarket. She was 21 and the most vivacious young woman I had ever seen, with a smile that was magical and completely entrancing. I asked her to dinner that night, and having seen her, I made sure I was on time.

Dinner was at the Marshland's Inn in Sackville, then the most elegant dining room in the area. After dinner we toured the Radio-Canada International shortwave station on the Tantramar marshes, where we learned about the technical intricacies of beaming to the world Canadian programs produced largely in Montreal and Toronto. Louise and I talked into the early hours of the morning, not only that night but every night for the next three weeks. After the second week, my mother confronted me.

"*Wie loifst du arim alle nachte biz zwei azager—mit shikses?*" ("Where are you running around every night until two o'clock—is it with Gentile girls?")

Ironically, the only time my mother ever questioned me in this regard was about a relationship that would have been legitimate in her eyes. Towards the end of the third week of courtship, I was parked on the street talking to Louise when my mother walked by. I started the car to get away, but she was too quick and jumped into the back seat. My mother, a vain and proud woman in many ways, loved beautiful things, a trait I must have inherited. She stroked Louise's long black tresses, which were draped over the back of the seat.

"*Zog mir, das iz a Yiddishe madel zu a shikse?*" my mother asked me. ("Tell me, is this a Jewish girl or a shikse?")

To my amazement—until then I had no idea she knew the language—Louise started speaking to my mother in impeccable Yiddish. It was enough for my mother.

"*Aza maidel lost man nicht duruch—oib du gaist nicht chasana haben mit ir vell ich dir araus varfen fon shtieb.*" ("A girl like this you don't let get away—if you don't marry her I'll kick you out of the house.")

I realized then and there that I was outmanoeuvred and outclassed. The next day the formal engagement was announced, and within five months we were married.

After the engagement, towards the end of September, Louise wanted to return to Los Angeles, where she worked in the head office of a ladies' clothing chain. I was determined that she stay in Moncton, fearing that her return to glamorous Los Angeles might awaken her to reality and she might not want to come back. I also wanted to make plans for our home and all that this entailed. Louise, however, was concerned about her salary, so I asked her how much she made. Forty-eight dollars a week was the reply, to which I countered I would put her on my payroll at seventy-five dollars a week, which I began paying immediately and, as a sentimental lark, continued to pay all our married life. Her mad money, we called it.

Her mother returned to Los Angeles alone, and Louise and I began looking around at houses on the market. When we could not find anything suitable, we decided to build a house on Jones Lake in the city. The comfortable bungalow in which we always lived and where I continue to live alone was built for about $75,000 on land bought for about $5,000. The wedding date was February 10, 1951, but we lived in a local hotel until the house was completed in the spring.

Louise was born in Montreal, during a time when her family lived in Quebec City. After her father's business there faltered, he moved the family to New Waterford, and it was in Cape Breton that Louise spent her formative years. Having moderately prospered in the retail clothing business after the war, the father again moved the family, this time to Los Angeles, where he expected to retire. This background gave Louise a rare combination of big-city sophistication and the unspoiled virtues and solidness of small-town Cape Breton. She could be equally relaxed and at home in a Buckingham Palace or a coal miner's hovel.

Along with her striking physical beauty, she had a charm, wit, sense of humour and graciousness that captivated all who met her. Her effect on others was apparent to me from the start. In my bachelor days I had been inveigled into helping with local fund-raising for the Canadian Friends of the Hebrew University. Sam Risk, the national executive director of this charity, was in town on the occasion of our engagement and succumbed to Louise's charms. When he got back to Montreal, he must have raved about her to his boss, Allan Bronfman, the founder and national chairman of the Friends charity. Bronfman learned from Risk that Louise and I were stopping in Montreal on our way to our honeymoon in Florida, and he sent word he wanted to meet us.

From the old Mount Royal Hotel, we crossed over to Seagram's—this was before Sam Bronfman eased out his brothers—and were ushered into Allan's office. I had heard Allan had a weakness for pretty women, but his reaction to my wife was instantaneous surrender and a bit overwhelming, even though as a blooming bride she was indeed breathtaking. Allan insisted we come to his home for dinner that evening. He sent his driver for us, and on that cold night the elaborate fur blanket provided for our feet was a helpful luxury.

Dinner was served by a stiff and proper butler, who after each course stood at attention behind the dinner table, without the flicker of an eyelash, waiting to cater to our next needs. It was the first such experience for both Louise and me, and I made a small blunder when I refused a V.O. cocktail before dinner, saying I never touched the stuff. In one of the many lessons in etiquette and diplomacy she was to teach me, Louise dutifully accepted a drink and sipped it.

The Bronfmans had lost a daughter in the last year to suicide, attributed to post-childbirth depression, and we were the first dinner guests in their home since the tragedy. Bronfman's wife, Lucy, found my wife's vivacity lifted her own spirits, and she thanked us profusely for coming. Allan only wanted to know if there were any unattached sisters. When I told him the youngest daughter was still single in Los Angeles, he pestered me to arrange for her to meet either of his sons, Peter or Edward, a request repeated for some time after we returned from the honeymoon. I did ask the young sister if she might be amenable to a contact, but she already had a boyfriend in Los Angeles and showed no interest.

I only met Allan once more, at a fund-raising dinner in Montreal, when at his request we were seated at his table. During the evening he opened his wallet to remove a hundred-dollar bill, and my wife, who had a delightful brat in her makeup as well, peered over to say, "I always wanted to see what the inside of a Bronfman wallet looked like."

Louise became a sensation in Moncton and was sought after by all elements in the city for aid, advice, community work and socializing. An attractive and intelligent woman might be viewed with coolness or jealousy by other women, but my wife's warmth and personality attracted everyone to her. In our first summer we spent a Sunday afternoon at Blair Steeves's cottage, and among the other guests was Erna MacManus, a musical woman who sang in a choir on local radio. At the end of the afternoon, in which she had engaged in much conversation with my wife, Erna took me aside.

"I knew you were a perfectionist, but I never thought you could achieve such perfection in a wife," she said.

As a result of Allan Bronfman's persuasion, I continued an interest in the fund-raising efforts for the Hebrew University for a few years more. An early organizer and fund-raiser who came to us in this connection was Dr. Bernard Cherrick, a suave and dapper gentleman, educated in England and possessing the impressive English accent. He became another in the myriad of fans of my wife. On his first visit he arrived in the afternoon to address the small group we had arranged to participate, and he left the next afternoon. My wife picked him up on his arrival and delivered him back to the airport the next day for his departure. On the way to the airport he asked my wife to stop the car in the middle of the road. Somewhat startled, she obliged. He stepped out of the car, walked around to the driver's side, took her hand and kissed it, saying he wanted to mark a significant anniversary: the twenty-four hours since he had met her. This act of gallantry accomplished, he returned to his seat and they proceeded to the airport.

Dr. Cherrick returned almost annually for many years to follow, when on his North American trips, even though the funds raised in our little community could never justify the time and expense of such visits from year to year. Such is the power of a woman and the weakness of a man.

Of the many other fund-raising visitors to stay with us at our home over the years were Gerda Weissmann Klein and Itzhak Perlman. Gerda Klein recently appeared on the American television show "60 Minutes," with the absorbing story of her survival of brutal Nazi oppression and eventual rescue by an American soldier who became her husband. The story on TV was spellbinding, but less so than when she related it to us in person two decades ago.

Itzhak Perlman was only a kid of 14 when he stayed with us, closely supervised by a rather hawkish and domineering mother, who seemed to fret as much over his valuable violin as she did over the budding virtuoso himself. It was painful to see the young kid pluckily move around with leg braces and crutches as the result of his bout with polio.

My friend Babbitt Parlee also became a fan. Whenever the circus came to town, he would call Louise at five o'clock in the morning and the two of them would go down to the railway siding to watch the animals being unloaded.

Louise's personality was outgoing and engaging; mine was reserved and perhaps even dour in certain social circumstances. I could not dance; she was an expert and loaded with rhythm. She tried desperately to teach me the rudiments of the waltz and foxtrot, but my two left feet presented a formidable challenge. Louise became so accomplished in culinary arts that she set the pattern for all budding hostesses, who soon sought her help. I used to say she could serve a simple sandwich so attractively that it would be more appetizing than a banquet prepared by a master chef.

We had moved into our new house without a stick of furniture or any drapery, and with a borrowed bed from a local furniture store run by Mike Baig. Wooden orange crates served as night tables, and for more than a year the floors were rough plywood. Louise took her time furnishing, to make sure each piece complemented her overall plan for design and decoration. She had extraordinary artistic talent and an uncanny eye for spotting treasures generally overlooked by those less sophisticated, trained or gifted in this regard.

Early on, we were visited by one of those pesky itinerant art salesmen who plagued most small communities in those days. This fellow hung several canvases on our extensive and bare walls and asked us to live with them for a few days, when he would return for our decision. Louise was taking art lessons at Mount Allison University, where two of the teachers were Alex Colville and Lawren P. Harris, son of Lawren Harris of the Group of Seven. She asked Colville and Harris to come to our house to advise her on the worth of the salesman's paintings. Their advice was to get them off the walls and not waste money on vulgar commercial art.

If Louise wanted to gain an appreciation of art and form the nucleus of a collection, she should start with local artists who had talent, her teachers said. The works would be inexpensive and the artists' careers would be helped along by our purchases. As Louise learned and became less constrained financially, her interest could expand into the national field and perhaps beyond. She heeded this advice, and having a natural and perceptive artistic eye herself, it was the format for her accumulation of art over the next three decades.

My only regret is that I was a barbarian and did not always follow my wife's instincts. In later years I wanted to kick myself for not having made an important and available acquisition that at the time looked extravagant. We had an exceptional canvas from Alex Colville hanging on our walls, direct from the artist, for which he was asking $6,000. This seemed to me an exorbitant price for a local artist, as well as a challenge to my income, and my wife reluctantly returned it. Years later, when we were better able to afford the painting and approached Colville again, we were told we had to deal through his agent in Europe, even though Colville lived only a few miles away. By that time, the $6,000 canvas would have brought twenty times that.

Colville is an exceptional painter, but, unlike many artists who live in rarefied worlds of their own, removed from economic reality, he has a shrewd business sense. And like any good business head, he learned how to effectively market his product in line with conditions of supply and demand. He was the chancellor of Acadia University when I was given an honorary degree there, and he and his wife, Rhoda, graciously entertained us at their Wolfville home on the occasion. He and I are contemporary in age, but happily, his contribution to our society still continues at a pace that many of us lesser beings may only view with admiration.

Lawren Harris became a closer social friend as the years progressed. When he came for dinner one night, he brought one of his father's paper sketches for a painting, which we suitably framed and prized.

Ralph Bell was one of Mount Allison's great benefactors, and when his wife died, he asked Lawren, before the funeral, to paint her portrait. Lawren agreed and asked Bell for a recent photograph from which he could work. This wasn't enough for Bell, who insisted that she be sketched from the original. With that he delivered Lawren to where the body was resting, opened the coffin and stood, overseeing, while the shocked artist painted the preliminary sketch.

Shortly before Lawren's father died, the two men attended a large, important retrospective of Lawren Sr.'s works. As they passed in front of the paintings, most of which had left his father's hands long ago and which he had not seen for years, the father uttered not a word. When they finished and walked out of the gallery, he at last broke his silence, saying to his son, "God, I must have been great."

When his father died, Lawren became heir to a third of the estate's paintings, which were shipped to him and stored in the vault of the Owen's Art Gallery at Mount Allison. My wife and I were privileged to view them in the vault and to select any of the works at what would be ridiculously modest prices today. Here again I let my economic practicability overcome my wife's common sense. Many of those paintings have how been traded at five to ten times the prices we could have enjoyed. We also lost the pleasure of hanging the paintings in our home and sharing them with our family and friends.

In retrospect, how much better it would have been had I been guided by my wife's artistic instincts rather than by my own obsession with the accumulation of a financial common stock portfolio, which eventually becomes valueless paper.

One of the great regrets of our marriage was the absence of a family. After struggling with the problem for several years, we sought professional help, and in the days well before modern fertility clinics, we both endured the primitive and embarrassing testing of the day. The charting of temperature to help indicate the period of ovulation seemed to be the only technique available, but all it did was serve as a romance-killer. Fortunately, medical science has progressed in this field, and considerable help is now available to couples facing this problem, which can often create domestic turmoil.

After years of disappointment we faced the prospect of adoption. It wasn't an easy decision for me, and I had to do a lot of soul-searching; but being in my thirty-eighth year, it became a matter of some urgency. The first girl we adopted, Debra, came to us when she was less than a week old and was the picture of what one dreams about in an infant. She at once became the focal point of my wife's life and, surprisingly, quickly won over her hard-boiled father.

When our daughter was only a few months old, my wife had to go to New York with her niece. A qualified nurse was engaged to look after the baby, but a couple of hours before my wife's departure the nurse called me to say that a personal crisis prevented her from coming. Not wishing to disrupt my wife's plans, I did not tell her about this dislocation and let her go off with a clear mind. I determined to handle the situation on my own, and looked after the baby myself for the rest of the day.

Feeding and bathing a baby were a completely new experience for me, which I struggled through as best I could. When the baby settled down, I made phone calls to try to locate reliable nursing help, but this proved more difficult than I had expected. My wife would call nightly to ask how the baby was faring and how well the nurse was doing, and I reported glowingly to her on both counts. After the third or fourth day of not being able to find a nurse, I gave up and thought it best to stay at home until my wife's return. Besides, I was beginning to pride myself on my newfound talent for infant care. This occurred at the peak of my productive professional earnings and was probably the most expensive baby-sitting cost in the country.

When my wife returned and heard my confession, I earned sufficient brownie points to make the loss of earnings worthwhile. I basked in her accolades as she repeated in amazement that the baby had never looked better or healthier and seemed visibly to have put on weight in one short week. Floating from these compliments, I suggested that Louise relax while I gave the baby her supper. I opened the can of strained baby food, poured it into the dish and began the feeding. My wife interrupted me, saying I had forgotten to heat the food.

"Heat it?" I said. "Why?"

My wife was aghast. "You don't mean to say you fed this poor child cold baby food for a whole week?"

I sheepishly admitted that I had no idea that the canned food required heating. Even though the baby had apparently thrived on the cold food for a week, my baby-care duties were brought to an end.

Our first girl proved to be such a contented child that we began to question all the warnings we had been given about sleepless nights and infant screaming. Our baby slept through the nights with hardly a whimper. We took her with us almost everywhere, even to restaurants, where we would plunk her down in her basket on the table, with never an interruption. Once, when she was about four months old, I sneaked her a little ice cream off my spoon. She smacked her lips while I was lectured.

Emboldened by this favourable parenting experience, we adopted another girl, Natalie, with only a respectable nine months intervening. That's when we learned what all the warnings were about. Our new baby screamed from the time she arrived and almost continuously for the better part of a year. I often thought that if she had turned out to be as easy as the first, there might have been a third, or more. Ironically, the youngest, the wailer, grew up to have a more placid disposition than her older sister.

I could write a treatise on the pros and cons of adoption. It is particularly difficult to assess when one parent is a perfectionist, with a fetish for achievement. Standards and expectations can become a mindset and cause disappointment to the parent and frustration for the child. The statistics on disappointments in families with natural children probably equal those of families who adopt, but a question cannot help but flit occasionally across the mind of the latter. In either case, the memories of pleasure in both natural and adoptive families probably outnumber by far the moments of pain.

When our first girl was little more than two, her uncle Simon loved to play with her, and he had a born talent for entertaining kids. His business at the time was slot machines, which he had installed around the town, mostly in small convenience stores and shops of that kind. One day he took our little darling with him while he made the rounds to his machines. One location was run by Stubby Ferguson, who had something in the nature of a slot-machine arcade in the front of the shop and, it was rumoured, more serious gambling in the back. When Simon brought our daughter home, she was bleary-eyed and trembling with excitement.

"Where did Uncle Simon take you, dear?" my wife asked her.

"Tubbies," she replied.

"And what did you do there, dear?"

"Tum on seben," our innocent child replied as the mother had to be revived.

My wife usually made an annual trip to Los Angeles to visit with her family, particularly her mother, and I occasionally went along. Often a friend of the family invited me to the Hillcrest Country Club, an exclusive Jewish social club and a haunt of many a celebrated name in the entertainment world. Oil had been discovered on the club's land years before, and the original members, instead of having to pay hefty annual dues, received participating yearly cheques from the oil revenues. It was fascinating to see oil drills pumping away on the grounds, as passing golfers nonchalantly ignored them.

On one visit to the club, I was in the men's room, and standing at the urinal next to me was a face I recognized as George Burns. While we were engaged in our urinal business, he asked me where I was from.

"From Canada," I replied.

"What part?" he asked.

"A rather remote part of the country that you probably never heard of— New Brunswick."

"What city in New Brunswick?"

"Moncton."

"I never played there, but I played Saint John in my vaudeville days in the Twenties."

Burns invited me to join in a card game with his cronies, but I begged off, knowing that I was no match for those Los Angeles sharpies and would probably end up as a turkey, plucked of my meagre Canadian currency.

Standing at urinals often provides for interesting dialogue, and I once read that Howard Hughes made some of his biggest business deals in such surroundings. I recall a few even in my own career. A drawback for women trying to reach the upper echelons of business is that they are banished to their private cubicles, denied the advantages men enjoy for conversational interchange in public washrooms.

My wife's mother usually spent the summers with us. The stories of her escape from revolutionary Russia with her husband and two infant children were always enthralling, and her broken English and malapropisms added to the charm. One of her favourite expressions was "Patience is a virgin," but since she had five daughters to marry off, I wondered if this was contrived rather than accidental.

When a daughter was getting married to a man named Wiggins, one of the guests, a crony of my mother-in-law's, was also of European background and spoke with a broken English accent. As a wedding gift this woman sent a silver tray engraved with the initial *V*. The bride called the woman to find out who supplied the tray, to see if they might change the *V* to a *W*. This annoyed the guest, who asked, "How else do you spell Viggins but mit a *V*?"

For her mother's eightieth birthday my wife sent her two tickets to visit Russia and the scenes of her youth, the extra ticket being for any companion she wished to take along. My wife was enthusiastic about this exciting gift to mark a milestone in her mother's life, and was disappointed when the tickets were returned. Her mother said she had too hard a time getting out of Russia to ever want to go back.

My mother-in-law attended an Orthodox synagogue in Los Angeles and always boasted of the talents of her rabbi. His wonderful services and ser- mons were better than those of lesser congregations anywhere in the country, not to mention in our own remote corner. One year, however, the mother made no mention of her rabbi. My wife learned through her sisters that, as a fund-raising project, the Los Angeles synagogue had sold tickets on a raffle for a diamond ring, which raised about $40,000. The worthy rabbi, however, abandoned his family and disappeared with the ring, the money and his secretary. I prodded my mother-in-law to explain why she was making no laudatory comments about her rabbi during her visit that year. She kept mum at first, but when I kept harping on the question, she concluded that I was aware of the facts, and she blurted out: "It vasn't so bad. The secretary was Jewish."

Despite her strict Orthodoxy, she was not unbending. At our summer cottage at Barachois when our kids were small, she would help them collect mussels on the rocks at low tide, cook the forbidden shellfish in a pot on the beach and watch the youngsters enjoy the treat. I contrast this with my own mother's reaction one evening when my wife and I visited her on our way home from a restaurant. She asked us what we had eaten, and when I jokingly said "lobster," she shook her head from side to side and said to us: *"Auf eim glabe ich, nur auf dir nicht."* ("I believe it of him, but not of you.") In my mother's eyes Louise could do no wrong; I was questionable.

When Louise and I were married, she had been out of the country for at least five years and had lost contact with Canadian politics. A federal election was soon in progress, and to reintroduce her to Canadian public affairs I took her to hear all the party leaders when they came to town.

M.J. Coldwell, the leader of the CCF, was reputed to be a good speaker, and even though I did not adhere to his socialist philosophy, I wanted Louise to be exposed to all segments of our political life. We attended his meeting, but Coldwell did not make much of an impression on her. Nor did Louis St. Laurent, when we caught his speech to a Liberal party gathering.

The last leader we heard was George Drew of the Conservatives. He spoke fifty miles away, in Sussex, midway between Moncton and Saint John, presumably to draw people from New Brunswick's two largest cities. By the time we arrived, the meeting was in progress, with many people standing at the rear of the small theatre. An usher advised us there were a few seats available and led us down to the front row.

Babbitt Parlee was on the stage with other dignitaries and at the end of the meeting brought Drew down into the audience for some personal introductions. When they reached my wife, Drew said, "I know this lady's name because I already asked about her. From the moment she came in, she was the inspiration for my address."

With that, my wife's political persuasion was determined. George Drew, however, for all his acumen and finesse, did not win the election.

My wife and I became friends with the Conservative Hugh John Flemming, who stayed in power in New Brunswick for two terms, until the

Liberals under Louis Robichaud won the 1960 election. Although Hugh John had reduced the sales tax from 4 percent to 3, his planned $25-a-year levy for health insurance was his undoing. Had Babbitt Parlee been alive, the matter would likely have been handled with more intuitive political expertise and the government would not have lost on such an insignificant issue.

My relationship with Hugh John was cemented through a legal connection more than a political one. His son Fred was associated with the legendary American developer Zeckendorff, who built Place Ville Marie in Montreal, then one of the largest real estate developments in the country. Fred Flemming planned a similar, but much more modest, complex in Moncton and assembled an extensive number of properties for a site. The buildings were levelled and the land cleared, but because young Fred was developing the project on his own, Hugh John was asked to guarantee the loans. The complex never materialized, and when Fred was unable to carry the financial load, his father was called on his guarantee.

The sum involved hundreds of thousands of dollars, because the lands, once the buildings were removed, were worth only a fraction of their original cost. Even the original cost was in excess of the market values at the time of purchase, which is usually the case in a land assembly. Hugh John stood to lose a substantial fortune on his guarantee, since the market value of the land would be only a minor percentage of the accumulated mortgage interest, principal and taxes. He was extremely worried when he spoke to me, and I suggested he let the creditor go to a mortgage sale.

In a calculated gamble on my part, I appeared at the sale, without Hugh John, and started the bidding. Each time I bid, the solicitor for the mortgagee, thinking I had a real interest in acquiring the property and that he must have a live fish on the hook, outbid me. When the bidding got up to the full balance outstanding, I backed off and left the other solicitor stuck with his final bid. Hugh John walked away free, and the mortgage company was left with the property and the loss. The naïve solicitor should have backed off himself when he bid to the expected low price the land would bring. That way I or my client would have been stuck with the property, and the guarantor with the large deficiency.

Such legal gamesmanship requires strong nerves, and I only tried it a few times in my career, when the stakes were high—once in Saint John, where I salvaged more than $750,000 for my client at the expense of an Irving company. Hugh John thought I was a legal genius, and I never told him that the saving grace was owed more to another lawyer's gullibility, if not stupidity, than to any great legal ability on my part.

One Christmas, Hugh John sent us a portrait of himself, taken with a handsome young Robert Stanfield and an aging Winston Churchill at the opening of the London office that was to tend to the joint affairs of New Brunswick and Nova Scotia in Europe.

During Hugh John's tenure we were also invited to a reception in Fredericton to meet the young Queen Elizabeth II and her consort. K.C. Irving was there too, resplendent in striped trousers and black suitcoat. Irving had already become a legend, and my wife seemed more excited about meeting him than she did about meeting the Queen.

Having the rare gift of old-fashioned common sense, my wife became the confidant of all privileged to know her. And having excellent judgment, she was my complete support in virtually every aspect of life. With her vitality and entertainment skills, she also opened doors I had never dreamed of entering.

Our first dinner guest was Bernard Lockwood, the Maritime Life general manager from Halifax. He too was captivated, and he invited us to Halifax, where over the years we spent many a Christmas dinner with his family.

Soon the senior officers of Mutual Life in Waterloo came down on a business trip and stayed with us. Both the president of the company, Louis Lang, who was Catholic, and Eugene Pequegnat, the general manager, who was Baptist, expressed the wish to attend church services on Sunday. Louise accompanied Lang to early mass at St. Bernard's Church and returned in time to attend the ten o'clock service with Pequegnat at the First Baptist Church. Some people in the congregation told me later that Louise could be heard singing the hymns of the service loud and clear above the rest.

Shortly after this visit the Mutual Life legal work that had been lost to the Saint John office before I married Louise was restored.

From this point there began an enjoyable relationship with these two Mutual Life officers and their company. We were invited to the annual general meetings, always staying in the Pequegnats' charming older home in Kitchener, where Eugene would wake us early playing music on the living-room organ. The inscription engraved over the Pequegnats' fireplace always impressed me: *A chaque oiseau, son nid est beau.* (For every bird, his nest is the best.)

It was Eugene who saved me from drastic surgery for a back problem that laid me up with pain so severe that every part of my body ached. He encouraged me to try osteopathic healing, and it worked. For thirty-five years, no matter what, I have religiously performed the lumbar tension exercises the osteopath prescribed. As a consequence I have a healthy respect for osteopathic healing, and regret that it enjoys little status in the eyes of the Canadian Medical Association and virtually no status in Canadian hospitals. We in Canada are the losers. In the United States osteopaths operate their own hospitals and clinics, with full accreditation to carry out most medical and surgical procedures.

Even after he retired, Pequegnat would visit and entertain us with stories of his travels to exotic, faraway lands. On one of Eugene's last visits, when his first wife had died and he had married his longtime secretary, we were at our cottage. It was well into September and the air was chilly, but Eugene, who was by then in his seventies, announced the first morning that he was going to take a swim. I tried to dissuade him because of his years and the fact that the waters of the Northumberland Strait were cold in the morning, even in the heat of summer. But he prided himself on his physique and manly prowess, and no arguing could deter him. His wife and I went down to the water's edge and watched Eugene wade in. When he got in as far as his belt line, she called to him.

"Eugene, is the water cold?" she asked.

"I have no feeling from the waist down," Eugene said.

"Yes, I know, dear, but is the water cold?"

CHAPTER 5

Building Central and Eastern

Leonard Ellen was fresh out of high school in Montreal when he started travelling the Maritimes selling what he called drug sundries. He was the greatest salesman I ever encountered.

Louise and I met him shortly after moving into our new home, when we invited a few friends in for a social evening. The Freemans, who became our next-door neighbours, were in the retail ladies' clothing business and brought with them that night a few clothing salesmen from Montreal. At the end of the evening, when everyone had left and we were cleaning up, my wife told me she was not impressed with "that young guy Ellen," who struck her as a patronizing city slicker, with a condescending attitude towards us small-town yokels.

First impressions are often not lasting. But little could we imagine that night the impact Leonard would have on the course of my business life.

With his personality and good looks, he turned the occupation of selling into an art. Years after he had left drug sundries—I always joked that he was peddling prophylactics—I was with Leonard when he met a retired pharmacist in Nova Scotia, and they reminisced about the old days. Leonard had once sold the man a bottled liquid that was imported from France and billed as a guaranteed morning-after birth-control potion. The pharmacist remembered catching lots of hell from many a mama and papa who had relied on the magic elixir. Thanks to Leonard, the man said, the birth rate in the province had increased dramatically.

Leonard left the drug business to take on the more profitable lines of ladies' clothing. Other salesmen carrying similar lines took five or six weeks to cover the Maritimes, setting up sample rooms in every small town during each seasonal trip. But Leonard had the retail trade convinced that his lines were special and that buyers should seek him out. He set up sample rooms only in the largest centres, and the merchants were happy to come from hundreds of miles around for the privilege of buying his lines. Leonard could complete his sales trip and be back home with his young family within ten days, and he still sold much more volume than any of his counterparts.

Around 1952, Leonard sought my help with investing some of the small savings he had accumulated, an investment he preferred to make in the Maritimes, whose people he understood and appreciated. Even then Leonard was prescient. He was born in Quebec, but he had an uneasy feeling about having too much investment there, particularly in immovable bricks and mortar. The combination of Leonard's savings and my own, and the establishment of substantial bank connections, led to an extensive and exciting business story that spanned the next four decades.

One of my earliest bank connections was the Dominion Bank, which arrived in Moncton like a competitive breath of fresh air. Its venture into the Maritimes was welcomed in a city that for years had known only one branch each of the Royal, Montreal, Nova Scotia, Commerce and Provincial—five banking doors in total. The regional vice president, a charming older man named J.K. Muir, came down from Montreal for a reception, to which I, as a budding young professional, was invited.

"Where are you banking, young fella?" he asked me when we were introduced.

"Bank of Montreal, sir," I replied.

"How much are they giving you?"

"Giving me, sir? I don't quite understand."

"I mean, how much are they lending you?"

"I have no need to borrow money, sir. I earn enough in my practice to get by quite nicely."

"Hell, you can't get anywhere that way, without owing money. Go down to see Freddy Logan tomorrow morning and tell him I said to start you off at $150,000. And if you need any more, let me know."

Although I told Muir I foresaw no need for his help, I mulled over his advice in the following weeks and finally went to see Logan, the manager of the new bank. I arranged my first bank borrowing and never looked back.

The credit with Dominion, augmented over the years, helped me buy the Maritime Life stock. The initial credit was substantial for that decade after the war, when bank growth was relatively stagnant. The banks then were hidebound with old managers who had come through the Depression and still felt a $500 loan was a big risk. It was only after these old-timers died or were pensioned off that bank growth started to explode. In the meantime trust companies expanded and proliferated to fill the gap.

My wife and I got to know J.K. Muir of the Dominion Bank better when we invited him to dinner. My wife diligently prepared a special spread for the occasion, but J.K. was more interested in drinking Scotch. While he and I talked, and he imbibed, until after nine o'clock, Louise fidgeted uncomfortably, worrying that her hard work would dry up. After we finally did help him to the table, J.K. touched hardly a morsel of food but continued to not spare the Scotch—a crushing evening for an eager young bride.

The Eastern Trust Company was initially the best and most remunerative connection of my early legal career. With its head office in Halifax, Eastern Trust had an important branch network in the Atlantic provinces, including a small office in Moncton. In those days the Canadian National Railway dominated the city's commercial life, and the regional vice president was the czar of its business and social affairs. Walter Appleton, the regional vice president of the CNR, was a director of both the Eastern Trust Company and Maritime Life.

The railway supplied Appleton with an impressive white mansion next to the general offices of the company and not far from the station itself. On the same expanse of land was a more modest house for the number-two man in the local railway hierarchy. The land also boasted tennis courts and large hothouses, which provided fresh flowers year-round for the officials' homes and the railway dining cars. At the western end of the property was a small house for the head gardener. The general office building was itself an imposing multistoried brick structure built in the nineteenth century. In the stone that framed the main entrance was carved the name Intercolonial Railway, a remnant of the time before regional rail systems across the country were consolidated to form the Canadian National Railway.

In the glory days of the CNR in Moncton, a job in either the shops or the general offices was highly prized and generally considered a lifetime occupation, with comfortable pension provisions. Political connections were often used to obtain those jobs, and many a politician was ensured of loyal supporters through such intervention. When an opening occurred for the position of regional legal counsel, Walter was asked by Montreal head office to make a recommendation. He suggested Ivan C. Rand, already an eminent lawyer in the city, practising with Senator C.W. Robinson under the firm name of Robinson and Rand. Head office was eager to accept the recommendation but told Walter he would have little success attracting a lawyer of such distinguished reputation, especially with the $6,000 salary stipulated for the appointment. "I went to him anyway with the offer, and he grabbed it," Walter told me.

It is distressing to see the CNR in our present day decimated and eviscerated in our community so as to be a scarcely recognizable shadow of its former strategic importance.

Rand, one of Moncton's most illustrious sons, later became a judge of the Supreme Court of Canada, author of the famous Rand Formula in labour relations, one of the commissioners who participated in the Middle East partition that created the state of Israel, and the founder and first dean of the law school at the University of Western Ontario.

One of my fond memories is of an evening Rand spent with me, my wife and Greg Bridges, who was by then the chief justice of the Supreme Court of New Brunswick. Rand had recently lost his wife, and the dinner at our home seemed to provide him with a few welcome hours of relaxation. After dinner and late into the evening he played the piano—score after score of classical music—without looking at a written note.

Walter Appleton's presence on the board of Maritime Life was certainly of benefit to me in obtaining legal work, but his connection with the Eastern Trust Company was the most helpful. I cultivated Bob Howard, the new general manager of Eastern Trust after Fred Jones was terminated and Bert Fraser of Jarislowsky Fraser in Montreal became president. Tom Hanrahan, the essence of a gentleman, was head of the investment department. From time to time all of these men were entertained at our home.

James Jordan Fay, the local Eastern Trust manager, was much more interested in fishing, playing poker and enjoying other pastimes than in working and promoting business. Jim was from Bridgewater, Nova Scotia, a Dalhousie Law School graduate and a first cousin of Henry Hicks. Their mothers were sisters. Jim inherited some money because his mother had befriended a nurse from River Glade, a small community about twenty miles from Moncton. Like so many ambitious young people in the early part of the century, the nurse went off to New England, or the Boston states as they were called in our area, to seek her fame and fortune. She gained ample reward for her gamble. During her nursing career a Mr. Jordan, one of the owners of the famous Jordan Marsh department stores, became her patient, and she went on to become his wife.

Mrs. Jordan never forgot her roots, and in the Twenties endowed and built an impressive tuberculosis hospital in River Glade—a impressive complex called the Jordan Memorial Sanatorium, which still stands today as an important health-care institution. It was because of her connection with Mrs. Jordan that Jim Fay's mother christened him with the middle name Jordan.

New England's close relationship with our part of eastern Canada can be traced not so much to geographic proximity as to historical, social and ethnic affinity. My early practice of law emphasized this to me. I was astonished at the number of estates brought to me for probate that had heirs and beneficiaries of the deceased—brothers, sisters, aunts, uncles, nieces, cousins—living somewhere in New England. It worked in reverse as well, with many a correspondence coming from Boston law firms, with instructions and documentation for heirs and beneficiaries in our jurisdiction.

The first important wave of emigration to New England was before, during and after the First World War and consisted largely of English-speaking New Brunswickers. Many an ambitious young professional or entrepreneur went to New England to seek a more inviting economic climate. When I visited the famous Boston Quincy Market once, I saw hanging overhead as a salvaged antique a large metal sign advertising the eggs and poultry of a Hicks company. Hicks was an expatriate of the small community of McKee's Mills, north of Moncton, who made a significant fortune selling farm products in the old Boston market. His brother, who stayed to run the family farm in McKee's Mills, sold farm produce in the old Moncton City Market every Saturday, and he and my father traded with each other. Some of the descendants of the Boston Hicks family still maintain a comfortable residence near the old homestead in New Brunswick.

A later wave of emigration to New England consisting largely of French-speaking New Brunswickers began before the Second World War and provided skilled artisans and craftsmen for the war effort. Indeed, the number of transplants in such places as Waltham, Massachusetts, transformed some New England towns into near counterparts of Buctouche and other Acadian communities.

Mrs. Jordan of New England left Jim Fay five thousand dollars in her will, which he inherited while still in law school. It was a lot of money in those days, and Jim took full advantage of the windfall. It was this, many of his friends felt, that contributed to Jim's apathy towards work. While somewhat derelict in his attention to business, however, Jim compensated by being an interesting social companion. After a stressful day I would often call him up to go driving or visiting. Jim could sense my mood and knew when it was best to drive along quietly and when to engage in interesting anecdotes. When Louise came into my life, he was the first person I introduced her to. The next day he took her for a ride into the country to read her excerpts from *The Highland Heart in Nova Scotia.* I still have the book, with a wildflower she picked that day pressed in its pages.

Jim's secretary at Eastern Trust was the middle-aged Theora Getson, who, as a strict Baptist of the old school, initially looked with some suspicion on this ethnic intrusion who was enjoying so much of the office's business. She kept me at a distance as much as she could, but I worked doubly hard to gain her confidence. Gradually she warmed up and became one of my best boosters, recommending my legal services to office clients and to her personal friends. This was one of my great satisfactions, capped eventually by her naming me to look after the probate of her will and the affairs of her estate.

Jim Fay, however, was forced to leave Eastern Trust, and after domestic dislocations, moved with his new wife to Florida, where he lived out his final years. His most enduring legacy to me was the introduction to his cousin, Henry Hicks, who was then practising law in Bridgetown under the name of Orlando and Hicks and participating in the family lumber business with, appropriately, a casket and undertaking adjunct. We established what turned out to be a warm friendship, and Henry went on to a distinguished career in politics and academia, in which I shared a small part.

With the Eastern Trust Company connection, I competed effectively against Central Trust at every level, while happily accumulating Eastern common shares at around the twenty-dollar level, until I had about 20 percent of the company. Tom Hanrahan and I even approached E.H. Ritcey, the general manager of Central Trust, to see if Eastern might buy that small company, but we were not successful.

This little bubble was soon to burst. Bob Howard, Eastern Trust's general manager, would call me from time to time, asking me to let him have some of my stock. He said the company was expanding its branch network into Ontario and the west, and the stock was needed to qualify directors in the new locations. The stock would be replaced in due course, he promised. Although indignant that I myself was not asked to be a director, I obliged; I didn't want to do anything that might endanger the business relationship.

Bob gradually got most of the stock out of me at $23. When I woke up, I learned it had all gone to some major players in Nova Scotia, including R.A. Joudry and others who were either on the board of the Bank of Nova Scotia or associated with it. The stock was part of the nucleus of control that helped the Bank of Nova Scotia amalgamate the Eastern Trust Company with the Chartered Trust Company of Toronto to form what was called the Eastern and Chartered Trust Company, headquartered in Toronto. The price obtained for the stock was rumoured to be in the $70 range.

This was a bitter disappointment for me, not just because of the loss of business and the financial loss on the price of the stock. These both hurt, but more painful was that a venerable financial institution, the Eastern Trust Company, was lost to its Maritime roots forever. It was a crucial lesson in my young career and taught me the importance of being in charge, personally, of pulling the strings. And it was a lesson that, because of a combination of unusual and unfortunate circumstances, I was unable to use much later in life.

When Eastern and Chartered were merged, their combined assets were $600 million, and the move was hailed in financial circles at the time as the creation of a new financial giant. It had taken the better part of one hundred years for the two institutions to achieve this growth, which today would not be considered significant. It would make an interesting doctoral thesis for some graduate student to take the explosion in asset growth of our financial institutions in the past fifty years and correlate it with the previous one hundred years, in relation to inflation and devaluation in currencies, and the growth in money supply brought about by expansion in the national economy.

A short time after the creation of Eastern and Chartered Trust Company, new legislation prohibited chartered banks from owning or controlling trust companies. Eastern and Chartered was merged with Canada Permanent, and even the Eastern name disappeared forever. The Permanent itself was eventually absorbed into Canada Trust.

Legislative changes in recent years have again opened the door for banks to own not only trust companies but investment dealers. What were once known as the four pillars of financial services—banks, trusts, security brokers and insurance—used to be considered inviolate in their own areas of activity, with no encroachment permitted from one to the other. Now, only the insurance industry stands as an independent, but weakened, pillar, and this too is crumbling through indirect incursion by banks.

It is hard to conceive that, as I began to practise law a half-century ago, banks were barred from engaging in the household mortgage market and indeed would only take a mortgage if it was intended as collateral security for a commercial loan. Such is the pervasive power of the banking industry that today this market is almost completely dominated by the banks.

Banks, as many have learned, can be fickle friends. The Dominion Bank, the first institution to lend me money, eventually became nervous about the loan for my purchases of the Maritime Life. This was long after the departure of the manager and supervisors I had known in the beginning. The loan was much less than one hundred dollars a share, but since the stock was unlisted, trading only over the counter, the new managers said they could not put a proper value on it. They kept requesting reductions in the loan until it was obvious they wanted it retired, which I scrambled to do. Not long after, the stock brought more than eight times the amount of the bank's exposure. So much for the sagacity and perspicacity of bankers.

The story of how the sale of the Maritime Life stock came about is an interesting one. In 1963, Bill Schwartz, the president, had invited me onto the board of the company in what was my first board appointment. Maritime Life was very small but was slowly extending its business into Upper Canadian markets. As business expanded, the company needed more and more capital.

In the life insurance field, the more new business written, the bigger the deficit initially, and the greater the need for capital to support the expansion. We could have done this with a rights issue, but the stock by this time was closely held, with 47 percent in my own camp and most of the remainder in the hands of the other directors, including Schwartz, Allan Foulis and other Haligonians. We were prepared to support our share of the rights issue or any call on the stock, but those Halifax directors who were getting on in years did not want to take on the additional long-term financial burden.

Nor were they warm to our offer to support an issue and thus obtain more than 50 percent of the stock and absolute control of the company. An outside purchaser who would take them all out at a substantial gain seemed much more palatable.

The company had assets of less than $50 million at the time and was only a minor player on the life insurance scene. Many of the larger Canadian insurance companies were keenly interested in the acquisition but would not give the assurance that the company would not be completely absorbed. For the Halifax directors, a commitment to preserve the company's Maritime name and identity, as well as its Maritime head office, had to be a condition of the sale.

John Hancock entered the scene from Boston through a call made to me by Peter Mitchell, the New York manager of S.G. Warburg. After lengthy negotiations in the Bonaventure Hotel in Montreal, the price was finally agreed upon. We had been sticking at $700 a share, and the Hancock representatives said they had no mandate to go beyond $650. We relented and said we would agree to split the difference at $675. The Hancock people had to retire to consult with Boston, even for such an increase, but after about thirty minutes they returned to our room.

"Well, Mr. Schwartz, you just made your stockholders an extra quarter of a million dollars," their spokesman said.

Schwartz, looking at his watch, replied, "Well, hell, you've kept us here for over half an hour. It hardly paid for our time."

The Hancock representatives came to Halifax and readily gave the undertaking to retain the local presence. There was, however, a legal impediment to overcome. The federal Insurance Act limited non-resident ownership to 10 percent for any single owner or 25 percent total non-resident ownership. Fortunately, Maritime Life had been incorporated by a special act of the Nova Scotia legislature that stated that all the provisions of the federal act would be applicable to the company.

A group of us, including Vic Lutnicki, a vice president of Hancock, and Arthur Weaver, a Canadian in Hancock's upper management, visited the premier of the day, Robert Stanfield, to ask for an amendment to the provincial act, under which all the provisions of the federal act would still apply, except for the clause limiting non-resident ownership. Stanfield was impressed with Hancock's sincerity and the amendment was quickly obtained. It was the last Canadian-owned life insurance company to go into non-resident hands.

Gerald Regan was the leader of a three-member Liberal opposition at the time, but lacking his own seat in the legislature, he observed the house proceedings from the visitors' gallery. As a courtesy and to ensure there would be no flack from the Opposition, we asked for his support for the amendment. Later he told me how flattered he was that we sought his cooperation at this low point in his political career. Regan and his wonderful wife Carole later came to be warm friends of ours.

Hancock has lived up to every inch of its commitment and much more. It had a fairly substantial group business in Canada, servicing the Canadian branches of large corporations it insured in the United States, and this business was incorporated into the Halifax office. Under Hancock's tutelage, Maritime Life has become an important financial institution, with assets now well over $4 billion, and is one of the largest employers in the Halifax community. The two gleaming glass towers on Dutch Village Road help attest to Hancock's role as the ultimate model of a responsible corporate citizen.

It was around the time of the Hancock takeover that corporate Canada, bowing to criticism and pressure, began to seek token females as directors. Maritime Life was not immune to this new wave, and it employed headhunters to provide a list of prominent women in the country who might be eligible to serve. The chairman and president interviewed several of the suggested names and settled on Dr. Reva Gerstein, the Toronto psychologist. The fact that the other members of the board were not consulted in the decision upset me at the time, but all of us quickly succumbed to Reva's charm, elegance and intelligence.

After Reva's first meeting the board retired to a luncheon, as was the usual custom, and this time it was held at the Halifax Club. The club had been a solid male bastion for about two centuries and, naturally, was lacking in female washroom facilities. I escorted Reva to one of the men's washrooms and stood guard at the door to bar any male intrusion while she powdered her nose. From then on I was delegated to be her father protector.

A retired bank official from Quebec who was then on the board also became infatuated with Reva, and after a few glasses of wine his basic Gallic nature was not to be repressed. Seated next to Reva and much to her horror, his hand was given to roam upon her knee and beneath her skirt. She endured this discomfort as the perfect lady she has always been, but from that day forward I always made sure I sat next to her as a protective barrier.

Reva recently retired as chancellor after a four-year stint at the University of Western Ontario. She also received what I believe was her sixth honorary degree, this one from her alma mater, the University of Toronto, where she once taught. Now in her eighties, she has lost none of her spirit and charm, and continues to be an inspiration to all who know her.

Several years into my business relationship with Leonard Ellen, matters at the Central Trust Company in Moncton heated up. A battle broke out between three directors and the general manager, E.H. Ritcey, and a bitter proxy war ensued. I still have the letter from Babbitt Parlee returning the shares I lent him to qualify for his appointment to the Central Trust board at the time of the proxy fight.

Ritcey won the war and the three directors resigned, throwing the stock they voted or controlled onto the market. The largest block of this stock was the E.A. Reilly estate. Reilly, a Moncton lawyer, was the founder of the trust company and the first president. He was also the first president of Maritime Life.

Ritcey arranged for the stock to be purchased by Louis Lévesque in Montreal, who held it for a while and then spent months trying to find a new home for it. It seems it was peddled all over the country until Leonard and I bought it from Lévesque's Trans Canada Fund, which then gloated all over the financial papers about its profit of $750,000.

Over the years Leonard and I tried to expand Central Trust by acquisition. One target was Acadia Trust in Truro, controlled by the Stanfield family, but we lost out to Montreal Trust. This was a bitter pill to swallow because the Stanfield family, a pillar of the Maritime community and the defence of its economy, preferred the Quebec buyer over our Maritime bid, even though ours was higher.

Several other early attempts at expansion were likewise unsuccessful, including a bid for British Mortgage and Trust, when the Gregory family, the owners, experienced grave difficulties. This stock went to Victoria and Grey, eventually ending up in the pot at Hal Jackman's National Trust.

In the early Seventies we bought a block of Montreal Trust itself from the Sir Herbert Holt estate and were almost equal in this holding with Paul Desmarais. But the Royal Bank held a critical block, and its going either way would have given practical control. To avoid embarrassment to the bank, which would have had to choose between two high-profile customers, we sold to Desmarais for what seemed a handsome profit at the time.

We had more success with Nova Scotia Trust, which we considered a natural fit; it covered Nova Scotia the way we covered New Brunswick. Gradually we accumulated a stake of about 15 percent and made approaches to the management, but Don Grant, the CEO, resisted all the way. Then R.B. Cameron, who owned a block similar in size to ours, decided to sell. We were told the Nova Scotia Trust directors tried to take Cameron's block but could not, or would not, come up with the financing. When it was offered to us, we grabbed it. Even so, our agreement to purchase was delayed for several weeks by the vendor, who wanted to give the Halifax crowd every opportunity to act.

Cameron's block gave us about 32 percent, and we asked for a meeting with the full board of Nova Scotia Trust. At that meeting the only friendly face on the board was Dick Logue of Sydney. The next day Don Grant and his cohorts ran to the provincial government for legislation that would limit our voting to 28 percent.

We decided to go for a knockout bid, and with the help of Bill Ritchie of Scotia Bond we persuaded Halifax lawyer Harry Rhude to act for us. Throughout most of that night there was an open telephone line between Moncton, Halifax and Montreal. The stock was trading in the low $30 range, and our offer the next day came at $75. John Coleman, the Joggins, Nova Scotia, boy who was then number two in the Royal Bank hierarchy, arranged the bankrolling. When the offer hit the street, the Haligonians capitulated and came running to tender to it.

Thus was born the Central and Nova Scotia Trust Company. Our financing for all of this was not without its hitches. Our regular bankers were not eager to participate, whether because of the credit or because they didn't want to ruffle the feathers of the Halifax burghers on the Nova Scotia Trust board. Hume Ellis, the Central Trust president at the time, had recently moved in from the main branch of the Royal Bank, and it was he who suggested we contact Coleman, the chief general manager at the Royal in Montreal. Having never dealt with the Royal Bank, we were hesitant. If our own bankers, who knew us, showed reluctance, we felt it would be even more difficult to convince a new bank player. However, Ellis made the appointment with Coleman, and Leonard Ellen went to see him.

Coleman, just about the most capable banker ever produced in Canada, was well briefed by Ellis and his own people and had carefully studied the file of information before him. His story of the meeting is that Leonard made an admirable presentation, after which John told him, "You've got it." But Leonard, the inveterate salesman, continued his pitch, to which John said again, "You've got it." Leonard continued to sell so intensely that he seemed oblivious to John's words of approval. Finally, after calling in Tom Dobson, one of his right-hand men, John announced he was going overseas the next day; Tom would look after the matter should there be any dislocation in John's absence. This terminated Leonard's presentation, although John sensed some disappointment that it had not been a tougher sell.

Maritimers take considerable pride in the career of John Coleman, who, from the humble background of a Nova Scotia hamlet, rose through the ranks to become one of Canada's preeminent bankers. His father worked for the coal company at Joggins Mines, and his mother, a Comeau, was a French-speaking Acadian. John was raised by his mother as a Roman Catholic, and such was the religious rancour at that time that after John's parents married, some of his father's longtime friends would cross to the opposite side of the street to avoid acknowledging him.

John went to work at 16 in the bank's Amherst, Nova Scotia, branch, and although he virtually ran the Royal at his peak in Montreal, he was never made president. Earle McLaughlin kept the titles of president and chairman for several crucial years of John's career, and I often felt it was John's religion that hindered his appointment. If this was the case, I am happy that society has progressed substantially in the last quarter-century, at least in this regard.

If you were to seek the ultimate portrait of a banker with a heart, John Coleman would fill the bill to perfection. He was a humane and ever-polite gentleman, but God help anyone who betrayed his trust; he would stand for no deviation from propriety or integrity. Such was the capacity of the man and his far-flung reputation that when John retired from the bank, he was asked to sit on the boards of more than thirty-five companies in Canada, the U.S. and Europe. He sat on the boards of Chrysler Canada as well as Chrysler U.S., and was a member of the committee that hired Lee Iacocca to take over the management of the automaker at a time when the company's very survival was threatened.

Today, well into his eighties, John still sits on five or six boards, and his wise counsel continues to be valued. He still makes the trip to Joggins every summer to visit his parents' graves and contribute to the upkeep at the parish church where he was baptized. He is often accompanied to the cemetery by Anne Murray's mother, from Springhill, who grew up with John and whose parents are also buried at Joggins.

By the time Central and Nova Scotia Trust was created in 1974, Leonard Ellen had long ago given up his clothing line and established a lumber-brokering business, helped, I suspect, by the many connections he made during his years of travelling through Nova Scotia and New Brunswick. His company prospered and quickly established an international reputation, with business not only in Canada but in the U.S. and U.K. as well. It is still an active and viable company, from which, I assume, Leonard draws most of his livelihood today.

Never over the course of our business relationship did Leonard and I enter, or even consider, a legal partnership. We had confidence in each other and were close friends as well as business associates. We even took our vacations together. He was much more aggressive in business in areas where I was inclined to be conservative, and it was this combination that helped bring us success.

Leonard's tall, athletic build and good looks, combined with overflowing charm, made many a woman cast a second glance. He was always immaculately dressed and could have posed in an advertisement for a man of distinction. His personality and congeniality attracted people from all walks of life, and his athletic proficiency made him a sought-after golf and ski partner, whether by bank presidents or his grandchildren. I never learned to hit a golf ball, let alone to risk life and limb on a ski hill.

Leonard also had a compulsive determination to overcome any obstacle in his path to success. His ego seemed fed by a feeling of inadequacy over not having a college education. A smashing success in the business world could compensate for this, and eventually Leonard came to bask in the adulation of his contemporaries in the Jewish Montreal scene—all financially comfortable, but most in the retail and mercantile businesses they inherited from their fathers. Leonard broke into the hallowed precincts of the financial world on his own, without any parental handouts, starting as a teenager selling drug lines.

One evening Leonard and I had dinner with Fredericton lawyer Ewart Atkinson at the Eden Rock Motel in Fredericton, which we owned at the time. Ewart had built up a large and lucrative divorce practice throughout the province when adultery was about the only grounds for marriage dissolution. He had his hand in every scheme of tricks for proving adultery, and he also knew the human frailties of many of New Brunswick's staunch and upright citizenry. Leonard had invested in a modern lumber mill in Boiestown, on the Miramichi River, and the official opening was the next day.

At the table with us was a senior official from the banker of the project, who had come down from Montreal to attend the ribbon-cutting. The banker had recently undergone a prostate operation, which apparently had some detrimental effect on his libido. As Ewart, then probably in his seventies, regaled us with tales of the stable of lovely ladies available to ensure the efficient operation of the divorce machinery, the expression on the banker's face easily gave away his orgasmic excitement, whereupon Ewart said to him: "Would you like a date? I'll have her there at your room at nine o'clock."

After dinner we all went to the banker's room to await the nubile lass. As nine o'clock came and went, each passing minute was like a year to the banker. Leonard called Ewart to see if there was a hitch in the arrangement; no stone should ever be left unturned to keep your banker happy. Assured that everything was in order, Leonard returned to our vigil at the motel-room window. Finally, at nine thirty, a car drove up. The banker, under the impression that Ewart had made similar arrangements for Leonard and me, kept repeating excitedly: "She's mine, she's mine. Yours is coming later."

Out of the car stepped a somewhat plump, garishly painted woman. As she walked into the room, she apologized for being late, explaining that she had to put her kids to bed. She was the wife of a soldier from nearby Camp Gagetown. Leonard and I discreetly made our exit and returned to his room, but less than ten minutes later a knock came to the door and in walked the banker with a sheepish look. Never a word was said about his encounter. An old Yiddish expression aptly sums up this adventure: *araus gevorfene gelt* ("money thrown away"). After that, whenever Leonard and I recounted the tale in family settings, our gleeful expression became: "She's mine, she's mine. Yours is coming later."

At the opening of the sawmill the next day, K.C. Irving closely examined all the new machinery for pointers that might improve his own lumbering enterprises. A reception was held at the Tuck-a-Way Lodge, overlooking the broad expanse of the Miramichi. Leonard was taken with the location, and having been asked often about salmon-fishing trips by some of his lumber customers, he inquired about renting the lodge. Arrangements were made for a lease, and the rent was paid.

Leonard offered the lodge to several of his customers at certain times during the season, but all those who had pestered him for years had other commitments on the specified dates. As the year went by and the lodge was not used, I drove up for a few days so that the rental payment would not be a complete loss. When I entered the premises and saw mice scampering across the floor, I turned tail and drove back home. Another example of *araus gevorfene gelt*.

In the early Seventies I interrupted Leonard's lumber career when I persuaded him to enter the stock brokerage business. Almost a decade earlier the board of Maritime Life had interviewed several investment firms to administer our stock and bond portfolio, in the end choosing C.J. Hodgson and Company, a securities house with headquarters in Montreal. Archie Hodgson, the scion of the founder, made the presentation that impressed the board, and would present periodic reports to us on the management of the account. He and I came to have quite a rapport. Getting along in years, Archie soon turned over the ownership of the business to his senior employees, who proceeded to run it down to the ground. With the firm's future at stake, Archie called me for advice. He was distressed because his pension, on which he relied for retirement living, was tied to the earnings and prosperity of the investment company and was thus now in jeopardy. I promised to speak to Leonard in Montreal and have the two of them meet to see what salvage arrangements could be worked out. It was this meeting that launched Leonard in the investment business.

We buttressed the investment company with the needed new capital, and Leonard went in to take active management. He studied for weeks on end to prepare for the investment-dealers' examination so that he could become a full-fledged broker. With a couple of brokerage acquisitions, including T & A Richardson in Toronto, the company soon became an important player in the medium-sized investment-dealer business in Canada. Fortunately, too, Archie Hodgson's pension was rescued and Leonard became his white-haired boy.

With the creation of Central and Nova Scotia Trust, Harry Rhude came on board as chairman, giving us that rare combination of a disciplined legal mind and practical business acumen.

It had not been easy to get him to act for us in the purchase of Nova Scotia Trust, since he was a director of the company and felt he could be in conflict. Bill Ritchie had suggested other lawyers, including Ian MacKeigan, later a chief justice of Nova Scotia. But I was impressed with Harry's ability during previous legal associations with him and was determined to obtain his services. It was perhaps my greatest coup in the art of persuasion when I got him to send in his resignation from the Nova Scotia Trust board to clear the way for him to act. Time and events proved that my judgment in this regard was completely on target.

Legal documents were piled a foot high and spread more than ten feet across when we closed the purchase of United Financial Management in Toronto a short time later. The company marketed the United Group of Funds across the country, and the vendor was Waddell, Reed Inc. of Kansas City, Missouri. Representing the vendor was a battery of lawyers, including three or four American lawyers and some Canadian legal talent. All were verbose, as is often the case with lawyers who feel they must show their client how diligently they are protecting his or her interests.

We, as purchasers, had only Harry Rhude. Less than half an hour into his professional and confident presentation, the other lawyers knew they were in the company of a master. It was inspiring to see how quickly, even among his legal peers, Harry's dominance was recognized.

The officers of the vendor company seemed to be in a hurry to get their hands on the purchase moneys, and we learned that they were nearing a deadline for payment of a two-million-dollar fine levied by the Securities and Exchange Commission for a misdemeanour. We did feel uneasy handing over a man-sized cheque that would be rushed onto the next plane to Washington for payment of a regulatory penalty.

Included in the United Financial Management package were a small life insurance company and a small trust company, which were disposed of in due course, covering most of our purchase price. The funds company itself soon came to have a value many times the original purchase price and became an important part of our financial services structure.

Earlier, I also enjoyed an important business relationship with the Nova Scotia Savings, Loan and Building Society. The company planted its roots in Halifax in 1850, and since it was structured along the lines of the old English building societies, it had no share capital. In later years, to get access to capital to enhance its growth, the company obtained legislation to become a stock company and changed its name to the Nova Scotia Savings and Loan Company. As stock became available from time to time, Leonard and I picked that up as well, eventually holding about 30 percent of it.

We acquired a similar stake in the Eastern Canada Savings and Loan Company, headquartered in Halifax and founded in 1867. For years this company's business had been a mainstay of my practice, and I was invited onto the board in 1965. This was my second board appointment, and I religiously attended the meetings, held every Thursday at two o'clock. I would fly to Halifax on a Viscount every Thursday morning and return in the evening. The return fare was $28 during all those years; today it is more than $350.

Harry Rhude at my behest also came onto the Eastern Canada board. He was an amateur artist, and at the end of the meetings I often collected the drawings he had doodled on his notepad and left behind. Harry was at the top of the heap in his law profession at Stewart, MacKeen, Covert and sought after in numerous quarters as the foremost business, commercial and corporate legal brain in eastern Canada. He was also a director of Sobeys and National Sea Products, and during the Seventies both were trying to entice him to work for them full time. Harry was harassed on all sides by demands for his services and worked punishing hours trying to keep everyone happy.

When Harry eventually chose to come aboard full time with us, it was less a tribute to my abilities than to those of his wife, Elsie. She was worried that the incessant demands on his time were hurting his health. Sensing her concern, I enlisted her help in getting him to retire from the law office and accept a major corporate challenge, which would mean a lighter workload and a less hectic schedule. I also got Elsie to persuade Harry to come in our direction rather than to Sobeys or National Sea, where he might face more travel and physical stress. The power of a woman triumphed again.

Harry was a tall, handsome man, without an ounce of extra flesh on his frame. After his distinguished service in the Royal Canadian Air Force during the war, he enrolled in law school at Dalhousie. But his health was never robust, and in his law school days he developed tuberculosis. In his final year of law Harry was confined to a hospital bed, unable to attend any classes for the whole term. He nevertheless studied the texts in his hospital room and wrote the final exams, finishing at the head of the class with marks that are an enviable target for achievement to this day.

During his years of practice he lectured part time at the law school, his most prominent subject being taxation. John Crosbie, the former Conservative cabinet minister, once told me he owed much of his success in law and other endeavours to the disciplined teaching of Harry Rhude.

Cigarettes were a constant companion with Harry and, with his lung ailment, a forbidden habit. He was always lighting up, despite the lectures from his family and friends. In later years, when it became essential he quit smoking, and he himself was convinced of the necessity, he made a determined effort; he no longer kept cigarettes on his person or in his desk. The craving was so strong, however, that he would wander out to beg a cigarette from anyone around or, failing this, sneak out to buy a pack and smoke in secrecy. I have never had a cigarette in my mouth, but I believe it must be a most powerful addiction if a person with the intellect of Harry Rhude, completely aware it was killing him, was not able to conquer this curse.

The Rhude era at Central brought exciting challenges and accomplishments. With Harry, the management and image of the trust company were dramatically transformed, and responsible planning was instituted for profitability and growth. We amalgamated with Eastern Canada Savings and Loan, creating assets now running into the billions instead of the hundreds of millions. I was particularly pleased that this amalgamation, unlike some of the others, was accomplished without dissension. My years on the Eastern Canada board and the confidence this might have engendered, together with the respect held for Harry Rhude throughout the business and professional communities, must have helped.

Donald Smith, who later became Nova Scotia's consul general in the United Kingdom, was the president of Eastern Canada, and Hal Connor its chairman. They were persuaded that the days of a company limited strictly to a savings and loan business were in jeopardy. Recent changes in regulations that allowed chartered banks to engage in the residential and retail mortgage market had completely altered the competitive picture. The banks, with their vast capital resources and extended branch networks, were creating fierce competition for mortgage product, as well as for deposit sources. This seemed likely to make an anachronism out of a regional savings and loan operation acting purely in an intermediary function, fighting for deposits with which to fund mortgage loans.

Many times, forward commitments had been made to be funded weeks or months later, when cash flow permitted. As well, regional institutions were often forced to pay higher interest rates to entice deposits, which meant narrower spreads to be competitive in the more desirable segment of the market. This, with the attendant squeeze on profitability, created pressure to consider less desirable, or riskier, product at higher rates to maintain the spread.

Eastern's amalgamation with Central offered a diversity of financial product, an extensive base of fee income, a much larger branch network and the usual synergies in operations. Unlike statutory legislation governing the amalgamation of trust companies, no statutory authority existed for the amalgamation of a trust company with a savings and loan company. Since both Central and Eastern held federal charters, a special act of Parliament was needed.

Nova Scotia senator Irving Barrow piloted this bill through the Senate, and Herb Breau, the member of Parliament from Gloucester in New Brunswick, was equally helpful in the House of Commons. We did have a few anxious days, though. The bill to transform the Industrial Acceptance Corporation, or the IAC, into a bank was also before the Commons and was being subjected to considerable scrutiny by certain committee members who had left-leaning convictions and perhaps an innate antipathy towards banks. As a financial institution we were concerned that some of these feelings would work against us and cause an unwelcome delay. This certainly proved to be the case with the IAC bill and the proposed formation of the Continental Bank, which was postponed, after an unsuccessful debate, to the next session of Parliament.

We were not a target, however, and our bill got through expeditiously. In 1976 the Central and Nova Scotia Trust Company became the Central and Eastern Trust Company, and head office moved from Moncton to Halifax.

Around the time Central and Eastern Trust were amalgamated, I was invited onto the board of MICC Investments, which operated the Mortgage Insurance Company of Canada, the largest private insurer in the business and competitive with Central Mortgage and Housing, as the government insurer was then called. MICC eventually absorbed its only private competitor, Sovereign Mortgage Insurance, and became an aggressive and important contributor to the health of the Canadian real estate market. I took pride in the fact that this board invitation came not because of any investment stake

I had in the company, which at the time was minimal, but because the board and management felt I could make a useful contribution.

Often during my career, people across the country sought my counsel or financial direction; it seemed I had developed a reputation for being helpful. One such call came from Jim Pattison in Vancouver, when he was laying the early cornerstones of his business conglomerate. Jimmy's banker had pulled the plug on him, and he needed certain refinancing or the result would be catastrophic. After picking Jimmy up at the Moncton airport and discussing his problem, I took him home for dinner, after which he helped my wife with the dishes and regaled us with a recital on the piano. We enjoyed the music, but I told him that I, personally, regretted the precedent he had set in the kitchen.

Jimmy's financial requirements were a bit beyond our resources at the time, so I arranged an appointment for him with John Coleman in Montreal. The matter was cleared up, and Jimmy soon invited John onto his board, where I am sure John played an important role in helping to build Jimmy's empire.

At MICC, Reg Ryan succeeded Gardner English as president, and I soon developed a healthy respect for Reg's leadership, humanity and integrity— a respect I feel was reciprocated. Leonard felt that MICC could be a valuable asset in our scheme of things and wanted to make a bid for control. I resisted, mostly because I would have been embarrassed if Reg and his people thought I betrayed their confidence. I also worried about the effect such a move would have on the company's dealings with its other institutional clients, because MICC would be controlled by one of their competitors.

My resistance to the MICC investment led to the only dislocation Leonard and I ever had in our relationship. He was so upset that once, when he came to Moncton on other matters, he did not stay with us, as he always had, but registered at a hotel. Nor did he call me. I eventually relented part way, after consulting with Ryan, who felt comfortable that a less-than-control stake would not harm his company in its business with other clients.

Harry at the time was busy buying the Federal Trust Company, a small network of ten or twelve branches in Ontario, introduced to us through John Coleman. While these branches were not all that strategically located, they brought us our first ethnic branches, operating in the Chinese, Portuguese and Italian communities of Toronto and adding a new flavour and dimension to the trust operation. Harry approved of the MICC investment and felt that a move into this new area of financial service, which was an extremely profitable business, could improve his bottom line. In fact, during the years when inflation was enhancing real estate values, MICC was often embarrassed by the lack of claims as it reaped in growing premium income. When the odd claim did appear, it was welcomed and paid promptly to show some justification for the sale and value of MICC's insurance product.

Central's investment stake in MICC was originally 20 percent, so that Harry could equity account MICC's profits with Central's. This profitability went on for a few years, until the Trudeau government's unpopular National Energy Program devastated the Alberta oil industry and western real estate markets collapsed. MICC lost $235 million in less than two years, and this was reflected in Central's earnings, bringing its stock price down to under five dollars.

MICC had to seek new capital to bolster its regulatory capital requirements. Since Harry did not take part in this, Central's holding percentage in MICC was reduced and the equity accounting, with its effects on Central's earnings, was no longer required. The outstanding efforts of MICC management recouped the enormous losses within two years in what was probably one of the greatest turnarounds in Canadian corporate history to that time. Unfortunately, in the real estate market turndown of the Nineties, MICC did not fare as well, suffering losses, particularly in Ontario, that proved fatal.

In its days as a "cash cow," MICC came to have a substantial investment in Inter-City Gas Corporation, with its head office in Winnipeg, and that company came into our sphere of influence as well, with reciprocal representation on both boards.

On a holiday in Paris one spring, Leonard and I visited the Bourse, as the city's stock exchange is called, and for some excitement we placed an order for shares of Crédit Foncier Franco-Canadien, the only Canadian company we were familiar with that traded on the Paris exchange as well as on a Canadian exchange. When we got back home, we discussed this company with Harry as a possible acquisition. Crédit Foncier was more than one hundred years old, incorporated in Quebec but always controlled out of France, with its controlling block held by La Banque de Paris et du Pays Bas, or Paribas.

Crédit Foncier had between $700 and $800 million in assets, but, more important, it had an important presence across Canada, with particular strength in the west. After making enquiries through banking connections, Harry went over to Paris and, after considerable negotiations, made a deal with Paribas to buy control of Crédit Foncier in the $75-million range. The agreement was formalized, and Harry returned to Canada with the necessary documentation in hand and in order.

Raymond Lavoie was the president of Crédit Foncier, and he was well known to Leonard, who often golfed with him, although perhaps better known to me. He had sat on the MICC board, and from our conversations over the years I was impressed that he was a devotee of a free-market economy for business, unhindered by undue government regulation and interference. We considered Lavoie a friend. But when Paribas advised Lavoie of the sale, we were told that this friend and eminent free-trader hurried to Quebec City to get the Parti Québécois government of René Lévesque on his side and against us.

We were not concerned, since we had a legal contract and all the moneys were duly escrowed. In late 1978, to help ensure an orderly and smooth transfer and as a courtesy to the Quebec government, Harry, Leonard and I flew to Quebec City to meet Jacques Parizeau, then the minister of finance. Our appointment was for seven o'clock. After a quiet dinner at the Hilton Hotel we rushed over to the government offices to be in good time for the meeting. Parizeau kept us cooling our heels until after ten o'clock, the only minor relief coming from a chat with his secretary, who told us she was raised in northern New Brunswick.

When the great man finally did appear, he apologized for the delay, citing pressing governmental business. Parizeau was not uncordial as we explained our plans for Crédit Foncier. What we thought was a satisfactory reception and interview lasted about an hour, and we came away feeling confident. The next day, Lise Payette, the minister of consumer and corporate affairs, introduced legislation in the Quebec National Assembly prohibiting our purchase of Crédit Foncier.

This discriminatory legislation could have been fought and would probably have been disallowed, particularly if it reached the Supreme Court of Canada. But we were too bitter to take action. It seemed incredible to us that Crédit Foncier, with its head office in Montreal and most of its assets in other parts of Canada, could be controlled for more than a century by non-residents living in France, while a Halifax-based company, with one of its main shareholders a second-generation lifelong resident of Quebec, could not be deemed an acceptable owner.

We relinquished our Crédit Foncier shares to the Montreal City and District Bank, a Quebec-oriented institution that was to be brought forward as a saviour. Eventually this all ended up in Paul Desmarais's Montreal Trust.

A short time after this disappointment, my wife and I were at the fiftieth birthday party in Montreal for Leo Kolber, who later became a senator. Lévesque was still the premier, and with an obviously practised eye for the prettiest woman in the crowd, he asked my wife for a dance. After learning her name and where she was from, Lévesque put two and two together. "You're not his wife?" he asked Louise. When she answered yes, the discomfited premier interrupted the dance, brought her back to our table and spoke to me.

"I'm sorry, but you should have come to me," Lévesque said.

"We went to your minister of finance, who we felt was the proper person in the government to be consulted in a matter of this nature," I said.

"That was a mistake—next time you should come and see me."

"There will be no next time," I said emphatically.

Certainly there are numerous business opportunities to be enjoyed in Quebec, but my own experience convinced me that if you are not Québécois, you must act as if you're doing business in a foreign country. Meech Lake, in many ways, seemed to be an attempt to enshrine *de jure* what exists *de facto* in Quebec and Canadian society.

Like many Canadians, I was agitated when the government of Robert Bourassa enlisted the notwithstanding clause provided for in the Canadian constitution—a constitution already rejected by Quebec—to negate the Supreme Court of Canada decision striking down the Quebec language law, which offended the essence of the Charter's protection of individual rights. Some people have argued that we should not be too concerned about such episodes in the evolution of Quebec's "distinct society," since the province, after all, is not a banana republic likely to trample individual rights, and since minorities historically have always lived and prospered in Quebec. These arguments I would refer back to the Duplessis era, with its infamous Padlock Law and the Roncarelli restaurant lawsuit, launched after a liquor licence was cancelled and the owner put out of business because of his involvement with the Jehovah's Witnesses. Luckily, in those years the courts and the rule of law, not the politicians, were the final word.

In present Quebec society I feel a bubbling undercurrent of racism. It's a disturbing feeling and one I believe is beginning to be shared by many other concerned Canadians. In 1992, in *Summer Reflections*, the playwright and author Vaclav Havel, now the president of the Czech Republic, wrote of the possible breakup of Czechoslovakia into two republics, one Czech, the other Slovak, because of cultural and language differences. What a catastrophe this would be, politically and economically, for both, he wrote. It is uncanny, from his account of the clashes between the two groups, how closely that situation parallels the current state of affairs in Canada. Havel's intelligent arguments did not prevail, however, and passion overcame reason.

Few nationalist movements have not achieved success in the last half-century. If Quebec nationalists succeed in breaking away, I fear a fascist or semi-fascist state will be created within a decade of the event, and that Montreal will become another Belfast.

In my young days, business usually required five or six visits to Montreal for every one to Toronto. A few decades later, visits to Montreal for business purposes were eliminated. And on the occasional visit for a social event, it was distressing to see the decay of the downtown retail shopping area.

CHAPTER 6

The Crown Story

Our dream was to achieve national status for Central and Eastern Trust, and the experience with Crédit Foncier was not the only time Leonard and I were frustrated.

In the early Seventies we had begun buying shares in Crown Trust. Crown, with headquarters in Toronto, was a perfect fit. It was small enough to be purchased from our internal resources, yet had a branch network stretching from Montreal to the Pacific. Crown was strong in the corporate and personal trust business, where we were weak, and it was weak in the intermediary business, where we were strong. It also had an excellent reputation in the industry and on the street.

Leonard and I accumulated more than 30 percent of the shares in Crown Trust, using the Canadian Imperial Bank of Commerce to help finance the purchases, which were partly in our individual personal accounts and partly in a company we jointly owned. The CIBC was not our usual banking association, but we had a special reason for leaning on the bank in this instance. The estate left by John McMartin of Hollinger Mines fame owned 25 percent of Crown Trust stock, and Crown was a co-executor of the estate. Bud McDougald, a nephew of McMartin, was a director of the Commerce and the most powerful member of its executive committee. He also acted as chairman of what was called the advisory board of Crown, the real power directing the affairs of the trust company. A change in the Bank Act that prohibited a bank director from serving on the board of another financial institution had sent most bank directors scurrying away from trust company boards—Hal

Jackman being, I am told, the only bank director in the country to resign from a bank board to stay on a trust company board. The creation of the advisory board at Crown was a neat way to get around this legislative restriction and permit McDougald to continue to make all the important moves.

Advised that McDougald was the key to the McMartin stake in Crown, we wooed him for the better part of the decade. McDougald was revered in the financial world at the time as one of the "four horsemen" who created Argus Corporation. The conglomerate controlled a large part of the industrial and commercial giants that made up an impressive segment of the Toronto Stock Exchange, including Massey-Ferguson and Dominion Stores, which are no longer significant players in Canada. Argus in its day was the model for corporate acquisition. It would take a large, but generally minority, position in companies and effectively control them through board, and often management, appointments—a model that would be largely ineffective and an anachronism in the corporate climate of today. The other three "horsemen" were E.P. Taylor, Lt.-Col. Eric Phillips, who was McDougald's brother-in-law, and Senator Wallace McCutcheon. Conrad Black's father, George, was also associated with the Argus team.

During the quest for McDougald's cooperation over the McMartin shares, my wife and I came to have an enjoyable relationship with the man. He and I had many lunches at the Toronto Club, where his portrait hung in the main lounge and where he presided at his own table, reserved exclusively for him and not to be contaminated by lesser humanity, even when he was away. McDougald never tried to keep me hidden during these lunches, and with him I met some of the brightest lights of the Toronto establishment and business community. Leonard and I were always aware that we were perceived in some quarters of the financial world as "ethnic" outsiders, but we never considered this an obstacle that we could not overcome through our own integrity and acumen.

McDougald quickly became a dedicated fan of my wife and often asked her to adorn his table when he entertained special dinner guests. Louise in turn came to have a genuine fondness for him and looked forward to these social events. *Maclean's* magazine once ran a cover picture of Bud McDougald in one of his famous antique cars. Louise was engaged in the art of copper enamelling at the time and, using an enlarged version of the *Maclean's* photo, created a copper-enamelled portrait of McDougald, in full detail and colour.

This was a long and laborious task, requiring hundreds of hours of piecing, colouring and baking in a high-intensity oven. The finished product was a delight, and McDougald was overwhelmed. The portrait hung in his living room in Toronto and was transported each year to his winter home in Florida.

McDougald's imperial lifestyle was as fascinating to watch as the man himself. Our dinners at his homes in Toronto and Palm Beach usually included a CEO from an Argus company, but in Palm Beach, prominent names from the American establishment wintering there were also invited. Around Christmas, McDougald would delicately suggest he thought it fitting to dress up for the festive season, which meant black tie. Before dinner he usually took me aside, often to the garden, to fill me in on the background of the other guests, who on one occasion were Mr. and Mrs. Page Hufty.

Mrs. Hufty was an Archbold and she, not her husband, was the one with the money, McDougald told me. Her father had been a partner of John D. Rockefeller, and the Archbolds actually had more money than the Rockefellers, he advised me. The Huftys had a pretty, young daughter, Page Lee, whose picture was on the cover of *Town and Country* magazine that month, with two Arabian horses given to her by the king of Jordan. At dinner, of course, the magazine cover came up for discussion. Yes, the proud father said, his daughter was so popular the family never knew who would be next at the door to call on her; one night it might be King Hussein, the next, Teddy Kennedy. At this, McDougald leaned over to me and whispered, "It all depends on who your daughter is sleeping with as to whether you try to hide it or boast about it."

McDougald maintained an apartment at Claridge's Hotel in London and kept a limousine and full-time chauffeur there as well. He once told me that when he wasn't in residence in London, he let the Royal Family use his car and driver. He felt sorry for the family because they were "having a hard time financially, you know."

Members of the Royal Family were often his houseguests in Toronto, usually when they came for the Royal Winter Fair. When Princess Anne stayed, with her husband Mark (whom she later divorced), McDougald told me he didn't think the husband was "very much." On another visit Anne made an innocuous comment about the situation in Northern Ireland that so infuriated one of McDougald's housekeepers, who was Irish, that he was afraid of losing her. He placated the housekeeper after Anne left.

The Queen often consulted him, particularly about horses. McDougald's horse farm in Florida, which we visited, contained a large outdoor swimming pool for the horses, but both air and water had to reach a certain minimum temperature before the animals were allowed in for a dip.

Bud always dressed to fit the occasion, and the tassels on his shoes bore the Argus crest. His Toronto limousine had gold-plated hubcaps, presumably from ore mined by Hollinger, and on his Toronto estate the garage for several dozen of his prized antique cars was splendidly outfitted, with crystal chandeliers for lighting and silk curtains on the windows.

His antipathy towards Pierre Trudeau, then the prime minister, bordered on an obsession. A large block of the McDougald estate had been expropriated by the municipal authority, and when the plans were brought to him for his signature, so he could be compensated, he refused to sign. He held up the transaction for months because one of the new streets laid out in the plan was to be named Trudeau Drive. Only after the city gave in, by changing the street's name to Trudel Drive, was the signature obtained.

Joe Clark, the leader of the Conservative party and husband of Maureen McTeer, would never succeed, Bud said, because a man who couldn't get his wife to take his name would never be strong enough to run the country. Although a Catholic, Bud had strained relations with Cardinal Emmett Carter because the cardinal endorsed the boycott of California grapes at Dominion stores in a show of support for exploited migrant farmworkers.

Bud McDougald confided all these things. And all along he assured me that if Leonard and I bided our time and did not do anything rash—he mentioned Paul Desmarais's uninvited, rebuffed bid for Argus in the mid-Seventies—the Crown prize would eventually be ours. "I'm going to pop off one of these days," he would say to me. "You won't be harmed if I do."

Bud had no children, and the rumour at the time was that Conrad Black was the heir apparent, chosen to one day direct the affairs of Argus. When I questioned Bud about this, he was quick to reply that it was not the case, despite what Conrad himself might think and Bay Street might contemplate. Conrad was still young, Bud said, and had much to do to prove himself. When Black grabbed the reins soon after McDougald's death, it was natural to conclude that it was through Black's own ambition and determination and not through any process of natural selection.

During the winter of 1978, when Bud became ill and was confined to his room at his Palm Beach house, a call came to our house there asking us to visit him. My wife was otherwise engaged that afternoon, so I brought my daughter Debra instead. Bud looked wan as he came down to the living room in his dressing gown, but we had a pleasant chat, and I think he enjoyed Debra, since the company of handsome young people generally does give us seniors a lift. Bud said he was grateful and thanked us for visiting. Later I learned that we were the last people he asked to see socially. Within a few weeks, he was gone.

I went to Toronto for the funeral, and among the many who gathered afterward for a reception at McDougald's home was Conrad Black. Black, too, wanted the McMartin shares and moved quickly after the funeral. Emissaries, including Ainslie Shuve, then president of Crown Trust, were rushed around the world to sign up the McMartin heirs. Leonard and I sent a telegram saying we would beat any offer for the estate's shares, but it did no good. The McMartin stake went to Black.

Winning the McMartin shares gave Black *de facto* control of Crown, the key to his eventual control of Argus. Leonard and I then negotiated with Black for the better part of a year for his Crown stock, which had become redundant to him after it served the purpose of access to Argus.

On a visit to his father's Toronto home, where Black lived at the time, I was impressed to see on the hall table a copy of the *Jerusalem Post*. Conrad and his wife Shirley were busy scanning the newspapers for stories announcing their marriage, one of which carried the headline "Tycoon marries." The *tycoon* designation appeared to afford Black much pleasure. But the Montreal newspaper that carried a picture of "the modest bungalow" in which his mother-in-law lived seemed to displease Shirley, who also expressed concern about pressure on her mother from photographers and reporters.

At lunch, which was served by a butler, Black associate Peter White expressed the opinion that perhaps the Crown stock should not be sold. "Every wealthy man should have his own trust company," he told Black.

We also invited Black to dinner in Palm Beach and included his guest, Brian Stewart of the CBC, in the party. Black's lawyer at the time was a rather obscure sole practitioner named Igor Kaplan, and I once asked him why he, instead of a big name from an established Toronto legal office, got the job. "I think it is because he is a true, genuine Jewophile," Kaplan said.

During our negotiations I met David Radler, who was heading up the Sterling newspaper interests, then quite modest compared with Black's international newspaper empire of today. Radler's copious mop of black hair was impressive, and I was a bit envious, perhaps because of my own balding pate. His close association with Black further impressed on me Igor Kaplan's "Jewophile" comment. Perhaps this is also a fulfilling factor in Black's present wife, Barbara Amiel.

Black soon became a director of the Canadian Imperial Bank of Commerce and a member of its executive committee, taking the seats left vacant by McDougald's death. In the meantime, it became apparent that the bank held just under 10 percent of the Crown stock, the maximum it was legally permitted to hold, at that time, in a trust company. In our negotiations for the purchase of the now Black-held stock, and in a vendor's natural zeal to obtain the maximum possible price, it was intimated to me that our bid could perhaps be increased if the bank could be persuaded to accept a lower price for its holding, so that our overall cost would be the same. I expressed my doubts that the bank would consider a lower figure than the price paid for the larger block, but that in any case, we could only deal with all shareholders on an equal level.

An agreement to buy the Crown stock was finally reached early in 1979 and reduced to writing. It was not to be executed, however, but kept in the desks of each side's lawyers for about six months. Only later did we learn why Black wanted the delay: he had made a commitment to the McMartin heirs that, if he sold his Crown shares within a year, they were to participate in the profit.

Before our critical closing date for the purchase, Izzy Asper and Gerry Schwartz, then together as business associates in CanWest Capital, made an unsolicited offer of $44 a share for Black's Crown stock. This was several dollars above the purchase price provided in our own agreement with him. The CIBC's 10 percent holding in Crown was pivotal to control, but despite all our efforts it was included with the sale of Black's shares to Asper and Schwartz, giving them control of the trust company.

All this occurred a little more than thirty days before new rules were adopted to protect minority shareholders in a purchase of control, under which Asper and Schwartz would have had to offer to buy our Crown shares, at the same price paid to Black and under the same conditions.

The quoted price of the Crown stock fell from about $35 to the $12 range, and the Asper group had the chutzpah to offer us $10 a share for our stock— not that they needed it, they said, but to help us out. With the market price of

One of my first photo opportunities, with my mother, Molly, in 1921.

My parents, David and Molly, seen here soon after moving to Moncton, New Brunswick, circa 1926.

My brother, Nathan, and I pictured here with our pony in 1926. This photograph was taken just outside of my father's barn in Moncton.

This is a picture of the building on Main Street, Moncton, in which I was born, just before it was demolished. The brick building to the right is still standing though most of what was on the left is now largely the location of the new City Hall.

The interior of my father's grocery store at 702 Main Street in Moncton, when it was still a tobacconist. It was in an apartment above this store where my family lived and where I spent most of my formative years.

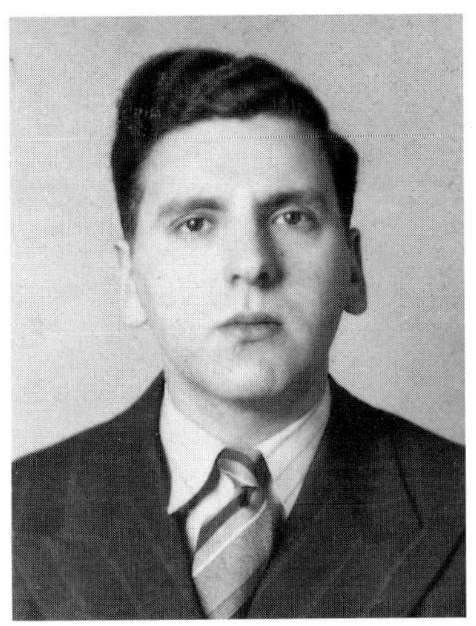

Off to Dalhousie University in Halifax with $150.00 awarded in scholarship money. Circa 1938.

My wedding to Louise, February 10, 1951, at the Queen Hotel in Moncton.

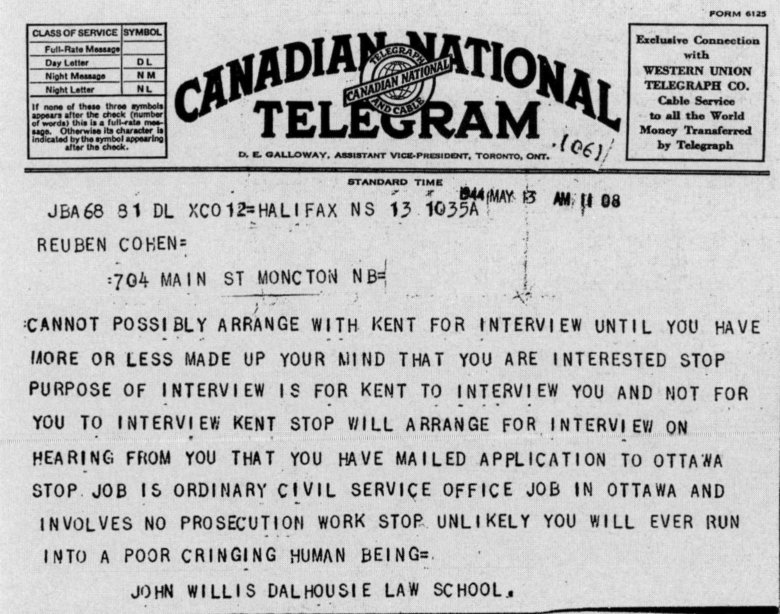

Telegram from John Willis, then Acting Dean of the Dalhousie Law School, dated May 13, 1944. Note the reference to the prospective interview in Ottawa. After only three years under his tutelage, he was quite aware of some of my personality characteristics.

A family portrait, circa 1973. From left to right is my youngest daughter, Natalie, myself, my eldest daughter, Debra, and Louise seated in front.

Myself, Louise, Henry Hicks and his second wife, Gene, photographed here at a garden party at Buckingham Palace in London celebrating the 80th birthday of the Queen Mother, in1980.

Taken at the Acadia convocation in 1983, from left to right, are Chancellor Alex Colville, myself, and then president William Perkin.

My wife, Louise, in 1985, just before she became ill. Louise would give me a portrait each year on Father's Day to hang on my office wall. This was the last one I received from her. She was 56 years old at the time this picture was taken.

My wife, Louise, with then Prime Minister Pierre Trudeau, taken at the 25th anniversary of Canada World Youth. On the right is the minister of fisheries from New Brunswick, Herb Breau.

Seated here with Rita MacNeil, singer/songwriter, and Frank McKenna, then premier of New Brunswick in 1988, after we each received honorary degrees from the University of New Brunswick. In the background from left to right are: Jim Downey, then President of the University of New Brunswick; Violet Aitken, then Chancellor of the University of New Brunswick; Gilbert Finn, then Lieutenant Governor of New Brunswick; and Colin McKay, President Emeritus of the University of New Brunswick.

Leonard Ellen and I pictured here on the slopes of Courcheval, France, circa 1989.

My installation as an Officer of the Order of Canada by then Governor General Ray Hnatyshyn in 1991, an elevation from a member of the order bestowed in 1979.

Jim Pattison and I pictured here on Jim's yacht in Vancouver, circa 1995.

A 70th birthday party for Harrison McCain, pictured here blowing out his candles. Standing in the background is Jim Downey, now President of the University of Waterloo, November 1st, 1997.

the stock decimated and its quoted value well below our borrowing against it, the CIBC called our loan. We had to hustle to pay the bank, and we sat for three years on the outside looking in, locked into a seriously depreciated, expensive and unproductive asset. If anyone ever needed a lesson about the magic of 51 percent, this one was a classic.

The Crown saga is told in detail by Patricia Best and Ann Shortell in their exceptionally well-researched book, *A Matter of Trust*, published in 1985. My only purpose here was to fill in some background. While most of the material in *A Matter of Trust* is essentially correct, I do question the ethical concern the authors raise about our unsigned agreement to buy Black's Crown shares after a certain deadline had passed. "It couldn't be a formal agreement, or Black would have to hand over the profit to the McMartin estate," they wrote. "It didn't seem to arise that there might be a conflict of interest in two major shareholding groups essentially planning to circum-navigate an agreement that was made to protect one of the estates the company [i.e. Crown] was counselling." In fact, Leonard and I were in no way privy to the agreement between the McMartin heirs and Black concerning the profit from a quick sale of his Crown shares.

Our financial loss on the Crown affair was too large to take sitting down. Leonard and I felt betrayed by the CIBC, which had welcomed our business while knowing all along, as we learned later, that our persistent effort to win control of Crown was unlikely to succeed. The CIBC had a duty, we believed, to insist that our shares be included when the bank sold its 10 percent to Asper. We asked ourselves what would happen if players our size—not large, but not small—did not stand up to be counted. What chance then would a little guy have in an apparent injustice at the hands of a financial goliath?

We took up the challenge and sued the CIBC, much to the snickering of the establishment in the financial and legal communities. Indeed, it was difficult to get a Toronto legal office to act for us, such was the fear of incurring the wrath of the financial world. After several turndowns we were advised to try Alan Lenczner at McCarthy and McCarthy, who agreed to act—but not, he later told us, without a confrontation with senior members of the firm who questioned the wisdom of his decision. Alan, however, felt strongly that it would violate his duty and integrity as a lawyer to deny service to a client out of fear of repercussions from a powerful lobby or potentially lucrative client group.

I have always believed that the fundamental basis of law is this: where there is a wrong, there is a remedy. But the great weakness in our legal system was demonstrated again when our lawsuit against the bank, like any major lawsuit, took years of emotional and physical stamina and the expenditure of huge financial resources to find the remedy.

The bank appealed to the Supreme Court of Canada, but we won the day in 1985, and at every English common law school in the world the case is now required reading on the law of fiduciary responsibility.

The utter duplicity of McDougald throughout our relationship was made plain at the trial and caused us a great deal of anguish. It was at McDougald's behest and to foil us in our quest for Crown control that Neil McKinnon, the CIBC chairman, arranged to buy Crown stock, so that the bank's holding reached just under 10 percent. Knowledge of the CIBC's purchases was limited to the chairman and top officers in charge of trading, and the pivotal stock was to be acquired patiently and quietly, without pushing up the share price. The bank increased its original Crown holding of fifteen thousand shares to about eighty thousand shares, at an average cost of about $18. In their book, Best and Shortell set out the crux of this ploy as revealed at the trial:

> An April 1973 internal memo made it clear to the bank's investment department that this stock had sacred-cow status. "The impression which I received from the chairman's comments," noted vice-president T.L. Avison, "was that we were holding this stock, quite apart from its intrinsic value as an investment, for reasons of policy, and therefore no sales should be contemplated solely on a basis of market or price consideration."

It saddened me that someone of McDougald's business and social stature could so crassly betray a confidence and friendship. With the present-day fetish for strict corporate governance rules, it is highly improbable that any single director now could wield such powerful influence over the affairs of a financial corporation or other major company. That era passed with McDougald, I hope. Page Wadsworth, who was a successor to McDougald's friend McKinnon as chairman at the bank, gave honest and forthright testimony at the legal proceedings. I have never encountered a gentleman of greater integrity.

While I looked with suspicion at the time on any further dealings with the CIBC, I must confess I now maintain what little is left of my personal banking at a CIBC branch conveniently located for me. Nor do I hold any malice towards Conrad Black. He might have had some moral obligation to us in the circumstances, but unlike the bank, he had no legal or fiduciary responsibility. In fact I applaud his string of successes as much as I admire his erudition and his language facility, even if it is pompous at times.

In the heyday of our relationship Black once asked me to his annual Hollinger black-tie dinner, at which Henry Kissinger was the speaker and the guests came from most of the top echelons of the corporate world. I was also grateful for the reference to Louise in his recent autobiography, *A Life in Progress*, when he referred to her as my "beautiful and talented wife."

In 1982, while the lawsuit against the CIBC was still being fought, I was in Halifax one day at a Maritime Life meeting when Joe Burnett called from Toronto to ask if he could buy our Crown stock. I had done legal work for Joe in the financing and construction of shopping centres in our area and knew him to be an aggressive, hard-headed entrepreneur. His call was like manna from heaven, and he flew down immediately to close the deal at thirty-six dollars a share, which substantially mitigated the damages the CIBC eventually had to pay us. We thought we were extremely fortunate to obtain the sale, but we did not know at the time that approaches were being contemplated to acquire the Schwartz and Asper control block at a much higher price.

When Burnett did buy the control block later in the year at around $62 a share, we agonized over the $10 million or so we lost in the spread of the price paid to us and what Asper and company got—another strong lesson in the value of control. Joe Burnett, in an edition of the *Financial Post Magazine* in the mid-Nineties, was cited as one of the fifty wealthiest people in Canada. Though he bested me beautifully in that trade years ago, I was happy to read of the exciting success he has achieved all on his own. Burnett lost his young wife to cancer, I am told, and I feel a sad affinity with him in this regard.

What quickly ensued after our sale to Burnett provided high and gripping drama in Canadian corporate, financial and legal circles for months to come. In a subsequent hearing the regulators would not accept Burnett as a purchaser of a trust company. Ever enterprising, Burnett had his purchase taken over by Leonard Rosenberg, an apparently acceptable buyer who was also the owner of Greymac Trust and a director of the Canadian Commercial Bank. The famous Cadillac Fairview apartment flip followed in the next few months, the Ontario government seized the assets of Crown and Greymac, and criminal proceedings began.

We bid on the Crown assets, but along with most of Bay Street we expected that the prize would go to Hal Jackman and his National Trust. In an ironic twist, we were chosen, the call coming while Leonard, Harry Rhude and I were at a Royal Bank annual meeting in Montreal. We were told we should be represented in Toronto the next morning to work out the particulars of an agreement. Since Harry had planned to return to Halifax that night, he had no luggage. But as soon as we left the meeting, Leonard ran to buy Harry a toothbrush and a change of underwear, and we hustled him to the airport.

The seventy-two-hour marathon to complete the documentation for the Crown purchase had all the lesser humans present either asleep or semi-conscious in their chairs. Harry, however, persevered without closing an eye. The formula and the document he negotiated that weekend became the precedent used by the Canada Deposit Insurance Corp. and other government authorities for similar transactions.

Harry got back to his hotel room at eight o'clock Monday morning and showered, and before nine o'clock he was in the Crown head office. In 1983, more than a decade after starting the pursuit, we had fulfilled our dream of a national institution reaching from St. John's to Victoria.

The Crown Trust executive offices were on the thirty-eighth floor of First Canadian Place, with the main banking floor on the ground floor of the complex, which was a development of the Reichmann family's Olympia & York. Crown had only recently moved from its old head office nearby on Bay Street. Apparently, the old Crown property was of value to the developers in their overall plan for the area, and during the Asper and Schwartz regime, O & Y agreed to buy the building at a very favourable price; in return, Crown was charged a less-than-market rental rate for its new offices. The lease from O & Y to Crown stipulated that no assignment of the long-term lease was permitted, so that the tenant could not profit by renting out the banking floor at market rates.

The Ontario government, meanwhile, passed legislation making Central the lawful successor to Crown wherever the Crown name appeared in a legal document—as an executor named in a will, for example. But O & Y claimed that Central's arrival at First Canadian Place was an assignment of the lease with Crown and demanded the going rental rate. This meant an increase of hundreds of thousands of dollars and probably millions to the balance of the lease. When Central refused to pay the increase, O & Y took legal action to have us evicted for default.

The matter was litigated in the lower courts and was eventually scheduled to reach the Supreme Court of Canada. Harry Rhude, who disliked lawsuits despite—or perhaps because of—his exceptional legal background, agreed to a compromise on the rent. Olympia & York still got Crown's old Bay Street property at a discount but without having to compensate for this with the original decrease in the rent.

The Reichmanns enjoyed the ultimate reputation at the time for integrity in the business world, and it was said that their word was their bond. Although I have never met any of them personally, my only business dealing with them, remote as it was, left a bitter taste.

Shortly after the Crown purchase, Leonard and I asked to meet with Bill Davis, the premier of Ontario. The meeting was most cordial and opened the door to a warm relationship, which has left me with a healthy respect for Davis's integrity, ability, good sense and, most of all, humanity. At the time, Davis introduced us to Dr. Bob Elgie, the minister responsible for corporate affairs, saying Elgie was both a graduate doctor and a graduate lawyer but, unable to make a living at either profession, was forced to become a politician. This dual training eventually stood Elgie in good stead: after leaving politics he headed the newly established faculty in medical-legal studies at Dalhousie University.

Eddie Goodman, long known as a backroom boy in the Progressive Conservative party, arranged the meeting with Davis. When Eddie published his autobiography, *Life of the Party*, a few years ago, I asked Davis for his opinion. "Until I read the book, I had always thought that I was the premier of Ontario all those years," he replied. I was pleased to see Eddie Goodman's distinguished service to our country recognized by his recent appointment to the Privy Council.

Politics

No part of Canada takes its politics more seriously than the Maritimes. It is a sport that has been played over the years with probably more interest, enthusiasm and sometimes venom than any other activity.

Take the experience of Leonard Jones Jr., son of the lawyer my mother tangled with in 1936 and who was responsible for renaming my Russian cousins. Shortly after Jones was elected mayor of Moncton in the Sixties, the city was visited by a rabid fascist anti-Semite from Quebec. He advertised a meeting to be held in the Brunswick Hotel, which I attended with Rabbi Lippa Medjuck. Jones was sitting in the front row.

When the speaker was well into his virulent tirade, Jones interrupted, took the floor and told him that people of many faiths and races had lived for generations in the community, in goodwill and harmony, making valuable contributions to the city and prospering themselves in the process. He did not appreciate "people like you coming into our city trying to stir up hate, dissension and animosity," Jones said. "My advice to you is to be out of this town by ten o'clock tomorrow morning, and if you're not, I'll try to see if we can arrange to have our police escort you out."

With that, Jones left, the meeting broke up, and Rabbi Medjuck said to me, "Whenever that man Jones runs for any public office, he will always have my support."

This is the same Jones who, a few years later, gained a reputation as a racist because of his confrontations with Acadians over what Jones perceived as inequities in the official version of bilingualism. He was branded an anti-

French bigot. The feelings became so inflamed on both sides that, in 1969, Jones refused to hear representation in French at city council meetings, and French-speaking university students deposited a pig's head on the doorstep of his house. The unhappy consequence of all this was a deeper cleavage between the French- and English-speaking segments of the city, with Jones the darling of the English right.

Jones later won the federal Conservative nomination for Moncton, but the party's leader, Robert Stanfield, evidently felt Jones was too hot a property. Stanfield refused to endorse Jones as the Conservative candidate, so he ran as an independent and won more votes than the Conservative and Liberal candidates combined. In that election Stanfield came within a meagre number of seats of upsetting Pierre Trudeau's Liberal government. Many local people felt that with Jones on his side, Stanfield could have won a few more seats in our area and become prime minister.

From my own experience with Jones, I believe the racist label was unfair. He was not opposed to bilingualism but to its method of rapid implementation, which he felt discriminated against the English-speaking majority. Jones favoured second-language instruction early in the school curriculum, so that within a generation virtually all young people would be able to apply for the myriad advertised jobs that required bilingual employees. Jones's failing was a lack of diplomacy and political finesse. He was dogged and bullheaded, and when backed into a corner he retaliated with an angry determination that served only to aggravate. Both sides were to blame in the clash over language, but Jones should have shown a greater degree of judgment and courtesy. He chose not to run again for Parliament after serving only one term.

Jones's busy law practice, paradoxically enough, served a large and faithful Acadian clientele. As mayor for more than a decade, he was one of the ablest administrators in the history of the city, a fact that was recognized by many in the Acadian community who voted for him each time. He was also a tough lawyer, who fought every inch for his clients. No matter how big a reprobate, Jones's client was always right and his opponent in the wrong.

In his later years of practice Jones was hit with charges under income tax regulations, which he fought unsuccessfully. He believed that the pressure for the charges came from French-speaking members of the Commons from the area, including Roméo LeBlanc, the member for neighbouring Westmorland-Kent who went on to become governor general. Not long after the income tax controversy Jones sold his practice and retired to Alberta to be near his daughter.

New Brunswick political life in the Sixties was dominated by Liberal Louis Robichaud, whose administration was notable for instituting the program of Equal Opportunity. The southern, more prosperous parts of the province were pretty well cared for in the fields of health and education, but in the northern, less prosperous and largely Acadian areas, schools and hospitals were in a grim state. The Equal Opportunity program removed responsibility for education and health from local authorities and concentrated it in the hands of the provincial government. Many people in the south, myself included, felt the transfer of powers would raise the level of services in the north at the expense of reduced services in the south; and this, by and large, was the effect. Our school structure in Moncton today does not seem as professional or dedicated as it was in my school days, and the financial restrictions in hospitals have been a concern for some time.

In fact, Equal Opportunity in New Brunswick was similar in many ways to the federal equalization program introduced by John Diefenbaker. The poorer provinces were to be helped by the largesse of the richer provinces, with the goal of a more uniform level of social services throughout the country. Unfortunately, the more affluent part of New Brunswick was not prosperous enough to bring the less affluent to its level, so it had to slide downhill, just as the richer provinces now have difficulty maintaining the flow of funds into federal coffers to maintain a national plan of social services equality.

Robichaud's first election campaign must have been in some important measure financed by K.C. Irving. The morning after the 1960 election I was at the Moncton airport waiting for a flight when Louis arrived, flush with the joy of victory, and was rushed into a small plane. People in the airport recognized it as an Irving-owned plane and said it was on its way to Saint John, where the Irving headquarters are located.

Much later in his tenure Louis had a falling-out with K.C. over the spoils of mining and smelting operations in northern New Brunswick, which Irving coveted and which Louis helped deliver to Upper Canadian rivals. Shortly after this episode I was travelling from Boston to Saint John on an Air Canada Viscount when my seating companion, quite by accident, was

K.C. himself. The airline food was unappetizing and I only picked away at it, but K.C. ate heartily, leaving hardly a crumb on his tray. K.C. told me he faced a dilemma in the coming provincial election: he was a lifelong Liberal, but he found it difficult to support Robichaud.

The Robichaud era came to a close with the election of 1970, but its demise could be foretold. The Progressive Conservatives, after the debacle of Charlie Van Horne's leadership in the late Sixties, had turned to Richard Bennett Hatfield. He was a bright, young and seemingly fresh and unblemished leader, still in his thirties and named after R.B. Bennett, the New Brunswick native who was prime minister in the early Thirties. Youth, even if untried, often has an untarnished appeal over the warts that seem to accrue to an incumbent administration of some years' duration.

Robichaud's confusion, for whatever reason, at a meeting in Moncton of an organization for mentally disabled children became a well-known embarrassment. He kept referring to the guest speaker, Mrs. Hubert Humphrey, as Mrs. Johnson, the wife of U.S. president Lyndon Johnson.

Louis loved a party, as did Hatfield, but the latter's inclination in this regard was not to become apparent until much later. Louis used to come to our house for dinner and, more often, visited us at our summer home, where his wife's brother was our next-door neighbour. Louis and I once discussed the ethnic restrictions on membership in Riverside, the major golf and country club serving the Saint John area. He was incensed to hear that such discrimination existed in "my New Brunswick," and determined to do something about it. Not long afterward Riverside's doors were opened, whether as a result of his intercession or the routine civilizing of our society.

Louis's visits to our cottage, like Richard Hatfield's later, were usually prolonged, running well into the early morning hours. My wife, as the gracious hostess, would smilingly endure them to the end. I generally tried to retire shortly after midnight and always felt more relaxed when I left her entertaining Richard Hatfield than Louis.

The 1970 provincial election was my first and only active participation in political affairs. Richard asked me to serve on a committee to help with the Conservatives' election financing. I demurred, but he came a second time, getting the same negative result. On his third visit, I consented. When I later asked him why he persevered, Richard said that, while I was evasive, I didn't actually say no.

The finances of the Conservative party were in such a mess that the telephone company would not install a constituency telephone unless payment was made in advance. The bills left by the flamboyant and extravagant Van Horne were well in excess of $500,000. Newspapers and radio stations, with large unpaid balances, refused to accept any advertising without deposits up front. With these drawbacks, no advertising agency would touch the account, and even the telegraph office would not send a telegram for the party on credit.

Creditors who had lain dormant for years now issued writs for the collection of old debts, and Richard, as the new leader, was several times included as a defendant. I wondered at the time whether these moves, after a delay of so many years, were made in the expectation of a better chance for recovery in the middle of an election campaign or because the creditors were encouraged by the Liberals, who wanted to embarrass the opposition. Acting in all these suits were prominent Liberal legal offices in the province.

The first thing the Conservative party's so-called finance committee arranged was a war chest of $150,000, borrowed from a bank in Saint John, with two other signatures besides my own, those of Jim MacMurray and Larry Machum. Armed with funds, we arranged settlements on some of the claims with creditors who would agree to a compromise; and applications made to the courts were successful in getting Richard Hatfield's name removed as a defendant in the others. The way was thus cleared to concentrate on the election campaign itself.

Hatfield won and stayed in power for seventeen years. The day after the election he called to give me his private phone number, assuring me it was available to me at any and all hours. In the final years of his administration I wrote him four times about a matter of benefit to Mount Allison University before I finally got a reply. In this regard I always think, perhaps uncharitably, of a quotation from the Hebrew Ethics of the Father, Chapter 2, verse 3: "Be on guard against the ruling power, for they who exercise it draw no man near to them except for their own interests; appearing as friends when it is to their own advantage, they stand not by a man in the hour of his need."

The Hatfield years provided many an event of interest as well as concern. I continued to attend meetings of the finance committee to ensure that contributions were used to reduce and eventually pay off the $150,000 note. When we were off the hook for this, I retired.

In the late 1970s, long after this participation had receded in my memory,

I was visited by the RCMP. Two officers came to my office with a warrant to search for any files and information pertaining to political contributions. They took what documents they wanted and departed. This was almost a decade after I had innocently participated in the back rooms of the New Brunswick Conservative party. Charges in the nature of influence peddling were subsequently laid against two of the fund-raisers. One charge was later dismissed, largely on a technicality involving the admissibility of evidence. The other charge, against Francis Atkinson, the son of my old friend Ewart Atkinson, brought a conviction and a large fine. During the course of these proceedings my name came up intermittently in the evidence and appeared in newspapers and news broadcasts. The worry, anxiety and embarrassment this caused me was incalculable.

My advice to anyone who is ever invited to partake in the game of back room politics is—don't. You'll never know how participation in the utmost of innocence can come back to haunt you. What you think is a useful contribution to the body politic can often bring misery rather than satisfaction. My only active involvement in political affairs is something I have come deeply to regret.

Richard Hatfield was probably the most sophisticated leader ever to grace the New Brunswick political stage. Widely read and travelled, he had a phenomenal interest in all aspects of artistic expression. He was an interesting conversationalist, with an absorbing curiosity about music, drama, literature, painting, native culture—almost everything in the sphere of human creativity. Tall, handsome and debonair, Richard was sought after by many admiring, aspiring but unsuspecting damsels, whom he would escort to social functions when he needed a partner. He could be equally at home at a rural New Brunswick political barbecue as in the salons of Paris or the opera in New York.

During his early administration Richard gave competent and dedicated government, without any hint of scandal. His political popularity came to engulf even the northern Acadian population, which in 1982, for the first time in history, abandoned its Liberal allegiance to return a majority of Conservative members. Richard was the consummate politician, but as his tenure extended into so many long years, his warts and vulnerability became more prominent, until he was hounded from office, losing every single seat in the legislature.

In his early years as premier, Richard maintained a discreet lifestyle, but in the final years he seemed to throw caution to the wind, almost as if deliberately inviting electoral disaster. At a reception and dinner in Saint John for Prince Charles and the Princess of Wales, his introduction to the royal prince was simply repeating "love, love, love." Rumours were just beginning to surface of friction between Charles and Diana and it must have been Richard's intention to counter these stories. Richard's performance left the audience bewildered and embarrassed as New Brunswickers. The poor prince managed what I thought was an extremely capable response.

After the dinner, my wife and I joined a judge and his wife in the bar of the hotel, and as we discussed the extraordinary event of the evening, the then leader of the Liberal Opposition joined us uninvited. After several drinks his diatribe against the government was most vehement, though not entirely coherent to the rest of us. When he finally left, I was left with the bill. The judge said to us, "You know, when I was younger I always had the urge to go into politics, but felt that I didn't have what it takes, but after listening to our premier and the leader of the Opposition tonight, I think I was wrong."

Richard loved to travel, and it was sometimes said that he was out of the province more often than he was in it. He visited us a few times at our home in Florida and was an immediate hit with our American friends.

Richard was often a dinner guest at our home and a delightful, sparkling and interesting conversationalist whose company was always enjoyed by all present. He would consult my wife on details of special social etiquette, and in 1984 asked her to coordinate arrangements for the Queen's visit to Moncton and to host a reception at our house for the royal party retinue. Attending this was the secretary of state in the Mulroney government, in charge of state visits, and when he arrived I offered him a cocktail. He at first demurred, saying, "My background is that of a Presbyterian minister, and we Presbyterians are born to suffer." By the end of the evening, I am happy to report, the suffering Presbyterian made probably the biggest dent in my bar bill.

My wife was once in Jerusalem with a group of women from Canadian Hadassah-Wizo, of which she was vice president at the time. After hours, the women were relaxing in a bar when Richard appeared out of the blue. We all know how gratifying it is to unexpectedly encounter a face from home when we are far away, and Louise was delighted to introduce him to her friends. He danced and entertained them well into the early morning, leaving the healthy bar chit to be picked up by Louise.

Other warts began to appear. His habitual annual Christmas vacation to Marrakesh, Morocco, began to raise a few eyebrows, as did rumours of questionable entertainment at his Fredericton residence. Gossip about Richard was not a revelation to me due to an incident that had occurred a few years before.

Richard usually stayed at our cottage during the opening of the annual Shediac Lobster Festival. We employed a young mother's helper from the area, Monique, who was about fourteen. After Richard left, Monique was cleaning up his room when she came running to us, tittering, and handed me a book that the Premier had left behind, a paperback called *The Photographer*, with Rodney Smith named as the author. The front cover showed a photographer with camera snapping three unclad young boys. The back cover set out in bold print a résumé of its contents as follows: "Hank was a photographer who loved little boys—the younger the better. And when he got a magazine assignment to photograph teenage studs in 'action' he was more than happy to accept it. He selected four boys, aged thirteen to sixteen, and put them through their paces before his camera. The kids made love in every position and pose. ... And when the photo session ended, Hank sampled each and every youth, forcing them to pay homage to his throbbing maleness." I hid the book away in one of my desk drawers, the repository for so many items of the last half-century. I should probably have thrown it into a fire long ago, but some inexplicable compulsion made me keep it. I resurrected it for the first time after all these years to copy out the words from the back cover.

The final straw for voters was seeing Richard charged with possession of marijuana at the time of the Queen's visit. While he beat a conviction, his political time clock had run out. Just before this final election I facetiously told Richard that only two moves might provide him with a glimmer of electoral salvation. One would be to announce that the marijuana really belonged to the Queen, and that he had been the gallant subject in trying to protect his beloved monarch. The other would be to marry, not just any woman, but someone in the order of a Jacqueline Onassis.

The Liberals were elected in 1987 with nonexistent opposition, a political phenomenon that was a first in the history of the province. About five or six months before the election Eddie Goodman asked for my prediction on Hatfield's chances, and I told him there would be a complete wipeout.

"Come on," Eddie said. "That's not possible. There will always be a few safe seats."

When I repeated my prediction, Eddie questioned my political acumen. I explained that my conclusion was based on a recent conversation with a retired legal secretary, Ermina (Sears) Dennison, who had once worked in my office. Ermina came from a longtime Conservative family in Dorchester, New Brunswick, and had worked in her early years for William Emmet McMonagle, the lawyer who ran numerous times before he was elected mayor of Moncton in my younger days. When McMonagle ran as a Conservative in a federal election in the early Forties, Ermina coordinated the campaign and worked tirelessly for him.

Just before Hatfield was incinerated, Ermina was retired and living in an upper-middle-class neighbourhood with a tradition of electing Conservatives by a healthy majority. Although a lifetime, dedicated Conservative, she told me she could hardly wait to vote Hatfield out of office. And if that was her feeling after years of devotion to Conservative politics, I was convinced there would be no safe Conservative seat in the province, including Hatfield's.

A few years after Richard died, his friend Nancy Southam contacted me when she was planning her book *Remembering Richard*, a collection of tributes to Richard from many of his friends. While I had many pleasant times with Richard and valued him as a personal and genuine friend, I felt uncomfortable taking part in the publication and reluctantly declined.

My business and other responsibilities in Halifax brought me in touch with political figures of Nova Scotia, particularly Liberal Gerry Regan and Conservative John Buchanan when they served as premiers. We saw more of Gerry after he retired from the provincial scene and became a federal cabinet minister. Gerry always included us in state functions and meetings of any significance in which he was involved, including one that provided my only visit to Meech Lake, whose name was later to become inextricably linked to our constitutional history.

When Gerry's federal career ended, I arranged to have him appointed to the board of directors of our mutual funds management company, which paid quite handsome directors' fees. I enjoyed seeing him on occasion and getting the advantage of his assessment of federal political affairs. He was not a great admirer of Lloyd Axworthy, a former cabinet colleague, probably out of concern for what he felt were Axworthy's too-leftist leanings. When Axworthy was touted as a candidate for the leadership of the Liberal party, Gerry told me that if "Axworthy were chosen as leader of the Liberal party, I would leave the Liberal party, and if he were elected prime minister of Canada, I would leave Canada."

Gerry once invited me to a tribute at the Halifax Club for Bob Coates, when the Nova Scotia Conservative was at the low ebb of his political career after resigning under a cloud as minister of national defence over a strip-club incident in Germany. About two dozen of us from New Brunswick and Nova Scotia were at this private affair, which Gerry hosted at his own expense. It is a measure of Gerry's humanity that he tried to give Coates a boost in morale when he was down, even though Coates was on the other side of the political fence.

Gerry's wife, Carole, is the essence of a lady, and their handsome and talented family is a singular credit to them both. Gerry's trial on sexual assault charges must be creating grievous concern and anxiety. It is regrettable that a statute of limitations cannot preclude matters of complaint from three decades or more in the past. The cost of his defence by Eddie Greenspan, one of Canada's preeminent criminal lawyers, must also be a tremendous drain on Gerry's financial resources. Greenspan is a nephew of my late friend Rev. Abraham Greenspan of Halifax, who played such an important and unforgettable role in the first of my young university days. Again one can see how Canada has been enriched by its immigrant population, and how frustrated their forebears must have been that they never had the educational or other opportunities to develop their talents.

John Buchanan is sometimes blamed for much of the reckless spending that left Nova Scotia with the financial burdens leading to today's extreme belt-tightening in the province. This is unfair. Buchanan was a politician of his time, and all administrations of the early Eighties were more or less guilty of the same expansive practices, with more or less the same results. I once told Buchanan I would not be overly concerned if he had to close a steel plant, or if a fish plant or two had to shut down, but Nova Scotia would really be in trouble if it curtailed its universities, each of which has played a unique role in the province's history; unhappily, such a day seems to have dawned. Buchanan, a Cape Bretoner, was a true booster of his province. If he had still been premier at the time, I felt our trust company might somehow have been salvaged, to continue its role as a key player in Nova Scotia's economic development.

Hatfield, Regan and Buchanan were all graduates of Dalhousie Law School. During their years in politics, two other Dalhousie law graduates served as provincial premiers: Alex Campbell in P.E.I. and Allan Blakeney in Saskatchewan. Clyde Wells and John Crosbie in Newfoundland also came out of Dalhousie. Beginning with R.B. Bennett, the Law School has been and continues to be a spawning ground for political aspirants.

Canadian public life has been largely dominated by members of the legal profession. Among the most charitable reasons advanced for this is that lawyers' training makes them more suitable to deal with matters of legislation and confrontation. I, however, often attribute this to other motives. Struggling young lawyers feel that participation in politics can help propel them onto a public stage, which gives them early and rapid exposure that might otherwise take decades to build in a confined legal practice. As well, the routine of a day-to-day legal practice, particularly a civil one, can lead to a degree of boredom, which the excitement of political engagement can helpfully assuage.

For those fortunate to reach the top rungs of the political ladder and enjoy office for a respectable time, there can be rewards. These lawyer-politicians are generally sought after by the larger legal firms, not for their legal capacity, which is often badly eroded by years of political activity, but as rainmakers who, from contacts made in political life, can bring in valuable business. They seldom engage in legal nitty-gritty but spend their time with corporate board appointments and massaging important potential clients.

In my addresses to law graduates at convocations, I have tried to impress upon them the importance of obtaining a good foundation in practice before letting themselves be bitten by the political bug. Political life can be transitory, and interrupting a professional career without having a foundation to come back to can be an expensive exercise. As Mark Twain said, there are two times in a man's life when he shouldn't gamble: one, when he can't afford to, the other, when he can. Politics is a fearsome gamble at almost any stage of a professional career. In this respect I have often quoted Winston Churchill's famous admonition: "War and politics are equally exciting, but politics is more dangerous, for in war you can only be killed once."

It is interesting to note the difference in impact that some politicians make on our lives. When Churchill died, I was affected emotionally as I lived again through the famous oratory that stirred and inspired the free world in its darkest days. I sat glued, with tearful eyes, to radio and television to hear once more the voice and words of indomitable courage that had sustained us all. My wife, who was only a child at the time of Churchill's greatness, seemed scarcely involved emotionally in his death. However, when John Kennedy was assassinated, she was devastated, and my own emotions came nowhere near those I felt at Churchill's passing.

CHAPTER 8

Service—Community and Beyond

My wife was savouring the display of pearls in the vault at Bulgari's, the famous jewellery emporium in Rome. For a good half hour I wandered along, feigning as much interest as I could, when out of the far corner of the vault an elderly gentleman approached. It was Mr. Bulgari himself, and he wanted to give us a personal tour. This was early in our marriage, and my young wife was bug-eyed over the jewels. Bulgari, obviously relishing Louise's enthusiasm, placed a bracelet on her wrist and said, "Take it home with you."

We were at the end of a European trip and near the bottom of our funds, and I told Bulgari we had not anticipated spending money on jewellery; we just wanted to see the wares. "Take it anyway," he said. "And pay me whenever you can."

I asked how he could trust such an expensive item to people he was meeting for the first time. "I see you are wearing a Rotary button," he said. "And that is good enough for me."

Rotary membership could have had an expensive downside for Mr. Bulgari even in the Rotary world of that era. The same trust that he displayed probably could not exist today.

No young professional in a small community can be immune from pressure to engage in community service. Early in my career I decided to limit myself largely to one community endeavour at a time and follow it through to a successful conclusion before turning to the next challenge. My first association was with the local Rotary club.

Rotary has more prestige in Europe than in North America, where membership is somewhat less restricted to the captains of industry, business and other fields. But in the days before television journalism came into wide use, the club's weekly luncheon meetings were a popular platform for delivering a message to the community. I spent almost forty years in Rotary, serving as president of the local club and later as a district governor.

Within Rotary much has been made of its worldwide fellowship and the good that inevitably flows from it. At an international Rotary meeting in Lake Placid, New York, I befriended Anant Pandya of Mombasa, Kenya. Anant was of East Indian background, and his family had a long-established hardware business in Kenya, where Anant was also a member of parliament. A knowledgeable and cultured man, he was once asked by Rotary International to represent its president at some official functions in South Africa. Anant was happy to oblige, only to find that because of his colour he would not be accepted by the Rotary clubs of that country. He was crushed and humiliated by the realization that Rotary, which was built on international fellowship, could not overcome the curse of apartheid in South Africa. He did not live to see the end of that blight.

For years the local YMCA was another of my community concerns, and I was privileged to be the president on its hundredth anniversary in 1970. By then it had been struggling with annual deficits and was burdened with an accumulated debt that threatened its service to the community. With bank cooperation, arrangements were made for the freezing of interest and principal retirement on a sustainable basis. We also initiated a capital endowment campaign, and with well over one million dollars now in the fund and suitably invested, the annual income should help the YMCA carry on its responsibilities for another century.

While president of the local Y, I went to the annual national meeting, where the hot topic of conversation was whether the word *Christian* should be dropped from the Y's name because of the multicultural constituency the organization now served. A large number of people spoke in favour of removing the word, but I spoke for its retention, saying I had consulted my local rabbi. He interpreted the "Christian" in the Y name as an intention to promote the precepts and ideals of the religion, not the religion itself, and said that if all mankind lived by these precepts and ideals, the world would more than reach its ultimate paradise. Coming from a Jewish adherent, my argument won the day and terminated the discussion; and now, more than a quarter of a century later, the YMCA still proudly carries the name that is an integral part of its heritage.

At the time I was president, the local Y was largely regarded by Acadians, who made up 30 percent of the city's population, as an English-speaking Protestant domain. But I helped arrange for the election of the first French-speaking president, and today almost half of the board members are Acadian. I also had a hand in the election of the first woman as president of the Y. These two elections must have made the staunch Methodist stalwarts who founded the Y in 1870 turn in their graves.

A few years ago the board of directors of YMCA Canada honoured me with one of their highest appointments, that of an "officer of the fellowship of honour," at a ceremony at Government House in Ottawa presided over by the chief justice of Canada.

Minor surgery for the repair of a fistula led me to another of my community endeavours: the Moncton Hospital. It was the busiest time in my career, and I decided to have the surgery done at the Montreal General Hospital, where I would be less known and less accessible to clients, visitors and others, including hospital staff seeking free legal advice. Months after the operation I received a form letter from the hospital soliciting funds from former patients and friends for its annual campaign. The letter impressed me, and I checked with the Moncton Hospital board to see if it might gain advantages from a similar program. At the time I did not foresee the results that the program would achieve in providing substantial benefits to the hospital and community. We incorporated Friends of the Moncton Hospital Foundation, as well as another corporate structure required for income-tax purposes, to handle commercial aspects of revenue raising.

The annual drive by the foundation was a modest success at first, but as the years progressed, contributions grew. The management company derived revenue from the silver salvaged from X-ray plates and from the parking concession and the TV rentals in hospital rooms.

The provincial government, as part of the Equal Opportunity program of Louis Robichaud, had taken over responsibility for all hospitals, so that equipment that would have been part of the hospital's budget in the past could now be denied or allocated to another part of the province. Equal Opportunity also abolished county councils, and the Westmorland county council found itself with about $300,000 left in its treasury. We snared the money and used it as the nucleus of financing to build a medical arts office building next to the hospital.

The building cost more than $2 million to construct, and in its early years was heavily mortgaged. Now, with the encumbrance considerably reduced, the free revenue has become significant in the hospital's financial planning, softening the impact of the government's restrictive allotments. In a recent capital campaign with a target of $2.9 million, the Friends contributed $600,000. As well, hundreds of thousands of dollars have been contributed by the Friends for the purchase of equipment the hospital could not otherwise have had, including its first CAT-scan machine.

The hospital foundation and the management company have become an integral part of the hospital's financial planning. I believe it was largely in recognition of my hand in this venture that I was invested as a member of the Order of Canada in 1979 and later elevated to an officer of the order. The three gradations in the Order of Canada used to upset the late Louis Levèsque, whose funding and contacts were largely responsible for the establishment of the Université de Moncton. Louis was made a member of the order, whilst many who had not performed a fraction of his service were in the higher classes. He told me that he felt the order as established was divisive, saying that if one is chosen to be initiated into the order, it should be for meritorious service that does not allow for measurement.

During the several years I spent on the board of Canada World Youth, I met its founder, Jacques Hébert, who is now a senator. Jacques is a friend of Pierre Trudeau, and during the Trudeau years Canada World Youth was sufficiently funded to carry on its work worldwide. In the Mulroney years federal grants were substantially curtailed, and for one area of the organization's work, Katimavik, eliminated. This led to Hébert's hunger strike on Parliament Hill, which lasted several weeks and brought considerable worry to his friends. Happily, the matter was resolved before any serious damage occurred to Hébert's health. While Canada World Youth has continued undiminished since then, only recently has Katimavik been revived on a somewhat limited scale.

When pressures on my time forced me to relinquish my hand in Canada World Youth, my wife took my place on the board and visited some of the areas where the organization carried on its work. In Ecuador, Jacques Hébert put the board members up at a vermin-infested fleabag for seven dollars a night. Most of the board members spent one sleepless night there before checking into better accommodation. The fleabag seemed not to bother Hébert, so my wife, determined to show she was just as tough and unspoiled, persevered at the dump for the whole trip. When she got home, every item of clothing and luggage from the trip was either fumigated or discarded.

Dalhousie University received most of my outside attention. Soon after Henry Hicks became president, he invited me onto the board of governors, an appointment that was required if I was to serve on its investment committee. Henry told me that I need not worry about attending meetings of the board, as he could run the university with its present board constituents, as long as I did not neglect the investment committee. For the thirteen years that I served, I only attended one or two meetings of the full board, but in all that time I missed only one monthly meeting of the investment committee.

At one full board meeting that I did attend, we dealt largely with the onerous problem of male visiting hours at Shirreff Hall, the women's residence. The student council wanted all-night privileges for the residence, but most of the conservative, straightlaced board members were horrified at the request and felt a midnight curfew was as far as they could bend. With both sides standing firm, Henry proposed a 2 a.m. curfew as a compromise. The board accepted the proposal with some reluctance, and the student committee withdrew from our meeting. Henry then advised the board that he had consulted his young son, Hughie, the night before for advice, and it was Hughie who suggested the 2 a.m. curfew, saying, "If a guy hasn't made it by two o'clock, he might as well go home anyway." The board chairman, a senior gentleman of the establishment, was seated in front of me, and I watched the back of his neck turn beet red from the top of his collar to the receding hairline.

In my student days male visitors to Shirreff Hall were confined to a ground-floor waiting room, and the women were summoned to meet them there. The whiff of a male presence was not permitted in the dormitory section, and women had to sign back in by 10 p.m. I assume no restrictions apply these days, and co-ed dorms are fairly standard. Sometimes I wonder if I should regret being born in an earlier generation, but I am dated enough to appreciate having lived in a more modest age, with an old-fashioned male respect for feminine mystique, nobility and virtue.

The Dalhousie investment committee assumed direct responsibility not only for the endowment funds of the university but also for the pension funds of the faculty and staff, with a total of around $300 million at the time. The endowment fund was of good size compared with other Maritime universities, but despite its ranking as the third-largest university endowment fund in Canada, it was considerably below McGill and the University of Toronto. Some canny investors served on the committee, including Don Sobey and the late Charlie McCullough.

The Dalhousie Medical Research Foundation was created by a gift of $1 million from Nora Balders on condition that it be matched by $9 million from other sources. The late Bill Sobey was the chairman of this committee, and I sat on it until the target of $10 million was achieved.

Henry Hicks attended the meetings of the investment committee, and we renewed the old bonds established in our younger days, when he was practising law in Bridgetown. Henry was a showman, with an ebullient personality and contagious enthusiasm. I once visited the Nova Scotia legislature when he was the minister of education in the Liberal government of Angus L. Macdonald. Spotting me in the visitors' gallery, Henry quickly obtained the eye of the Speaker to gain the floor. He then put on a display of ringing oratory, with appropriate flourishes of motion, all the while looking to the gallery for my approval.

Henry won the leadership of the Liberal party and succeeded Angus L., but he lasted only from 1954 to 1956, when the Conservatives came to power in an election that ushered in the Stanfield era in Nova Scotia politics. After his defeat Henry said he resembled the planet Earth: they were both flattened at the poles. Politics' loss was Dalhousie's gain, for his seventeen years at the university transformed the campus and all its facets.

In 1967, Dalhousie conferred an honorary degree on Queen Elizabeth, the Queen Mother. She proved to be a loyal honorary alumna and dutifully attended Dalhousie alumni meetings in London. In 1980, Henry invited me and my wife to that year's meeting, which drew about fifty alumni in Great Britain. At a reception, all in attendance were presented to the Queen Mother before proceeding to the luncheon, with the admonition that protocol required that no one leave the luncheon until after the Queen Mother departed. The meeting began about twelve thirty and its business was well concluded by two thirty. The Queen Mother, however, was having a great time exchanging pleasantries with those of us at or near her table and appeared in no hurry to depart. While many in the crowd were anxious to get back to their business affairs and took surreptitious glances at their watches, the Queen Mother didn't get up to leave until after four o'clock, keeping the whole gathering captive—all true alumni of Dalhousie, respectful of their gracious royal alumna.

We were back in Canada only a few days when Henry called to say he had been invited by Buckingham Palace to a garden party being held by the Queen to celebrate her mother's eightieth birthday. The Queen Mother had requested that Henry be put on the guest list and told to bring any other Dalhousie associate he might choose. Henry asked Louise and me to come. Having just returned from London, we were reluctant to go back so soon. But Henry was persuasive, and we agreed to go, certainly with excitement about the chance to enter the portals of Buckingham Palace.

The invitation we got from the Queen is unusual. It is stamped with the seal of the Lord Chamberlain, St. James's Palace, and addressed to my wife, but our residence address is followed by New Brunswick and then by Nova Scotia. My wife framed the envelope as a reminder that the Lord Chamberlain's office needed a few lessons on the geography of the Queen's fast-shrinking realms.

I arranged for a private aircraft to take us to New York, so we could board the Concorde for London. This was the only time I bested Henry in gamesmanship. We arranged to have our private plane taxi alongside the Concorde, where we were met by British Airways officials and customs officers. After being processed by customs, we exited one plane to board the other, without going through any terminals. Henry seemed impressed, but he was soon to outdo me.

As the Queen Mother walked through the receiving line at Buckingham Palace and reached Henry, she squealed, "Dr. Hicks, how nice to see you," threw her arms around his neck and gave him a big hug. I thought Henry would melt on the spot and I would have only a blob of fat to transport home. Turning towards us, Henry said to the Queen Mother, "And you remember the Cohens, of course," to which she diplomatically replied, "Of course," and passed on to the next guest in the line. It was obvious that Henry was the star.

"When you get back to Halifax make sure you tell everyone about this," he said to us.

Other members of the Royal Family, including the Queen, were present, but their receptions were all dutifully formal. If any of them had inherited the Queen Mother's ebullience and dignified charm, they might not be facing the crises that now engulf their lives and threaten the continuation of the House of Windsor.

Henry always stayed in London at the old Stafford Hotel in St. James, which he introduced to us as the favourite luncheon spot for Winston Churchill during the critical war years. It was antiquated, but this was a part of its attraction for Henry, especially the cat that reigned undisturbed on a chair in the small lobby sitting-room.

On one trip to London, I made it my mission to try to find a special prayer book for an American rabbi then in Moncton, who thought it would be a nice change to have the traditional Saturday morning prayer for the government replaced by the prayer for the Royal Family, which is used in synagogues in Britain. None of our local prayer books contained this royal prayer, and the rabbi asked me to look for the proper book the next time I was in London.

His request went completely out of my mind, with all the excitement of a London visit, until one night at a theatre performance when two young men wearing yarmulkes sat directly in front of us. This jolted my memory, and I asked them where I might find a Jewish bookstore that would carry the prayer book. By far the best place to try was Foyle's, they said. At about four o'clock the next day I thought it a good time to go to Foyle's. We were again staying at the Stafford with Henry and his wife, and we all had an early appointment that evening. With the instruction that I be back not a minute after six, I took a taxi to Foyle's, a fairly expensive fare over to Charing Cross.

Before entering the bookstore, I noticed a fruit stand with exceptional seasonal produce, including firm, black cherries the size of plums, and green-flesh Israeli melons, the sweetest in the world and seldom available in Canada. Fruit is the only food that I savour and crave, and I can seldom resist the temptation of a fruit and produce stand. This time was no exception, and I bought melons, bags of cherries and other fruit, which I knew we would all enjoy in our hotel rooms. Not wishing to be burdened with the parcels, I asked the vendor to keep them for a few minutes while I ran into Foyle's. Little did I know what was in store for me.

Inside, I asked where I might find the Hebrew department and was advised to go to the third floor. No elevator being visible, I climbed the wooden stairs to my destination. There, I was greeted by a middle-aged woman who told me the store carried several texts that would fulfil my requirements, but she recommended a Hertz publication. She proceeded to the shelf, got the book, opened it to the required page and read the royal prayer in impeccable Hebrew, translating it into English as she went. In utter amazement I asked the lady if she was Jewish, though no person could have looked more Anglo-Saxon. I learned she was an Anglican.

"Where," I asked, "did you learn such perfect Hebrew?"

"At Cambridge," she said, explaining that the store carried books in almost every language, and clerks had to be knowledgeable in the language of the section to which they were assigned. What a contrast this was to our part of the world, where most clerks, at least in the chain bookstores, are pimply-faced young kids trying to pick up a few extra dollars after school and don't seem to know the difference between a novel and a biography.

After buying the prayer book, I browsed through a small section of the third floor, oblivious of time, until I came to and was startled to see that it was already six o'clock. I ran outside to try to flag a taxi, but it was rush hour, and I stood in a panic for a good half hour before I found a driver to rush me back to the hotel and the appointment, for which I would be at least an hour late. It was only when I got back to the hotel and a stern lecture that I realized I had forgotten the bags of luscious fruit. The cost of the entire episode, including the book, taxis and lost fruit, came to well over a hundred dollars. On my return home I proudly delivered the prayer book, but to my knowledge it was never used.

Another trip to London coincided with the annual Canadian Club dinner, which brings together a large group of Canadians living in Britain. More than a thousand people attend this gala affair, which is usually graced by the incumbent Canadian high commissioner. On the night I attended, Lady Violet Aitken, then the chancellor of the University of New Brunswick, was my guest. She was seated on one side of me, and on the other side was Lady Ramsay, the wife of the heir who was to succeed to the Dalhousie peerage. On the way into the dinner I bought two rather expensive tickets on a car that was to be raffled that evening. At the table I asked Lady Aitken to choose either one of the tickets, which she did, and I gave the second ticket to Lady Ramsay.

None of the thousands of tickets I have bought in my life ever won so much as a ten cent prize, but as fate would have it, the ticket given to Lady Ramsay won the car. I thought poor Lady Violet was going to eat herself alive. When she was ready to go home, I got her the best bottle of brandy available to take with her, hoping it would help drown her disappointment.

Early in Henry Hicks's tenure as Dalhousie president, he precipitated an event that would further enhance his image with an important segment of the community. The Halifax Club, tracing its history back to the 1700s, may be the oldest club of its kind in the country. Giant portraits of royalty and nobility have graced its walls through the centuries. Well into the middle of this century the club continued its restriction against ethnic membership, thus barring many prominent professional, business and community leaders. This discrimination incensed Henry, who sent in a letter of resignation, giving his reasons and demanding the letter be posted on the lobby bulletin board.

The bulletin board displayed all pertinent notices to club members, including the names of members who were delinquent in payment of their accounts, which was a good barometer of those suffering economic dislocation. Henry's letter caused considerable consternation, because the president of Dalhousie University was considered a prestigious member. His resignation, with the publicly displayed reason, led to a quick resolution by the governing body. Many prominent Jewish citizens, distinguished in numerous aspects of community service, were quickly invited to join. Henry Hicks, with the heinous ruling broken, was persuaded to withdraw his resignation. Probably few people today have knowledge of Henry's hand in this episode, and I am happy to recount it as a further star in the crown of his cherished memory.

Sometime after Henry's first wife died, he began keeping company with Gene Morrison, a schoolteacher of mature years whom Henry's children always deferentially referred to as Miss Morrison during the years of courtship. When Henry and Gene were finally married and just returned from their honeymoon, they were in their bedroom when one of his sons answered a telephone call for Henry. To Henry's embarrassment, the young son replied, "I'm sorry, Dr. Hicks is upstairs sleeping with Miss Morrison." Old habits have a hard time dying.

My first honorary degree was from the Université de Moncton, which later gave my wife a similar honour. Founded in the early Sixties, the university rapidly assumed an important place not only in Acadian life but also in the economic, educational and cultural affairs of the larger community.

The university was the dream of Rev. Clément Cormier, who grew up in my old neighbourhood in the east end of Moncton. Father Cormier, a sweet and kind man, would be considered almost simple, or saintly, by today's standards of worldliness and financial affairs. But then, it would take a gentle dreamer, oblivious to the world's realities, to persevere and create a university against seemingly insuperable obstacles.

At the time of my honorary degree, my address to the convocation dinner was mostly in English, but I did struggle with some French remarks. One paragraph, about my marriage, was particularly well received:

J'ai parlé de mon amitié pour vous, monsieur le recteur, et c'est une chose qui me sera toujours chère. Maintenant, je veux parler un peu de mon épouse. Dans notre race, une grande importance est donnée à l'éducation, et la clef du succès, l'ambition de chaque parent juif, est d'avoir un docteur dans la famille—que ce soit le fils qui étudie pour en devenir un docteur, ou la fille qui est élevée avec l'idée d'en marier un docteur. Les avocats sont considérés comme étant bien plus bas dans le rang social, et si la fille ne peut faire mieux, si elle n'est pas très jolie, ou très intelligente, elle en acceptera un avocat. Je vous remercie de la part de ma belle-mère, car enfin sa petite fille pourra coucher avec un docteur pour la première fois. J'espère que c'est la première fois.

The French is roughly translated as follows:

I have spoken of my friendship for you, Mr. President, and it is a matter that I shall always cherish. Now I wish to speak a bit about my wife. In our race, a great deal of importance is given to education, and the key to success, the ambition of every Jewish parent, is to have a doctor in the family—whether it is a son who studies to become a doctor, or a daughter who is raised imbued with the drive to marry a doctor. Lawyers, as marital prospects, are considered well down in the social scale, and if a daughter is not that great, nor very pretty or very bright, she may have to settle for someone as lowly as a lawyer. I wish to thank you on behalf of my mother-in-law, for now her little girl will get to sleep with a doctor for the first time. I hope that it is for the first time.

After the interlude in French, I guarded my matrimonial backside:

You see now why, in talking about my wife, I felt it best to try to make those remarks in some language she would not understand. I only hope you French-speaking people here did understand. I tried my best. But I do want to thank my wife for the inspiration she has been to me for twenty-two years. In all this time she never stopped smiling and bringing radiance and joy to my personal life and that of this community. There now, in case my wife did understand my French, I have covered the risk with insurance protection.

The rest of my address that evening in 1973 dealt with the tensions in Moncton between French- and English-speaking people, aggravated by the stubbornness of the mayor, Leonard Jones.* I believe my words then have relevance in the larger context of our country today and the apparent barrier that divides Quebec and English-speaking Canada:

We have to acknowledge regretfully that there are some areas in which this university is considered a disquieting presence, and I feel it is the duty of all men and women of goodwill to speak, and hope-fully to act, in the continuing search for methods through education, and mutual trust, which may remove the iron curtain of separation and bring us closer together. We must recognize that as long as men are free and remain diverse religiously, racially and culturally, there will be problems and there will be tensions.

Discrimination in belief, in race, in language and in colour has existed for centuries. We could make the greatest contribution to understanding by agreeing in advance that our own fixed beliefs and practices are not alone the standards by which all should be judged. Human nature has a tendency to assume that our own view is the correct one, and if the fellow on the other side of the fence doesn't agree, then he is, of course, the prejudiced one.

Can we really pretend, any of us, that our religion, customs and insistence on exclusive language rights are not abrasive to others—

---

* Regretfully Leonard Jones passed away in June 1998.

whether Protestant or Catholic, Jew or Gentile in religion, or French and English in language? Of course, we're different, but must this difference continue to fester for years and years, to disrupt the growth, the peace and prosperity of our cities, of our provinces, and our country? Why cannot each of us take pride in his own origin and his own heritage without denying to the other fellow his right to speak or pray as he wishes?

The dogmas of the quiet past are inadequate for the turbulent present. We must think anew. We must act anew. We must ask each of us—and possibly ask a little bit more from the majority groups in this great country of ours—to bend a little, to not question another religion or another language. And we must, by encouragement and example, lead our children to learn the background and history of the people who make up Canada, so that they may grow to appreciate and to guard jealously the human right to exist in the culture of one's own upbringing.

Honorary degrees came in ensuing years from Acadia, St. Thomas, the University of New Brunswick and Dalhousie. At St. Thomas in Fredericton, I shared the platform with Rev. Theodore Hesburgh, the longtime president of Notre Dame University, adviser to seven United States presidents and once the subject of a cover story for *Time* magazine. We corresponded until his last letter told me of his retirement from Notre Dame and his plan to travel around the country in a mobile home. He thought this honour from St. Thomas was his 115th honorary degree, but his later autobiography, *God, Country and Notre Dame,* says he is in the *Guinness Book of World Records* as the recipient of 121.

At the UNB convocation I shared the platform with Premier Frank McKenna and Rita MacNeil, the Cape Breton songbird. The usual photograph of us, in full academic regalia, hangs in her studio in Cape Breton, and many visitors to this tourist attraction have told me of seeing it there, prominently displayed. This has become one of my very few claims to fame.

From my first days of earning an income I also took satisfaction in being in the forefront of charitable giving, whether to community and national causes or in response to the proliferation of religious-oriented demands. No request, large or small, went unanswered; I felt guilty turning down any solicitation.

Some people might say my willingness to give was a legacy of my Jewish heritage, which makes charity one of the three principal components of salvation, along with prayer and penitence. I have met a great many of my religious counterparts who were certainly not badly bitten by the charity bug. I have also met many who have been distinguished nationally and internationally by their charitable labours and dedication. On the whole, Jewish giving at all levels is probably higher than in the rest of the community.

Leonard Ellen was also active in community affairs, but I suspect the desire to promote and enhance his image and stature predominated over any deeply felt charitable passion. I suppose this is a common motivating human trait, and in the quest for personal glory, man throughout history has accomplished much good, as well as perpetrated much evil. Much better the former than the latter, and in the long run, whatever the motive, it's the good act that counts.

Leonard's attractive exterior cloaked another persona, which could be tough and hard if need be, even if he was not completely comfortable that way.

I had been asked to join the board of regents at Mount Allison University at a time when I was also on the board of governors at Dalhousie. In declining, I suggested that Leonard might make a significant contribution if he could be persuaded to accept. He served on the board for almost a decade and never missed a meeting, travelling from Montreal at the expense of considerable time and physical effort.

He and Art Crockett of the Bank of Nova Scotia played an important part in a capital campaign conducted by Mount Allison. Leonard expressed some concern about the deficiencies of the general chairman of the campaign, and felt that if he and Art had not taken over and followed up some national contacts, the campaign would not have succeeded. But shortly after the campaign Mount Allison conferred an honorary degree on the national chairman. This infuriated Leonard, who believed his contribution was far greater. When I tried later to have him join me in setting up a foundation to fund, in perpetuity, higher education in the Maritimes, Leonard would sneer, "You and your Maritime universities—you can have them."

At the time, he and I controlled the Enheat Company in Sackville, which included the old Fawcett plant next to the Mount Allison campus. The buildings were an eyesore, but the extensive piece of land could be a natural and given to the university, and instead of a blight of rundown old buildings on the approaches to Mount A, there is now an attractive grassed area, available for considerable building expansion if needed in the future.

After the gift of the land, many weeks passed without so much as an acknowledgement from the university. But with some delicate prompting the president, Guy MacLean, eventually sent a letter thanking Leonard and me and saying the gift would not go unrecognized. This was the last we heard of the matter, which further dimmed Leonard's view of Maritime universities. Finally, in a desperate attempt to change his attitude, I arranged a meeting with Don Wells, MacLean's successor, and Purdy Crawford, an important member of the board, now chancellor. I explained the difficulties in getting Leonard to participate in my educational foundation plan and entreated their assistance. Shortly after, Mount Allison invited Leonard to receive an honorary doctorate, a belated recognition of his years of unselfish service to the institution.

At the convocation dinner, Leonard, who is not usually a relaxed or comfortable public speaker, delivered an exceptionally fine and pertinent speech, which provided me personally with much satisfaction. I had hoped the ice was broken and later asked him to join me in a building project on the Dalhousie campus to bear our joint names. He emphatically declined.

Soon afterward, Leonard contributed $600,000 to an art gallery at Concordia University in Montreal that was to bear his name. I don't know whether to attribute this to his not wanting to participate in shared glory, or to a desire to bask in the accolades of his home community. I was crushed at the time, but the subsequent and rapid unfolding of events soon made the whole question academic.

Financial Days

In the early Eighties, Leonard and I were invited by Austin Taylor, then head of McLeod Young Weir, to participate with a group in the purchase of Royal Trust to shut out Robert Campeau in his attempt to take over that grand old lady. The meeting with Taylor was held in strict secrecy in a Toronto hotel room, and included many important names in the financial industry of the day. We declined to join, seeing no value in such participation to our scheme of development.

Shortly after Campeau's rejection in the Royal Trust takeover I had the odd trading relationship with him, as well as a few social contacts. He was an intriguing man, who started out as a journeyman house-builder and created one of the largest, and certainly one of the most profitable, real estate empires in North America. His success, I am sure, was substantially aided by his connections with the Liberal party. The government of Canada became the tenant of the substantial complex of office buildings Campeau built across the Ottawa River in Hull. The rental income from these alone must have been huge.

Campeau has an impulsive personality, and one day I received a call from his chief financial brain, Don Carroll, a Dartmouth, Nova Scotia, native, saying his boss was interested in purchasing a Sabre 60, a plane that our trust company was running then. Campeau had a similar aircraft, and in his search for a duplicate he had found that ours was the only one in Canada. We had bought the plane a few years earlier in Edmonton, at an opportune time and at an attractive, distressed price. In this, our first transaction with Campeau, we booked a profit of more than $1 million.

Later that year Campeau invited me and my wife to his Christmas party at his riverside home outside Ottawa. The guest list included Prime Minister Trudeau and Brian Dickson, then the chief justice of Canada. In his remarks that evening Campeau extolled Trudeau in the most flowing terms for the recent patriation of the constitution. The chief justice, at whose table we sat, quietly uttered "Hear, hear," at each obsequious expression of praise.

Campeau's home was impressive in architecture and internal appointments, and his extensive collection of superb Canadian art contributed much to the ambience and décor. My wife was somewhat appalled, however, that the coffee cream and the butter were served in small individual plastic containers, and that the sugar came in the paper envelopes found on restaurant tables. Apparently the catering was done by a local *auberge* that Campeau owned at the time, and the hotel's equipment did not include the silver utensils usually associated with fine dining.

When Bob was riding at his height after the takeover of the American retailing giants, he called me several times to invite me to dinner, in either Toronto or New York. I was not feeling in top form and demurred, but he would not take a no.

"I'm sending my plane for you to have dinner with us, and then have them take you home," he said.

"Bob, there's no need for that. We have our own air transportation, and I can easily get up."

"Yes, I know, but my plane is a lot better than your plane."

I readily conceded his point but persuaded him to let me slum it up to Toronto. His chauffeur picked me up at the airport and drove me to Bob's baronial estate on The Bridle Path, a house that was spectacular in most respects but lacking the warmth of the Ottawa residence.

After the usual formalities, the English butler summoned us to dinner. Midway through the meal the butler informed Bob that Betsy Bloomingdale was on the phone. He left to take the call, and when he returned he said he shouldn't have disturbed himself since she was calling for a contribution to one of her favourite charities. The call cost him $100,000, he said.

Later, the butler again came to the dining room, this time to announce that Donald Trump was on the phone. After taking this call Bob said he was not an admirer of Trump, whom he found too flamboyant. Trump's father, Bob said, was the one who really made the money, and he did it quietly, with hardly anyone knowing about him. Donald, on the other hand, was so publicity mad that he couldn't go to the bathroom without calling a press conference. At this, I thought to myself of the proverbial pot and kettle.

After dinner we two men retired to the drawing room, and Bob produced reams of computer printouts showing profit projections running into the hundreds of millions for the retail operations in the next few years. Computers, I cautioned him, are something like property appraisers: feed them the information you want and they'll turn out the valuation required. And there might be some significance, I said, in the fact that he bought Allied Stores on Halloween in 1986, and Federated on April Fool's Day in 1988. I hoped he wasn't superstitious.

Considering his accomplishments from humble beginnings, I had a lot of respect for Campeau. And I was sorry to see a proud man and his empire destroyed—and not just by what some felt was his ego, which required him to do something dramatic in business after his perceived rejection by the financial establishment in the Royal Trust affair. The greed of investment bankers and their zeal for hundreds of millions in commissions also played a role. Campeau was encouraged to pursue a path that was almost certain to lead to failure.

I have always been offended by the scandalous fees investment advisers charge when asked for opinions in corporate matters, such as rendering valuations in mergers and takeovers, or for advice to committees of a board that are structured to act independently of controlling directors or management. Million-dollar fees easily roll off these advisers' tongues, and compared with them, lawyers, with their often outrageous fees, look like pikers. And lawyers often spend considerably more time and effort to earn their keep.

It was Orville Erickson, an American once brought in by Hancock to straighten up a small mess at Maritime Life, who introduced Leonard and me to a life insurance company in Atlanta, Georgia. Orville was living in retirement in Dallas when he called to say that he'd heard the Atlanta company could be bought reasonably. The company was about the size of Maritime Life when Orville first went to Halifax, but he felt that with proper management it could grow even more quickly, considering the favourable area of the United States in which it was licensed to do business. Since the company was too far from home for us, Orville undertook to oversee its affairs, and having complete confidence in his ability we did not hesitate to back the venture and leave all the management details to him.

After spending the first months seeking out competent management people, Orville had a heart attack and died. A caretaker administration for the Atlanta company, with a president who withheld vital information from his board, soon created the possibility that we would lose not only the profit potential Orville had foreseen but also our investment. Luckily, Leonard found an elderly Louisiana man who had recently sold a bank in that state and was prepared to rescue us with whole skin. His name was Rousell, evidently of Cajun background, and he was well into his eighties. For the closing in Montreal, Rousell flew in by private jet with his lawyer, his right-hand man and his 28-year-old mistress.

Rousell was obviously eager to close. He had sent out to our bank a $2.5-million deposit days earlier, before the agreement to purchase and sell had even been signed. On the morning of the closing he was interested only in counting the share certificates to see if they added up to the required number. Then, plunking down the millions more required to finalize the purchase, he put the share certificates in his pocket and told his lawyer he was leaving for the airport to fly home; if the lawyer wanted to tarry over the documentation, he could return by a commercial flight. The lawyer was facing reams of documents that needed to be perused, which is usually considered necessary for due diligence and protection in such transactions. But the old man with the shares in hand was not interested in bothersome legal technicalities. Flustered, the lawyer hastily bundled up the documents, stuffed them in his case and ran to catch Rousell at the elevator.

Another fortunate episode occurred with Continental Trust, a small company that was part of the United Funds purchase. Initially, it had been incorporated only to serve as an internal trustee for certain of the mutual funds requirements, but management later expanded it to sell guaranteed investment certificates, using the funds generated to make property loans. Before the directors became aware of the problems, sour investments had placed the little company in extreme jeopardy and we were facing a significant loss. Here again Leonard found an eager purchaser from western Canada who forked over more than $10 million, which more than covered our losses. The purchaser was then unable to get regulatory approval to operate, and the company, together with the man's investment, went down the drain.

Because of these and numerous others incidents, my wife hoped that what she called "the Ellen luck" would last forever, so that we could all be blessed in its reflection.

In our search for asset growth or geographic extension for Central and Eastern Trust, Leonard and I pursued other financial institutions over the years.

I travelled to Edmonton several times to speak to the illustrious Dr. Charles Allard about his North West Trust. Later, when the company came under the bailiwick of Ralph Schurfield and his Nu-West real estate group, several trips were made to Calgary to try to negotiate with Ralph's people, a venture that proved equally unsuccessful. The meetings with Allard, while not fruitful, provided an interesting glimpse of this remarkable man, an eminent surgeon who became a legend as he amassed a huge industrial and financial empire. Allard's first wife was a native of Bridgewater, Nova Scotia, and they often spent summer vacations at her old home.

In my travels across Canada, I have been amazed at the number of people in every part of the country, many prominent in business and professional life, who have Maritime roots or connections. I have always admired those hardy Englishmen who, in the days of sail and long before steam, were able to conquer, settle or civilize a great part of the globe. Such a breed will likely never again exist, but I liken it in a lesser way to the thousands of Maritimers who left their roots to play an integral part in building so many parts of Canada. They have been active in most fields of human endeavour—political, educational, commercial, medical, legal, judicial, financial, industrial and scientific. I like to think that a vibrant nucleus of such a breed remains in the Atlantic provinces.

But it was in the Maritimes that Leonard and I faced the most acrimonious fight of them all in our quest to expand the trust company. The battle for control of the Nova Scotia Savings and Loan Company began in the early Eighties, and Leonard and I were pitted against two of Nova Scotia's most prominent families, the Sobeys and the Jodreys. The Machiavellian means used to defeat us, and the important allies, including the Bank of Nova Scotia, that the company directors were able to enlist in their determination to shut us out, led to one of the most bitter lawsuits in local annals. We won the six-year fight, with Toronto lawyer Alan Lenczner again representing us.

At one time, in an attempt to resolve the issue, Ottawa authorities appointed Purdy Crawford, then a leading Toronto lawyer, to act as a mediator. Our offer to sell our shares to the Halifax crowd at a lesser price than we were prepared to pay for their holding was rejected out of hand.

The details of the lengthy and complex litigation are admirably set out in the judgment written by Mr. Justice Peter Richard of the Nova Scotia Supreme Court, and are well worth reading. Not only does his ruling set out precedents for corporate and directors' morality, but it also reads almost as an absorbing detective novel, which at times will keep readers on the edge of their seats. The judge, I am told, began his legal career late in life after operating a service station for years. He headed the investigation of the Westray mine disaster, and his conclusions were most incisive.

Harry Rhude's health began to deteriorate dramatically in the early months of 1985. The annual meeting of Central and Eastern was to be held March 21, and the ever dedicated Harry was determined to try to leave his hospital bed to officiate at the business portion of the meeting; he would then quickly return to the hospital. A few hours before the meeting Harry called to ask if I would sit in for him. The booming voice that had once automatically commanded respect and attention was now reduced to little more than a broken, barely audible whisper. A few days later, he was gone. It was his smoking that had decimated his body and, with his final weeks in racking pain, destroyed him.

For the company *Insider* publication for April 1985, I was honoured to be asked to write a tribute. The following passages are the first and last paragraphs:

> A dozen or more years ago, I was visiting a large law office in Halifax, and at the time the partners happened to be interviewing ten or twelve candidates from Dalhousie Law School for articling positions. They indicated this was done on an annual basis, and I remarked on how dislocating it must be to an office to try to process this number of students every year, as we always found it difficult to have even one or two. The senior partner of the firm replied that by processing twelve or fifteen students a year over a period of ten or fifteen years, they hoped that surely they might eventually find "another Harry Rhude" out of the lot.
>
> Harry was practising law at the time, and I thought this quite a tribute for one lawyer to pay to a confrère with whom he competed in practice. This is only one of many stories that can be told to illustrate the legend of Harry Rhude, the lawyer. The name Harry Rhude has passed into our language as a generic term. The descriptive

phrase applied to an up-and-coming top-flight lawyer, that he (or she) is "another Harry Rhude," is now automatically understood to be one of the greatest accolades that can be paid in our legal world.

Now Harry is gone, his talents no longer available to us. The void is one that can never adequately be filled. His genius can never be duplicated. We were all enriched by his life of energy and dedication. We are all diminished by his passing. We can take comfort from the fact that his association and memory will be an inspiration for all of us who were privileged to share a part of his life.

CHAPTER 10

Grief

Harry was only 61 when he died, and as devastating as the blow was to the company, it was magnified a thousandfold for me personally in the loss of a confidante and friend. Little did I suspect the more personal tragedy only a few short months away, which would all but destroy my life.

Since the late summer of 1984, Louise had complained of an abdominal pain that was aggravated by walking and exercising. As the months went by, the pain became more pronounced, and frequent visits to doctors, including a gynecologist and an oncologist, did not provide a solution. Finally, in July of the next year, when the symptoms had become extremely painful, a laparoscopy was performed that indicated a malignant ovarian tumour. Almost a year had passed without proper diagnosis, a year that could have been vital in catching the problem in time. We now began the nightmare that was to consume our lives for the next three years, and mine to this day and forever.

After consultation it was decided to use medical facilities in Toronto, since the Moncton doctors were somewhat uncomfortable, whether because we were socially close or because they felt guilt over the delay in the diagnosis. It is too painful for me, even more than a decade later, to recall the details of the hell that followed. Only those unfortunate enough to have gone through a similar experience can comprehend and appreciate the agonizing hours spent in the surgical family waiting rooms, and the terror that attends the wait for a surgeon's report. Watching the ravages inflicted by series after series of chemotherapy, in many respects more debilitating than the disease itself, made me feel that the treatment should more properly be called chemo-butchery. Operation after operation, which Louise bravely consented to and courageously endured, led every fibre of my being to tremble in despair.

The hallways and rooms of the Toronto General, Wellesley and Princess Margaret hospitals became dungeons of gloom. The exhilaration and relief of those early and intermittent releases from hospital restored a taste of semi-normal living, but only for a short while. Most days I stayed in Louise's hospital room from early morning until midnight. In the weeks of extreme concern I stayed all night, trying to rest on a beat-up, black leatherette chair in the room.

After several weeks of such nocturnal vigils, and lunches usually consisting of a small yogurt or a muffin, I stood up early one morning to find the whole room reeling, with the floor teetering towards the ceiling and the ceiling towards the floor. The doctor, who had just arrived, caught me as I collapsed, and I was wheeled down to the emergency department, where my blood pressure was found to be so high that the emergency staff wondered how I had escaped a stroke. I have been on daily blood-pressure medication ever since.

I kept three nurses as specials on twenty-four-hour shifts for most of these years, but often when the nurse took her break at night, I crawled onto the narrow hospital bed to hold and hug Louise. Even with the miserable hindrance of draining and intravenous tubes, the warmth of these fleeting embraces provided cherished moments of solace and comfort.

One night the monitor showed heart failure, which quickly brought an emergency team into the room to restore the heartbeat. Shortly after, I was visited in the room by the resident doctor, who suggested that in cases of a hopeless cancer illness, instructions can be given to dispense with emergency resuscitation and to let the patient go peacefully. In front of my wife, the doctor coldly requested that I give such permission.

Anger is an emotion that I have rarely displayed, but I lashed out uncontrollably at this resident, telling him he might have the greatest medical training in the world, but without human sensitivity and compassion he would always be a mere technician, never a doctor. He hastily retreated from the room.

Even with my beautiful wife lying emaciated, with no semblance left of the bubbling vitality that lit up my world, I still held on to every thread of hope. I suppose I could never believe in euthanasia, although I could be persuaded to condemn the use of devastating chemotherapy to prolong a hopeless disease. One of my saddest regrets is that in the final weeks of Louise's life she was so heavily sedated, mostly with morphine, that there was no possibility of communication. I would have given everything for the memory of a few precious last words of intimacy. I pleaded with the doctor to cut down the medication, if only for a few hours, but it was to no avail.

The days and weeks that followed my wife's death are almost a blank in my memory. Whether because of the medication given to me at the time or a psychological barrier, I don't remember the funeral service or any of the people present. I was later told that Eddie Goodman came from Toronto and delivered a very warm, personal and touching eulogy. I doubt that I ever thanked Eddie for this kindness. He appropriately carries the name "good man." Eddie too was smitten with Louise from the moment he met her. Had we lived our lives in his city, he told me, she would have had all of Toronto at her feet.

There were hundreds of expressions of sympathy, most of them acknowledged by my daughter Debra, with the help of my secretary. I did not have the courage or the capacity to read a single letter, and they were packed away in a box. Someday I may have the emotional strength to unpack the box and gain some comfort from what I am sure are many sincere words of tribute to an exceptional life.

For weeks I was a zombie, not venturing out of my bedroom and scarcely out of bed. Medication was doled out to me, a pill at a time, for fear I might be tempted to overdose. My car keys were hidden, less out of concern that I might hurt myself than that I might cause injury to others. For months every knock on the door, every ring of the phone, stirred alarm, trepidation and terror. My few hours of medicated sleep were always terminated by my awakening suddenly, screaming into the night. A decade later this has abated but not ended.

With Conrad Black's autobiography, in which he speaks of his bouts of mental anxiety, and John Bentley Mays' account of his own battle with depression, it has become acceptable to speak freely of such afflictions. A generation earlier the tendency was to hide them in a closet. The expression of grief is a normal catharsis, but contemplating the enormity of my loss reduced me to a state of paralytic numbness. I could not eat, sleep or be consoled, and hidden in my room I refused to see people who wanted to help. I felt a suicidal desire to escape the agony of the despair. And along with this wish there was the universal question: why must roses, which beautify the world, die, while thorns, with little or no contribution to make, live on? As my mother used to say in times of trouble, *"Gaa freg bei gott a kasha."* ("Go ask of God a question.")

My boyhood friend, the psychiatrist Myer Mendelson, came from Philadelphia, offering comfort and consolation, and suggesting that I gather strength from all the wonderful memories. But I remember the comment of Northrop Frye, when he was offered the same advice after a similar loss: "To try to gain comfort from such memories is like telling a starving man to remember the wonderful banquet he had six months before."

With the passage of time I mustered enough courage to dress and walk to my office, at first accompanied by my housekeeper, but using back streets and alleys for fear of meeting someone who knew me and might want to talk. At the office I sat behind my desk, staring blankly into space for hours on end. After five o'clock, when everyone else had left, my secretary of thirty years, Norma Jones, would find me lying on the floor. Not knowing what to do or how to cope, she was sometimes reduced to tears. But never once did she leave before getting me into her car and delivering me home, sometimes staying to cook fresh vegetables from her home garden. Some weekends she and another woman from the office took me for drives in the country.

Gradually I learned to face the day by myself. But the mitigation of the paralysis of despair was followed by what is sometimes referred to as survivor's guilt. I felt guilt about any enjoyment, even from eating. A play, movie, social function, or even a comedy on TV, were impossible.

It was at this stage of my worst mental morosity that I had a visit from Pamela Wallin, who at the time was with CTV. She was touring the area to prepare a program on the Atlantic economy. I had always admired her elegance, and respected her talent as an incisive interviewer. I was flattered by her visit but when she learned that I would not submit to a television interview, she beat a hasty retreat, with the two cameramen in tow.

The process became one of trying to function again almost from scratch, to develop a pattern of existence in a completely changed world. My wife had assumed responsibility for almost all the details of my life—outside of business and my law practice, from the worries of which I always tried to keep her happily shielded. Almost like a spoiled child I had depended on my wife for most aspects of living. The first morning I went to work after our honeymoon, she looked at my tie and said, "Surely you're not wearing that tie with that suit." In my background, fashion and colour coordination were never a consideration, so from that moment, when my self-confidence was shaken in matters sartorial, I left my wardrobe to Louise. I never again bought an article of clothing on my own. I still haven't. My wife always draped three suitable ties over each of my suits, so that I could not choose incorrectly. Those ties, a decade later, are still there.

A few years ago I went to Montreal for Leonard Ellen's 65th birthday party, accompanied by my friend George Urquhart, a school chum of almost sixty-five years. We visited Brison and Brison, a men's clothing store that boasts Pierre Trudeau as a patron and where George was being fitted for a jacket under his wife's supervision. When a clerk asked if he might show me something, I thanked him and explained I was just waiting for my friend. The clerk walked away but came back ten minutes later to suggest I look at some of the new fashions. I demurred again, whereupon he complimented me on my tie. I was flattered for a moment, until he said the store had carried the Countess Mara line for years. "It was a fine line," he said. "We were sorry when the company went out of business fifteen years ago."

I had never even packed a suitcase for a trip. My wife always laid everything out for me, down to the cuff links, so I was lost here too. Food was another problem. Where I had once dined like a king, I now ate like a hermit. I had never eaten alone and had always used room service to avoid sitting in a restaurant or hotel dining room by myself. Now I sat alone, night after night, with a newspaper or CBC radio my only company. The details of trying to run the household, to which I had never given a thought, now assumed monstrous proportions.

By the fall of 1988, I began slowly to adapt and became less inclined to go out of my way to avoid meeting people. It was about this time that Eddie Goodman sent me a copy of his just published autobiography. His hand-written inscription read: "To Reuben—whose friendship I cherish but above all has taught me the depth of love that a man can have for a woman.—With deep affection—Eddie." It is amazing the healing effect a small expression of kindly sentiment can sometimes have.

CHAPTER 11

Petro-Canada

During the summer and fall of 1988, the months of my lowest mental apathy, Bill Hopper, the chairman of Petro-Canada, called several times to invite me to join his board. These were the days when I could not be persuaded to move from home base or show any interest in my business or other affairs. The odd time my secretary forced me to take Hopper's calls, I always thanked him for the offer and declined. Hopper was persistent, believing I would be a suitable director to represent the Maritimes after Harrison McCain's recent departure from the Petro-Canada board. But even if I were emotionally up to it, I told Hopper during one call, I would not serve.

"Why not?" he asked.

"I am so much against the government of Canada's being in the retail gas business that I never patronize a Petro-Canada service station as a matter of principle," I said. "And if I happen to run out of gas outside a Petro-Canada outlet, and the nearest competitor is ten miles down the road, I would gladly walk the distance to get a can of gasoline to avoid giving Petro-Canada the business."

"That is just what I wanted to hear, and all the more reason why I want you on my board," Hopper said to my amazement. "Besides, I've already had you Gazetted."

Such was his self-confidence that he had gone ahead with this requirement for an appointment to a Crown corporation. I had no idea that he had been striving for some time to persuade the government to privatize Petro-Canada, so the very reason I gave him for leaving me alone made him all the more determined in his pursuit. After several attempts he entered into a conspiracy with my secretary, Mrs. Jones, who was trying to get me functioning again and out of my mental lethargy.

David Smith, now a Chief Justice, was a young lawyer who had taken over the responsibilities of my legal office, and under the guise that he had legal business to look after in Ottawa, he and Mrs. Jones pushed me into going along. It was to be my first break out of Moncton in months. At the Ottawa airport, to my surprise, we were met by Bill Hopper, together with the then president of Petro-Canada, who whisked me away to a board meeting. Hopper had moved it from Calgary to Ottawa in order to trap me. Mrs. Jones was right in her assessment; this proved to be the first, slight opening for a ray of light to enter my gloom.

From my first exposure to Hopper it was instant rapport. I had never met so forceful and confident a character, and it was fascinating to watch his performance at company meetings. As the son of a diplomat, Hopper spent many of his younger years in various parts of the world. His career as a senior civil servant in Ottawa, including his service as deputy minister of energy, made him knowledgeable in the workings of the federal government and provided him with an extensive network of political connections. No one knew the ins and outs of the Ottawa corridors better than Hopper did, and few people in Canada were more familiar with the world oil market and its international players.

Hopper often spoke of his private dinners with Sheik Yamani, the head of the Saudi Arabian oil ministry and one of the architects of OPEC. I doubt that any oil or gas play of significance anywhere in the world escaped Hopper's attention. He was perceived by many, both within Petro-Canada and without, as autocratic and arrogant. But if these qualities existed, they only masked his humanity and compassion. He ran the company in some respects as a private fiefdom, which in its days as a Crown corporation might have been necessary for survival. I found Hopper's company and conversation, his humour and *joie de vivre*, a tonic at this critical time in my life. My exposure to him was therapy, which in a not so minor way jolted me into trying to face life again.

Hopper told me that he had had a Jewish girlfriend when his father was stationed in Washington. He was prepared to convert to Judaism until the woman's father broke it up, but in the interlude he learned to feel comfortable wearing a yarmulke. This served him in good stead when he dealt with Paul Reichmann during Petro-Canada's purchase of the Gulf Oil stations in the Ontario region. Hopper had several luncheon meetings with Reichmann in the Olympia and York offices, where the traditional kosher, but monotonous, tuna sandwiches were always served. Hopper ate them wearing a yarmulke, in deference to his host, and possibly as an aid to the deliberations. But when the negotiations reached a serious impasse, he broke the deadlock only by threatening to eat a ham sandwich and drink a glass of milk, without wearing the yarmulke.

Offshore oil at Hibernia and privatization were two of the momentous decisions involving the Petro-Canada board during the few years I was on it. Hopper was never a fan of Hibernia, considering it too big a bite out of the company's capital resources, which would limit its capacity to invest in oil plays having a more immediate return. Another concern was the gamble on the long-range oil price on world markets, in light of the high cost of the Hibernia product, even with enormous government subsidization. But Petro-Canada was under political pressure from its Ottawa masters to proceed. With great reluctance Hopper asked at a board meeting for a motion to approve a $1-billion commitment to the venture. There was silence around the boardroom table as directors looked uncomfortably from one to the other to see who had the courage to make the motion. I said I wasn't brave enough to move for the expenditure of a billion dollars, but I would agree to be the seconder if Ed Barroll, who was sitting opposite me, would be the mover. The motion was initiated and carried.

The road to privatization, with the initial public offering, was a much less burdensome decision, and was entered into with excitement by all members of the board, particularly Hopper, after his arduous months of negotiation and delicate prodding of federal authorities.

The most dramatic incident of my years on the Petro-Canada board involved the termination and departure of Bill Hopper. The history of the company has been well documented in Peter Foster's book *Self Serve: How Petro-Canada Pumped Canadians Dry*, which was published in 1992 and won the National Business Book Award. The book is a well-researched and fascinating account of the company from its creation, and also an intriguing story of the oil industry in Canada and its interplay with the politics of the country. My only complaint is with the book's vilification of Hopper, who is portrayed as the ultimate Machiavellian schemer. Adequate allowance is not made for the fact that Hopper would have to be more than ordinarily capable, if not cunning, to have survived the political vagaries of his seventeen-year tenure and the succession of political administrations and masters he had to serve. The author also failed to show another side of the man, the one marked with a humanity known by the many who experienced his generous warmth and sensitivity.

The softcover version of Foster's book contained an epilogue called "End of the Line," dealing with the circumstances surrounding Hopper's termination at Petro-Canada, which occurred long after the hardcover version was published. The details of the board deliberations set out in the epilogue are as accurate as if the author had been present with a recording machine. It is frightening to think that such a private matter in a major corporation's affairs could have been leaked so completely, especially since even the corporate secretary responsible for taking the minutes had been excluded from the boardroom.

I had a brief inkling of a rumble on the Petro-Canada board during an audit committee meeting. Tom Kierans, a recent appointment, offered the comment that, except for the very top, he was satisfied that the management of the company was as good as any other in the Canadian oil industry. Despite these words I had no idea of the convulsion that was to take place soon after, when we were summoned to a special meeting to deal with the question of company management.

The way it was all handled upset me. Four directors had met privately to lay out the strategy without any consultation with me or three others on the board. The first four presented us with an ultimatum: Either the Hopper dismissal would be accomplished or they would all resign, possibly taking some top managers with them, which would do the company more harm than would the termination of Hopper. I believe Kierans was the architect of the scheme and had done his work extremely well, especially at the Ottawa end, having made all the necessary political contacts and consultations. In effect he closed all the doors that Hopper had always been able to squeeze through. Hopper was cornered for the first time in his career.

The threat of the four resignations was strong enough to bring the other three directors on side to vote for the dismissal. I abstained, but not because I did not think Hopper should go once he had lost the confidence of the bulk of the board; my concern was with the process that brought it about. I felt some avenue could be explored that would let him depart with a degree of dignity and not too much loss of face. I suggested giving Hopper a leave of absence until the annual meeting, which was only about three months away, and announcing his resignation then with the customary tribute. This was shot down because, under Hopper's contract, a voluntary resignation carried a year's less compensation than a dismissal, and he would reject giving up some compensation just to save face. My suggestion that we try to amend the contract was quickly dismissed because it would have involved government input and waved a red flag in front of the public, which the government could not politically accept. I alone abstained in the vote for dismissal.

The meeting was among the most exhausting and troubling of my corporate career. The next morning the story was headline news across the country. Since then there have been rumblings that it was several heavyweight western politicians in Ottawa, including Harvie Andre, who wanted Hopper removed, and that Tom's appointment was the instrument for carrying it out. If this was the case, Hopper didn't have a chance to save himself with his usual Ottawa connections. I doubt this story, although anything is possible in the world of politics.

All appointees to the board had to be government nominees, and management had little or nothing to say in their selection. Even so, the warm reception Hopper gave Tom on his appointment now seems ironic.

Ed Barroll, a longtime member of the board, was chosen as a non-executive chairman to fill the vacancy, but since Barroll was approaching the mandatory retirement age, I expressed my feeling to Hopper and others that the chair was just being kept warm until Tom was ready. This proved to be the case, with a one-year interlude by Jim Black, who was 69 when appointed and had only a year to go. I take my hat off to Tom; I would always feel comfortable having him on my side. In many ways he's as capable and as shrewd as his father, Eric, whom I have respected since his very young days, when he lived in Moncton and called at my father's store as a salesman for Ogilvie Flour.*

---

* Hopper had during his tenure at Petro-Canada accumulated a substantial block of shares in Westcoast Energy of Vancouver, where he also served as chairman. From his very first entry on the board, Kierans questioned this investment and almost immediately after Hopper's dismissal it was disposed of in the $16.00 range. Had it been retained until the present market, it would have brought more than twice the sale price and afforded Petro-Canada a gain of several hundred million dollars.

The downsizing and other changes that have brought Petro-Canada up to, or above, industry profitability were instituted in the last few months of Hopper's tenure and in progress before he left, and would have been reflected in the bottom line had he continued. To his credit as well, Hopper assembled a superb top-management team, including the new CEO, Jim Stanford, whose exceptional management skills and industry knowledge were certain to provide continuing growth, expansion and profitability.

Our board meetings after Hopper's departure lacked the sparkle that Hopper's chairmanship provided. I have been off the board for several years, but looking back, I still take comfort in knowing that I did not completely abandon Hopper, perhaps out of gratitude for his lift to me in the time of my greatest despondency.

The Demise of Central

As I slowly began to re-expose myself to the business interests with Leonard Ellen, my heart was not in them as before, and my mind was too distressed to care.

Immediately after Harry Rhude's death in 1985, we had brought in Struan Robertson to act as CEO of Central and Eastern Trust. Struan had recently retired as president of Maritime Tel and Tel, and for some years was director of Manulife. We felt that his experience at the helm of a major Maritime industry, along with his legal background, would provide us with a competent leader.

Leonard had become obsessed with the creation of a holding company— in a sense, with aping the Edper–Hees Brascan group. He had gone to school with Edward and Peter Bronfman in Montreal and was entranced by the financial structure they had created. Leonard himself had once tried to gain control of Brascan, before Edper entered the scene. Eddie Goodman, who was on the board of Labatt, arranged for Leonard to meet Jake Moore, the Brascan chairman. Moore spurned this approach for a friendly buyout, possibly to his regret, since in the later Edper takeover of Brascan he was unceremoniously dumped.

Leonard, still smarting from the rebuff by Moore, was impressed with the Edper manoeuvring for Brascan, and often told me that Jack Cockwell, the brains behind the Edper–Hees machine, was the most talented and innovative business operator in Canada. If only he could find another Jack Cockwell, then he might equal or surpass the Bronfman empire.

Unable to find another Cockwell, Leonard pinned his hopes on Peter Cole. Months before Harry's death we were introduced to Cole through Tor Boswick, a broker at Gordon Securities, then the hotshot brokerage house on Bay Street. Cole was in the upper echelons of the Canadian Imperial Bank of Commerce but knew, I suspect, that he would never make the top slot. He was restless to find a substantial home where he could run his own show, and where an outstanding and dramatic success would prove that the CIBC made a mistake in passing him over. Our financial and industrial conglomerate, with its trust company, a mutual fund company, mortgage insurance company, energy company and important manufacturing facilities, was an enticing instrument to fulfil his dream.

A dinner meeting was arranged in Toronto so Harry could meet Cole and determine if he could help expand our operations, both nationally and internationally. Harry listened intently, but at the end of the meeting his quizzical smile indicated an unequivocal no. The matter lay dormant until after Harry died. Then it was revived, and with it, Leonard's dream of a holding company in the manner of the Hees group. Eddie Goodman was the emissary to make the contact with Cole, prompting Russell Harrison, then chairman at CIBC, to quip later at a fiftieth birthday party for Cole that we weren't brave enough to face him alone and had to engage Eddie to do it.

At the time, my wife was starting treatment, and if my mind had not been so occupied with her health, I might have exerted more opposition to the holding company. My reservations centred on the likelihood that a holding company would diminish the stature of the trust company, my primary interest. Leonard, however, was determined. And lurking always in my memory was his reaction when I had opposed the move he wanted on MICC, which almost ruptured our relationship. With my personal life so vulnerable I was in no mood to risk incurring his wrath again. In 1986, with Cole's added stimulus as CEO, Central Capital Corporation was born, eventually bringing all the individual corporate entities under its umbrella.

As a condition of Cole's employment at Central Capital, he brought with him Tom Hodgson, still in his early thirties and touted as a corporate brain. Hodgson, as executive vice-president, was to serve as Cole's alter ego. It didn't take long for them to generate excitement, and this, much beyond what could have been anticipated.

In the next three years they negotiated numerous acquisitions of financial firms, substantially increasing the assets under Central Capital's control and making it a substantial power in the financial services industry. With this growth, of course, came an enormous debt.

The biggest transaction was the purchase of Guaranty Trustco, which brought into the fold Guaranty Trust, Canadian General Insurance, Traders Group, Trans Canada Credit and some lesser entities. These purchases were negotiated over a single weekend, largely for cash, but also for a significant amount of paper. The irony was that Guaranty had been shown to us in the early Sixties, in the days of Wilson Berry and Moncton native Alan Ramsay, when it got into a financial squeeze through investments in low-interest, long-term National Housing Act mortgages. As interest rates escalated, the financial demands put the business in some jeopardy. We studied their figures in detail at that time, and concluded we could not generate the capital necessary to sustain the losses, and so passed on the opportunity.

Eventually, Guaranty came into the hands of Acres, an engineering company where Andy Sarlos worked as a financial officer. Andy is said to have arranged to put Guaranty into the hands of the McCutcheon family for a fairly minor consideration, and the family, whose founding father Wallace was one of the founders of Argus, sold Guaranty to Cole for more than $400 million.

David Rattee, who had come from the Continental Bank, was chosen to run the trust company operation, but after only a few months he was moved out, and Hodgson insinuated himself into the position. I asked many times why David was removed but never got a reasonable explanation.

Other acquisitions followed with whirlwind speed, including Capel-Cure Myers, a capital management company in Britain—founded in the reign of King George III in 1792—and an interest in the discount brokerage business. At one time Cole and Hodgson borrowed more than $500 million from Japanese banks, without collateral and with no principal repayment for five or six years. In Leonard's view this was a spectacular coup and a tribute to exceptional management.

During this borrowing and buying spree Leonard reached the height of his glory; he made the cover of the November 1988 issue of the Montreal Gazette's *Quebec Business* magazine with the bold headline, "How Leonard Ellen built Central Capital into a major financial empire." His face dominated the glass windows of every *Gazette* paper box in Montreal, promoting a four-page article inside titled "Elegant Acquisitor." The caption under the accompanying full-page picture said, "Ellen gives the impression that all his working life has been a preparation for these years of growth and prudent glory." In the article, writer Mark Abley paid Leonard the ultimate tribute: "People are beginning to compare [his] activities with the buildup of the diverse Bronfman fortune. And although Leonard Ellen's velvet reticence seems a world apart from the erratic, irascible brilliance of Samuel Bronfman, the comparisons may not be altogether mistaken."

With this, Leonard achieved his long-desired place in the sun and silenced those Montreal social colleagues who, largely in a spirit of envy, had sometimes attributed Leonard's success to my manoeuvring down east. Leaving little doubt as to the major player in the business, the article ended with one of Leonard's favourite sayings: "I think the good Lord has had his arm around me all of my life."

My wife always understood Leonard's temperament and could assess people more shrewdly than I. With good-natured teasing, she would say to him, "Ellen, tomorrow the world." Unfortunately, what she always called "the Ellen luck" was soon to run out.

When they were rolling and at their most arrogant, Cole and Hodgson purchased a large block of National Trust stock. Shortly after, Bill Somerville, a retired CEO of National Trust, arranged for Leonard and me to have a private dinner meeting with Hal Jackman, the controlling shareholder of National. To our amazement and chagrin, he told us that Cole and Hodgson had informed him they weren't stopping at the newly acquired block of National stock but wanted Jackman's control block as well. If Jackman would not deal with them in a friendly manner, they would manoeuvre him into a hostile takeover he was bound to lose.

Even more startling was that Cole and Hodgson had told Jackman they planned to acquire control of Central Capital from Leonard and me, either by friendly means or by whatever else might be required to achieve their objectives. This astounding information in itself would have warranted their immediate dismissal, but by then matters were progressing too precipitously to risk further dislocation.

The imprudent Financial Trust purchase, made without full report of the facts to the executive committee of the board, drastically changed Leonard's opinion of the management team. He was absolutely furious and gave instructions that there were to be no more purchases of any kind whatsoever—period. Unfortunately, it was already too late: Financial Trust was in such bad shape that Cole and company should have been paid to rescue the business rather than throw away $300 million buying it. I once asked Hodgson what possessed them to buy, without due diligence and examination, a company facing imminent collapse. His only reply, delivered in his imperturbable and expressionless mien, was, "I guess that was a mistake." So much for whiz kids.

And so much, too, for another breed. Leonard had persuaded Alan Lenczner, the brilliant litigation lawyer who had won two lawsuits for us, to leave his legal practice and join the management group. To Leonard's great disappointment, rather than being a moderating influence, Lenczner was soon at the front of the pack at the crap table. Brilliant litigation lawyers don't necessarily make management geniuses, although top corporate lawyers are often exceptionally successful in business, prime examples being Harry Rhude and, of course, Purdy Crawford, in his spectacular career at Imasco.

Cole's own management had become essentially one of cronyism; if you were a buddy, you were well in the door. Andy Sarlos was one such character, selling his investment company to Cole for millions of dollars in a deal that proved to be more dollars down the drain. In *Fireworks*, his 1993 autobiography, Andy told how he was instrumental in arranging Cole's acquisition of Financial Trust. Until I thumbed through the book, I did not know much about Andy's role in this disaster, and it reaffirmed my opinion of him as one of the wiliest traders I ever encountered. That soft, placid exterior masked as hard-headed an operator as could be found anywhere.

I was sorry when I learned of Andy's death in the spring of 1997. Andy and I met only three or four times, but I remember being amused at our first meeting by his thoughts on marriage and divorce in North America. The high incidence of divorce, he argued, could be alleviated by the European practice of taking mistresses, which would keep families from being broken apart and otherwise diminish the impact of matrimonial dislocation. And, he hastened to add, a mistress discarded should not be thrown to the wind but given every financial consideration to ensure she is not left in want, much as a wife in a divorce case.

In *Fireworks*, Andy offered his assessment of me and Leonard:

I greatly respected Reuben as an intelligent, cultivated individual and found him to be a generous person. As an active philanthropist, he planned to leave the bulk of his wealth to various universities and charitable organizations. On one occasion in particular, he opened his big heart to me: In the early 1980s, when HCI was facing possible collapse and the press was tearing me apart, Reuben reinflated my spirits and my self-esteem by arranging an invitation to have me speak to the Dalhousie University investment committee, of which he was a member.

Reuben had no political ambitions or expensive hobbies and liked to claim that the only interesting thing about him was his wife, Louise. They made a charming couple and were absolutely devoted to each other; when I knew them, they were living in the same Moncton house Louise had designed on the back of a paper bag prior to their 1951 marriage. It was close enough to Reuben's law practice that he could walk to work (and did). I felt deeply for Reuben when Louise developed cancer. Her long sickness and painful death naturally preoccupied Reuben and took him away from business. Unfortunately, this personal tragedy came at the time when Central Capital needed him most, and this was, undoubtedly, one of the contributing causes behind the company's collapse.

Leonard presented a very different and less palatable impression: he was stubborn, avaricious, and lacked the management skills one would expect from the owner of a huge enterprise like Central Capital. How two such different men stayed partners is a mystery to me, yet this odd couple enjoyed decades of friendship and partnership together. They operated strictly on trust and they proudly told people that never in their years together had "the scratch of a pen" come between them.

While I appreciated Andy's observations, he may have been too kind to me and too harsh to Leonard. Andy claimed, for instance, that as a result of his intervention in 1989, Leonard could have sold out to BCE Inc. for eleven dollars a share and saved Central Capital from its eventual collapse, but that he was greedy and held out for more. In fact, the negotiations with Jean de Grandpré, then head of BCE and a man Ellen knew well socially, would not have required such outside intercession. BCE was then in a program of active diversification, and if de Grandpré had not been retired at the crucial time involved, a successful sale might well have been concluded.

In August 1990, Peter Cole's tenure with Central Capital was terminated, and in April of the next year Ellen assumed the chairmanship in a desperate attempt at salvage. The company was then burdened with a colossal debt and millions of dollars' worth of injudicious investments, its position aggravated by the collapse of real estate values, particularly in Ontario. Serious efforts had been made to try to sell off parts of the assets to raise cash, but even where these were in part successful, they did not generate sufficient proceeds to forestall the impending downfall.

At one point I had heard that Cole and his minions were trying to raise money to keep their ship afloat by selling the energy business portion of Inter-City Gas and had retained a broker, at some multimillion-dollar commission, to find a buyer. At the time, Bill Hopper was also the chairman of Westcoast Energy, as it is now called, of which Petro-Canada had practical control. I suggested to Hopper that he might have some interest in this property, particularly with the utility end for Westcoast and the propane business for Petro-Canada. Hopper and I met in a hotel room in Winnipeg, the head-office site of Inter-City, and in fifteen minutes agreed on a sale price in the $780-million range, subject to the usual diligence inquiries and legal requirements. I am told that the broker received his outrageous commission; I have yet to receive so much as a thank you.

I would like to think that, had I been operating on all cylinders during the years of Central Capital's buying binge and the economic downturn that followed, the business catastrophe might have been avoided. One thing is certain: had Harry Rhude been in command, regardless of the severity of the downturn, the collapse would not have happened.

Leonard was certainly the catalyst that created the expansion and, at the time, the impressive growth of our business. He had the ambition and the energy, the drive and the gambling instinct required in every entrepreneurial success. Without him, I would probably have been content in my comfortable Maritime bailiwick, happily leading a life obscured from the national scene. Leonard and I were always considered a good match. He was the throttle that provided the enthusiasm and excitement; I was the brake that, with Harry's genius and able counsel, provided time for sober second thought. Regrettably, the brake pads wore down at a crucial turn in the road.

My own apprehensions had been growing since the amalgamation of Guaranty Trust with Central and Eastern. Always my dream was to prove that a major financial institution could emanate and be managed from the Atlantic area, achieve national status and provide excellent employment opportunities for the bright young people coming out of our universities. This would reverse in some small measure the drain of our best human resources that has hurt the region since Confederation. The amalgamation with Guaranty created Canada's third-largest trust company, in assets, behind Canada Trust and Royal Trust. For the new name of the trust company, I asked that we go simply with Central Trust and drop the Eastern that had been used to placate the old Eastern Canada Savings people. Because I did not want to leave my wife's hospital bed, I did not attend the meeting at which the new name was to be considered. Contrary to my wishes, the name Central Guaranty was adopted, apparently out of consideration for the Guaranty business and its customers in Upper Canada.

As I had feared, many important aspects of the trust company functions quickly moved to Toronto. First it was the investment department, then the accounting, until the Halifax office was reduced to little more than a regional satellite, emasculated of any real power or influence. Whenever I saw Struan Robertson, I castigated him for not standing up to the Toronto pressure and fighting to retain the head-office structure in Halifax, which was always my desire. Struan would only say that he thought the others knew better and he bowed to their seemingly greater knowledge of the trust business. This weakness of Struan's, I feel, influenced the unfolding of events. Struan's wife was sometimes present when I lectured him and always seemed to agree with my admonitions.

The transferral of management decisions to Toronto caused me so much anxiety that, at Central Capital's 1991 annual meeting in Halifax, I roused myself sufficiently to speak to the assembled shareholders. At that time things had started to unravel to such an extent that the stock price had slipped to a precarious four- to five-dollar range, from a high of at least three times that. The chairman, by then Robert Graham, mentioned in his remarks that 1990 was a difficult and disappointing year, attributable to the recession and its deleterious effect on employment and real estate values.

"While it is true," I said in my short address, "that these economic factors hit all financial institutions with drastic effects on their bottom line, we should have been smarter than the pack. The fact that we were not is attributable to what I call the Toronto syndrome. Over the years our investment department in Halifax was continuously eroded and eventually eliminated, with investment decisions becoming completely centralized in Toronto. I think this was a large part of the problem. I believe it is sometimes healthier to have investment decisions made a bit removed from the mainstream, where you can exercise a more detached judgment and not get caught up in the euphoria of an infectious investment climate that many times propels investment people to feel they must be as aggressive as their competitors down the street."

We always had an investment committee in Halifax, as well as a mortgage committee, made up of solid and responsible directors, largely from the Atlantic provinces, and I would prefer their prudent judgment anytime to that of slick traders on Bay Street.

In 1992, a court-ordered restructuring put Central Capital's assets into the hands of lenders, who then entered into the disposition of some of the assets. The loss of the trust company, which ended up in the hands of the Toronto Dominion Bank, meant the disappearance of an important player in the Maritime economy and was a bitter blow. With only thirty-five branches on the East Coast, an insignificant number compared with the combined branch network of the chartered banks in the area, Central held a preponderance of the savings, far in excess of any competitor. Had the trust company been able to achieve the same percentage of market penetration and customer loyalty in the rest of Canada, I believe it could have led the country in asset growth.

When Central disappeared, so did trust offices that had provided Maritimers with personal service, in their own communities, in the management of trusts and estates. Now the only trust operations in the region are centralized in Halifax.

Many older people had held their shares in the trust company for years, in some cases following a tradition of generations. And unlike the short traders in Upper Canada, who were out for a fast buck, these shareholders had a sentimental attachment to Central, regarding it almost as their own. When the problems at the trust company became manifest and it appeared its survival was in danger, people would stop me on the street and say, "Mr. Cohen, don't let them take our company away from us." *Our* company, they called it, not *yours*, so closely was it identified with the people of the area. I regret deeply the losses suffered by those small but loyal shareholders, particularly since so many had looked to me as a winning horse on whom they bestowed their confidence. My feeling that I let them down will always be a source of hurt and embarrassment to me.

How it happened so quickly and decisively, especially how the better part of a billion dollars in capital and reserves were wiped out practically overnight, I shall never understand. During my career I took part in investment decisions involving hundreds of millions of dollars without ever knowing what it was to lose a penny. On the contrary, virtually every investment, in every endeavour in which I was privileged to have a part, was profitable.

The collapse of the trust company was attributed largely to the implosion of property values, particularly in Ontario, but the company had faced other real estate downturns during its more than one hundred years of existence, including the more severe Depression. Each time, Central survived to build from success to success. Since all financial institutions in Canada suffered the same onslaught, I do not accept real estate values as an exonerating explanation for Central's failure. Indeed, the banks' write-offs, running into the billions of dollars, severely impacted their profits for a year or so, but they came back to record the largest profits in their history. Central could have done the same, I believe, had it been given the opportunity and a firm, prudent and knowledgeable hand at the helm.

It is still painful for me to see the many branch offices that I helped to build and nurture, often through my own vision and perspicacity, now clothed in the bilious green of an erstwhile competitor instead of the former rich and relaxing blue. When I have to be driven past such a location, I turn my head the other way to spare myself further anguish; if I have to walk by one, I cross the street to avoid the pain.

Since the difficulties of the early Nineties a new fetish has arisen, that of corporate governance, with stringent guidelines for directors' responsibility. "Where were the directors?" has become the new battle cry. My own experience over many years on the boards of companies large and small has convinced me that, if management wishes to conceal its tracks, no board, sitting intermittently, can be expected to have knowledge of mould developing in the corporate structure.

In our case I often railed at the quality of the earnings, which, although often impressive in quantity, seemed not to be hard earnings, from profitable operations; they were obtained mostly by income-tax considerations and asset-sales ploys. Since these were always sanctioned by the auditors, I had to retreat in silence. Auditors are in a far better position than directors to detect and ferret out early weaknesses, but they often appear hesitant to do so for fear of embarrassing management. After all, it is to management that auditors feel they owe their recommendation for reappointment, although they are fully aware their primary responsibility is to the shareholders, from whom their actual appointment emanates.

The most responsible function of a board of directors should be to see that the top management slot is filled with the right person, in the right place, at the right time. If this is done, everything else should flow smoothly throughout a corporate structure. Harry Rhude was the ultimate happy example in this regard.

Two factors, in my view, contributed significantly to Central's demise: the news media and the federal regulators.

From my earliest days I have been wary of the media and the damage they can do in their zeal for headline sensationalism. I was introduced to the media danger long ago, when as a young lawyer I appeared before Moncton city council to request an extension of municipal services to a sub-division in which a builder wished to construct one hundred new homes. One of the questions I was asked was whether the builder had arranged financing for this project. I answered that most of his previous development had been satisfactorily financed with mortgage moneys obtained from the Mutual Life Assurance Company of Canada, and I felt fairly confident Mutual Life would support him in this project as well.

The city council approved the application, and the next day the headline in the local newspaper was: "Mutual Life to build 100 homes." The local life sales office of Mutual Life was deluged with calls from people wanting information about the homes to be sold. Of course, when the flurry hit head office in Waterloo, I was in hot water, and it took a lot of explaining to keep from losing what was at the time my biggest client. A couple of years ago I bumped into Ouida MacLellan, the reporter I had called and scolded for that story so many years ago. She now lives in Calgary as Lady Touche, and all seems to have been forgiven on both sides.

This early lesson with the media taught me to tread carefully in relationships with what can be either a most formidable creative or a destructive power. If you are their darling at the moment, the media can be effusive in their accolades; if they perceive you on the ropes, they can be ruthless in hastening your destruction.

When the problems at Central first became apparent, the national media quickly headlined the difficulties with so much force and venom that any hope of recovery dissipated, their news coverage creating a run of depositors that eroded the financial supporting base. The local media then stepped in with vigour to seal the downfall.

To my great sadness and discomfort, as I walked out of my office early one afternoon, I saw television crews filming and asking questions of customers going in and out of a nearby trust branch. Did they fear for their savings? Were they withdrawing their accounts? One morning a CBC radio program offered a CBC coffee mug to the first caller who could identify the name of the New Brunswicker associated with the building and collapse of the trust company. These are tough weapons to fight against and their bullets almost impossible to evade.

As for the second factor, I believe that with a degree of cooperation from the federal regulator, the trust company could have been rescued. In the days when the regulator's office was in Ottawa, and under the management of such stalwarts in the field as Dick Humphreys, for many years the superintendent of insurance with responsibility for financial institutions as well, such cooperation would have been forthcoming. Humphreys was always keen to promote the well-being of local institutions, as a counterbalance to the national institutions in ensuring the health of the financial industry in Canada. The change to the new regulator, known as OSFI (the Office of the Superintendent of the Financial Institutions), seems to have changed the regulator's philosophy. Now the approach seems to be, "Stick strictly to the book and bring an end to the problem as quickly as possible—all the time keeping your own backside covered."

Michael Mackenzie, the head of OSFI at the time of Central's demise, is reputed to have said the trouble with the financial industry in Canada is that we have too many banks and not enough bankers. His quick action in our case suggests a determination to remedy the flaw he perceived in the system. For the trust company, his goal was to obtain new ownership with pockets deep enough to eliminate all worries for his office. This philosophy certainly helped alleviate pressure on OSFI, but I question whether it helped the competitive structure of the industry, particularly on a regional basis. If Dick Humphreys's attitude had prevailed, I believe the trust company would be alive still, serving a most important competitive function and probably racking up the healthy profits banks enjoyed in the ensuing economic recovery.*

At a time when I was already suffering deep emotional wounds, the business failure created insurmountable financial burdens. In an attempt to protect local small investors from harm—those who had trusted in me and whose faith I had done everything possible to sustain—I denuded myself of assets. What little flesh was left on the skeleton was rapidly and unfeelingly pecked away by the friendly bankers, leaving scarcely an ounce on the bones.

Ever wary of bankers, I had always planned to have free and unencumbered assets with which to meet any banking eventuality. Unfortunately, these assets, once worth well in excess of $100 million, lost their value almost overnight. My careful planning proved fruitless, and in my twilight years I faced blows to my pride and integrity that I had never in the worst scenario contemplated. A lifetime of building and caution had quickly come to naught, and the crime for which I had been brought to my knees was that of emotional weakness. Perhaps Nietzsche, the German philosopher, was not far off the mark when he wrote that the ethic by which to live is to "assert yourself—the only vice is weakness, and the only virtue is strength."

Depression, whatever the cause, is a difficult malady, creating in my case a complete paralysis of the will to live and do. Instead, I was to be led, and to leave to others the business and professional responsibilities I had carried quite effectively all my life. This was a serious mistake, as the severe consequences proved. Many of us overestimate the value of our contribution; in my case, I think I underestimated it.

It has not been my purpose to set out the sorry and complex details of Central Capital's demise, for God knows they were covered in the media *ad nauseam* at the time, and to think of them even now causes me pain. My endeavour has merely been to offer some insights, from my personal assessment of the background, and to suggest some nuances at play that perhaps are not obtainable elsewhere.

---

*   Indeed, the recent sale of the Casualty Insurance Company, Canadian General, to General Accident, for over $700 million, would have paid off virtually all the indebtedness to the domestic banks and left the bulk of the conglomerate, including the trust company, intact, and permitted all shareholders to come out with a full skin, if not indeed a profit. The same circumstances could probably apply to the Royal Trust Company, when that fine old institution was delivered into bank hands with substantial resultant losses to its shareholders.

While the business downfall has the ingredients of a tragedy, the loss of investment income is perhaps a more minor personal calamity when one is past the age of seventy. The real tragedy for me, and the *cause of much* anguish, is that my plans for a charitable foundation, structured to provide for the enhancement of post-secondary education and much of it as a memorial in perpetuity to my wife, were frustrated. In addition, charitable bequests that had been made on a five-year commitment left me facing a moral obligation of more than several million dollars. The lesson to be learned from this last is that older people should never make extended charitable commitments but limit themselves to contributions from year to year, as circumstances permit. These are problems with which I am still wrestling.

The blow to Leonard's ego and pride must have been equally powerful, and in some social aspects perhaps more so. In the halcyon years he called me almost daily to savour our victories and to impart news of family and community. For years, his would be the first call on my birthday, at New Year's and on other such celebratory occasions. Now, I never hear from him. "I've had my day in the sun," Leonard told me on one of the last days I saw him. On another occasion, when I called to consult him about severe pressures I was facing locally, which should have been of equal concern to him, he replied, "What do you want me to do, move down there?"

In the fall of 1995, I tried to reach him for his input on an emergency matter of considerable importance to me personally and of somewhat lesser consequence to him. I finally located him at a hotel in the western United States, where he was taking part in a golf tournament. He said he would be back in Montreal on the weekend and would call me the following Monday. More than two years later, I have yet to receive his call. It is true that Parkinson's disease has left Leonard with a pronounced tremor in one arm, and a colon operation for removal of a malignant growth led to a series of chemotherapy sessions. These problems, I am sure, have occupied a good deal of his attention. I am told he still winters in Florida and continues to golf there at his exclusive country club.

The last time I saw Leonard was in September 1995 at an affair in Montreal to mark his seventieth birthday and fiftieth wedding anniversary. While it was a lavish celebration, it did not faintly measure up to his sixty-fifth birthday party, when he rented the Place des Arts hall for his private guests and personally conducted the full Montreal Symphony Orchestra. *Sic transit gloria.*

CHAPTER 13

Chancellor of Dalhousie

Lady Beaverbrook, the incumbent chancellor of Dalhousie University in 1989, had not set foot on campus since her installation seventeen years earlier, much to the regret of university authorities.

My friend Henry Hicks visited her on occasion in England, but she had told him early on, around the time of student protests on American campuses, including the riots at Kent State University, that she was staying away from Dalhousie because she was afraid those "horrid students" would throw things at her. Henry assured Lady Beaverbrook that there was no such unrest at Dalhousie, but she was not persuaded. Her absence continued year after year, despite Henry's diplomatic suggestions that she might wish to step down.

The university administration would not take any unilateral initiative to remove Lady Beaverbrook as chancellor for fear of losing important financial contributions, one of which, in the order of $2 million, came when the law building had to be restored after a fire. She was the widow of both Sir James Dunn, who made her Lady Dunn, and Max Aitken, who made her Lady Beaverbrook, and as such she was the key to both the Dunn and Beaverbrook foundations. While the Beaverbrook Foundation was almost depleted, the Dunn Foundation was still healthy and the source for the law school contribution.

Then, in the fall of 1989, Dr. Howard Clark, the president of Dalhousie, called to ask me to consider the appointment as chancellor. Although I told him that my emotional and physical condition would prohibit my serving, Henry Hicks also spoke to me, and those closest to me at home encouraged me to take the position, hoping it would alleviate my mental lethargy. I was honoured that my alma mater wanted to recognize me in this way, but in the end a more important factor led me to reconsider.

During the Thirties and Forties all major universities in Canada and the United States instituted a quota system that limited ethnic enrolments in their professional schools, particularly in medicine and dentistry. Dalhousie University—not McGill, the University of Toronto or the University of Manitoba—stood almost alone in accepting students into its professional faculties on merit, without any restrictions based on race, colour or religion. Many medical doctors and dentists were afforded careers that would otherwise have been denied them. And since they practised in many parts of Canada and the U.S., their professional services would have been lost to their communities as well. Indeed, for many years Dalhousie's most loyal and generous alumni association was in New York City.

Dalhousie is proud of this significant chapter in its history, and the pride is shared by its far-flung alumni. If the university offered me its highest ceremonial office, I would be a poor debtor indeed if I did not accept.

During my chancellorship, Dalhousie attempted to set up a chair in black studies, which would have been the first such chair at a Canadian university. Funding in the range of $2.5 million was required for the project. Clark and his vice president of development met with the appropriate cabinet minister in the Mulroney government responsible for such requests, the Honourable Gerald Weiner, and were turned down with the reluctant explanation that if he had a hundred times his actual budget allocation, he would not even then be able to meet all the worthwhile requests that came to him. I asked Clark to arrange for a further meeting with the minister, whom I had never met, and which I might attend. This was quickly arranged, and Clark, the development officer and I met with Weiner in his Ottawa office; in the initial conversation he casually dropped a word of Yiddish. Picking up on this, I proceeded to converse with him in Yiddish for about ten minutes—his was impeccable, far better than mine—while Clark and his officer sat in silent bewilderment. At the end of our conversation, Weiner stood up and said to Clark, waving his hand across his belt line, that the chances for the contribution were about that level, but then, waving his hand over his head, he said that "after listening to your chancellor your chances are now away up here." When we left the office, an elated Clark asked how I had so drastically changed the minister's mind. I replied that I had recounted to him in Yiddish the story of Dalhousie's unique position in all major Canadian universities, in the dark chapter of iniquitous quota systems. Only a short while after this meeting, Weiner came to Halifax, hosted a luncheon, and presented the substantial cheque that provided the seed money that eventually enabled the first Canadian chair in black studies to be established at Dalhousie.

When the chancellorship invitation was made, I asked Henry how he would resolve the matter of Lady Beaverbrook's departure. "Oh, I've already done that," he replied. "I went to see her to tell her I had an exciting proposal for her, and that when I retired as president, the university appointed me as president emeritus, which is an honour I was to have for life and which can never be taken away. I told her if she would agree to step down, I might be able, if I played my cards right, to persuade the board to bestow a similar honour on her, and that as chancellor emeritus she would have a singular honour for her life."

Lady Beaverbrook bought the offer, and the door was opened to a new appointment. Here again Henry showed his talents as the ultimate diplomat, statesman and politician. When I left the chancellor's post after four years, Howard Clark asked me to accept the appointment of chancellor emeritus. I must say I regarded the offer with considerable suspicion.

Lady Beaverbrook was of Greek heritage, and while I never met her, I assume she must have been a woman of substantial capacity to have snared two formidable men and two peerage titles. Wags said at the time that the English monarchy was more powerful than God: it was able to make a Lady out of her twice, while God was not able to do it once. In her later years Lady Beaverbrook was a recluse. On his visits to her estate Henry was surprised to see plaster crumbling from the ceilings, while she expressed fear of being left in want. This latter concern seems to be common among elderly people, who become obsessed, no matter how affluent they are, with not having enough to see them through.

While she attended only one convocation, Lady Beaverbrook left the university a valuable legacy: for her inaugural dinner she sent over about twenty cases of the finest wines and champagnes. And with them came the makings of an interesting confrontation. The president of the university at the time, Dr. Alex Kerr, had been a Presbyterian minister and was death on liquor, so much so that he was given to searching the men's locker rooms for it. If he uncovered a bottle that faintly smelled of alcohol, it was curtains for that student. Kerr advised Lady Beaverbrook that there must be some mistake, since no alcoholic beverages could be served at any function on campus.

"It is my dinner," replied Lady Beaverbrook, "and I wish the event to be properly celebrated."

"There will be no liquor served in this university while I am president," Kerr said.

"There will be this service while I am the chancellor," Lady Beaverbrook said.

The wines were served, and the cases that were not used were kept in storage for state occasions. In fact the remnants of that shipment were served at my installation dinner almost two decades later. On today's campus, bars exist in many locations, from the Faculty Club on down. And the confrontation between Lady Beaverbrook and Alex Kerr, as I often reminded Howard Clark, serves as the precedent that the chancellor's authority supersedes that of the president.

Dalhousie's tradition of chancellors goes back only to 1967. Two of the university's distinguished friends and alumni, Isaac Walton Killam and Sir James Dunn, both Maritimers, had died a few years earlier, leaving substantial estates from which Dalhousie had hoped to benefit. To its disappointment, neither will made any such bequest, with the government of Canada being the greatest of the beneficiaries when it garnered windfall succession duties in excess of $200 million. To its credit the government of the day did not apply these funds to general revenues, but used them to establish the Canada Council for grants to the arts.

Dalhousie, however, felt like a family heir left out of a will. It thought that a well-connected chancellor might have helped avoid this loss of charitable recognition and could now ensure that it did not happen again. C.D. Howe was the first chancellor, and a happy choice it was. The American-born Howe had taught briefly in the engineering school of Dalhousie. During the Second World War he served in the federal cabinet, and his ministry did much to convert a country with a largely agricultural and resource-based economy into a modern industrial and scientific society. The C.D. Howe Institute, whose important work has helped perpetuate his name in Canada, is but a minor recognition of the debt owed to his outstanding contribution.

As the Dalhousie chancellor, C.D. Howe did his work effectively. When Isaac Walton Killam's widow, Dorothy, died, the bulk of her estate was left to charitable institutions, with Dalhousie a prime beneficiary, participating in bequests totalling more than $30 million. The Killam money transformed the campus, and the Killam name is associated with many aspects of university culture, including lectureships, scholarships and impressive physical structures. It was the Killam money, along with Henry Hicks's years of exposure to political abandon, that spurred him to even bolder adventures in expansion, which left the university with an operating deficit of $35 million at his departure in 1980. In the long run this burden may already have proven worthwhile.

I had little idea of what I was expected to do as chancellor, and little precedent to follow in view of the void in active participation during Lady Beaverbrook's years. I did not wish to attend regular meetings of the board, although I was permitted to do so. I was also assured that I need not worry about the general operation of the university. Nor did I wish to be a purely ceremonial chancellor, which on inquiry I learned was the practice at many campuses across the country. Some universities did say they had exceptionally active chancellors, who insinuated themselves into almost every aspect of their institutions' affairs, but this was often to the discomfort of the administrators.

When I took office, I was disturbed to see the disrepair and neglect of many of the buildings since my student days a half-century earlier. Walls were scarred, paint was peeling and concrete was crumbling. President Clark assured me that the university was aware of the problems, but the deferred maintenance costs required about $3 million a year, which was not available. The thought came to me to inquire about annual alumni giving, which I was advised was not significant—about $500,000 or less. With about sixty thousand alumni, an average annual contribution of fifty dollars each would accomplish the target of $3 million a year.

We set out to establish or reactivate alumni chapters wherever in the world our alumni numbers warranted. With the president and his wife, representatives of the alumni association and other dedicated officials, we covered Canada from coast to coast and also visited several American cities, Bermuda, Hong Kong, Singapore and Malaysia. As a result, annual alumni contributions tripled to about $1.5 million, although this was still only a little more than half the $3 million I had hoped for.

In our travels on behalf of Dalhousie, I was heartened by the warm feelings that most of our alumni have for their alma mater. Those who pass through her hallowed halls and into the highways of the world seem bound to Dalhousie and to one another by ties that can never be broken—the memories of four years or more of youth, hope and ambition. And just as Dalhousie is proud to call them her own, the alumni are proud to carry Dalhousie's name wherever they are in the world. They share feelings of affection, debt and gratitude for the university's contribution to the enrichment of their lives, friendships and careers. We found the feelings were stronger the farther removed the alumni were in time and distance, particularly among the professional school graduates.

The one jarring note we encountered was the complaint by a fair number of alumni that their children had been turned down for admission to Dalhousie, only to be accepted at other universities and go on to successful careers. In a few unique cases, three generations had attended Dalhousie University and this chain was broken when the fourth generation was turned away. These links, when broken, can seldom be repaired, and this is to the detriment and loss of all involved.

Dalhousie, with its location by the sea and its distinguished tradition of scholarship, has often been referred to as the Harvard of Canada. At alumni meetings in the U.S., I twisted this around, referring to Harvard as the Dalhousie of the United States, much to the delight of our American alumni. I also told them that we would gladly exchange endowment funds with Harvard, if that could be arranged.

In Southeast Asia the reception by our alumni was exceptionally warm. The round of elaborate lunches, dinners and sightseeing tours was arranged with impeccable detail. At our dinners the traditional whole suckling pig, roasted to perfection, was generally the opening salvo, followed by numerous courses of Asian delicacies, many of which I found hard to pronounce, let alone eat. The alumni there are loyal and grateful, and most are extremely successful.

This was also my first exposure to our Canadian consuls general in the countries of the Commonwealth, and I was greatly impressed by the work they do to promote Canada's interests. My belief that these were mostly sinecure jobs, occupied with social activities, was quickly erased. In Singapore our consul general, Gavin Stewart, had a luncheon for us to which he also invited leading members of the government, one of them being our alumnus. John Bell, the consul general in Malaysia, helped us develop important links with medical colleges in Kuala Lumpur that would see thirty-five Malaysian students study at Dalhousie at full tuition rates, underwritten by the Malaysian government. At an evening meeting of our alumni, John Bell concluded his remarks with this delightful anecdote about Dalhousie:

I had the pleasure of undertaking a most exciting and adventuresome expedition to the Malaysian state of Sarawak in Borneo, the world's third-largest island. We flew to Kuching, where we arrived late that night. The next day at dawn, we boarded a Dornier plane for Bintulu, where we were whisked off by helicopter to the interior for the ground-breaking ceremony for the mammoth Bakun hydroelectrical project and the inauguration of the 110-room "resort" on what had been virgin forest only forty-five days earlier. The prime minister officiated and then most people left by the way they came—that is, by helicopter.

When we found that there were no more helicopters left, we decided to take a small boat, go downriver to the little community of Belaga and spend the night; thereafter, my colleague would continue with a nine-hour express boat trip to the mouth of the Rajang River at Sibu, and I would return to the Bakun camp and depart by helicopter.

At last, when we arrived in Belaga, the sun went down and there were no rooms to be found at all. We went into a small restaurant, had a meal of noodles, wild boar and fresh river fish, and did a bit of an appraisal of our plight. It seems that our precipitous decision to spend the night in Belaga had been poorly conceived. There we were, at what seemed like the end of the world, with no place to spend the night. There was one other person sitting in the little restaurant, over in the corner, who shouted to us, "Where are you from?" "Canada," was our reply. "Oh," he said, "I'm a Dalhousie graduate, class of '84, engineering."

Suffice to say our problems were solved and accommodations arranged. The following week I got a nice letter from the individual listing all the Dalhousie alumni in Sarawak, two of whom my colleague met the following day when he finally arrived by express boat to Sibu. I managed to get back to Bakun and flew out by helicopter.

If Lady Beaverbrook's greatest legacy as chancellor was the breaking down of the liquor barrier, mine may be the breaking of the tradition in honorary degree selection. One of my first convocation duties was the conferring of an honorary degree on Ed Broadbent, then the leader of the New Democratic party. I did not have any bias against this choice because of

Broadbent's leadership of a socialist party; after all, as I told him, my mother had belonged to a labour union. But I did question what advantage the university would get from the degree, since it was probably Broadbent's first and last visit to the campus. Many universities have a policy of recognizing people in politics only after they have left office. I also learned that most other people chosen for honorary degrees at Dalhousie were academics, usually the heads of a faculty at another university and promoted by a Dalhousie faculty counterpart.

This discovery led me to the uncharitable suspicion that academic honours could be reciprocal, with university faculty heads promoting each other. In any case, little recognition appeared to be given to benefactors or potential benefactors of the university, or to people who might otherwise have rendered distinguished service to it. Howard Clark advised me that the president, the chancellor and the board of governors had no input into the selection, which had always been in the hands of the faculty senate. Clark also intimated that leftist-leaning elements in the faculty were so powerful that trying to honour anyone with business or money connections was harder than getting the proverbial camel through the eye of a needle.

After inquiring, I learned that other Maritime universities gave their boards of governors the final authority on honorary degrees, so I asked Clark to set up a meeting for me with the Dalhousie senate to talk about changing the selection process. Clark agreed, although he felt I was wasting my time, so jealously guarded was the senate prerogative. At the appointed hour, instead of the dozen faculty people I expected to meet, more than 400 showed up, with chairs placed in the hallways for the overflow. I learned that more than 800 of the 1,700 or so faculty members were in the senate, but the turnout for me was many times the number at a normal senate meeting. Individually, academics can be delightful, but a collection of more than 400 at once can be intimidating.

After negotiating for more than an hour and a half, we came up with a compromise. An honorary degree selection committee was to be formed, consisting of the chancellor, the president, and two representatives each from the board of governors, the senate, the alumni association and the students' union. The committee would meet early each year to review the submissions, which come from all constituents in the university, and make recommendations, reserving to the senate the power of veto. This new formula has worked well, with honorary degree recipients now representing a broad range of endeavours.

In my years as chancellor I conferred about fifty honorary degrees. The academic recipients usually appeared blasé about the proceedings, but it was enlightening to see the pleasure shown by captains of industry, who are usually phlegmatic about their entrepreneurial achievements. I often wondered whether it was the recognition itself that made them enthusiastic or the expectancy of being able to attach the title of doctor to their names, with the prestige they might have felt this entailed.

An honorary degree is, in some sense, considered akin to the Order of Canada or to a knighthood or peerage in Britain. If used cautiously and sensibly and never abused, it has the potential for attracting valuable benefactors to an institution. Powerful and influential recipients can demonstrate their satisfaction in many ways to improve the welfare of a university.

In my own case, I have always refrained from using the title of *Doctor* and feel uncomfortable when I am called "Doctor" while visiting university campuses. It reminds me of Stephen Leacock's story about the time when he was still basking in the glory of his first honorary degree and he took a cruise, signing the ship's register *Dr. Leacock*. There was a pretty young woman on board who caught every male eye, including his own. One day the ship's steward came running to ask Dr. Leacock to attend to the pretty young woman, who had fallen and injured herself. Leacock ran to her cabin as fast as he could, only to find he was beaten to the punch by a doctor of divinity. An honorary doctor is not the kind that can do somebody any good, at least not in healing, but a doctor of divinity could be useful in helping to heal the soul.

Former prime ministers Joe Clark and Brian Mulroney both attended Dalhousie. Clark left after his first year, perhaps finding law not to his liking, and Mulroney left as well, reportedly after having some academic problems. This suggests you need not be a top scholar to achieve political success or political notoriety. In past years it was common to confer honorary degrees on sitting politicians, but the practice was abandoned by most universities, which found that conferring such degrees on active politicians could come back to haunt and embarrass a school. Dalhousie has not honoured Clark, Mulroney or former Nova Scotia premiers Gerry Regan and John Buchanan.

One day when I was away from Moncton, a letter containing an outrageous attack on me by the Dalhousie student executive arrived at my office. My secretary, Mrs. Jones, placed the document face down on my desk and called me on my return with a warning not to read the contents until Monday. She did not want the letter to ruin my weekend. But on Sunday of that weekend Howard Clark called me with panic in his voice to say that this correspondence, which I had not seen and of which he was sent a copy, was just the expression of a small group; it did not represent the university at large, which appreciated my contribution to its welfare. He seemed to be trying to intercept either my apoplexy or my resignation.

On Monday, I finally read the communication, the most scurrilous attack I have received in my life, and I shook with disbelief. Mrs. Jones stood by to make sure my escalating blood pressure did not bring on a stroke. And she vowed to resign if I ever set foot on the Dalhousie campus again, or if I gave it any more of the time, talent and treasure that she, more than almost anyone else, knew I had expended on its behalf.

The letter in its mildest content threatened me with prosecution for intimidation and harassment, and with a complaint to the human rights tribunal. To add to my discomfort, the student newspaper I received a few days later carried a front-page article complaining of my abhorrent behaviour and demanding the board dismiss me as chancellor. Shortly after, "Maritime Magazine," a Sunday morning CBC radio program, came on the air from Halifax with a story about harassment. A Dalhousie professor spoke in an interview of how a silly old man in a position of authority had harassed helpless students at a university convocation. The victimized students, the professor said, were virtually powerless to do anything about it. All my life I have adhered to the proverb that it is better to have your name appear in hell than in a newspaper, so I was more distressed by the newspaper story than by being called a silly old man by an eminent member of the Dalhousie faculty.

I tried for weeks to track down the basis for the vicious condemnation, but finally Clark was able to give me a handle on it. At convocation ceremonies I always tried to introduce a bit of levity into what can otherwise be dreary proceedings. I stopped to chat with the students I knew, whether in person or by family background, and I lingered with students who had exceptional results or other special accomplishments at the university. Where appropriate, I tried to introduce comic relief; there hadn't been much of that since Henry Hicks paraded onto the platform wearing his flowing gown and open sandals over his heavy white woollen socks. I felt it was important to give time to the students at convocation; after their hard work, it did not seem fair on this great day in their lives to herd them quickly through like sheep. Many people told me in person or by letter that they appreciated my efforts in this regard.

Before the convocation in question, I was called by an old friend who had been the chief financial officer of a company with which I had been associated for about fifteen years. His daughter, whom I had known since she was a child, was graduating in dentistry, and my friend asked if I would linger with her at the presentation long enough for him to get a picture or two. I said I would go one better and give her a peck on the cheek for daddy. He was delighted, and I was pleased to accommodate him.

After the presentation the next candidate was a young man, and I said to him, in what I thought was humour, "I'm not going to kiss you." That was my crime. It was offensive to students of a certain sexual persuasion, and I was therefore branded as homophobic.

This episode, which eventually blew over, diminished my enthusiasm for the office, but it in no way lessened my loyalty and dedication to the university. At the next convocation I sat silently and glumly in my chair and let the president and vice-chancellor confer the degrees. But the passage of another six months and the healing of wounds helped restore my confidence, and I returned to the official convocation duties.

The new religion that has taken over our campuses is characterized by the buzzwords of zero tolerance and political correctness. As chancellor I encountered it at my first law school convocation, when I commented on how pleased I was to see that "girls" made up more than half the graduates and how different it was from my days fifty years before. This statement was greeted with howls and hisses from the women, and I should have learned my lesson there. Shortly thereafter I sought counsel from a contemporary young lady as to what were the proper words to use. *Ladies*, she informed me, was too cavalier. *Females* was taboo since its prefix "fe" did not remove the stigma of its derivation from "male." The proper and safe term to use, she advised, was *You guys*. That, she assured me, would never get me into trouble.

I only hope the new parameters of politically proper communication and behaviour do not materially restrict the very basic concepts upon which universities were founded and for which they have existed for centuries. The very word *university* derives from the same Latin root of *universe*, which

Webster defines as "the whole body of things observed or postulated." Universities have long been the bulwarks for the free exchange of opinions and ideas, for debate and discussion. Any concepts that could conceivably threaten these freedoms, in even the least degree, should be scrupulously monitored and closely examined.

It has been said that university campuses should be immune to the introduction of blindfolds, earmuffs and muzzles, or, as one commentator has warned, to the danger of becoming "islands of oppression in the midst of a sea of freedom." The thing that bothers me the most in this new era is the danger that we as a nation may be losing one of our most valuable assets: our sense of humour.

After presiding over five spring convocations and four in the fall, I came to the end of my term as chancellor in 1994. I was glad to be relieved of the physical demands but have fond recollections of the 10,000 or more young graduates whose hands I shook and whose heads I capped.

Howard Clark left the presidency soon after my own departure, and the affairs of the university are now in younger and quite capable hands. In the back of my mind, however, is the suspicion that, had my personal financial affairs not deteriorated, I might have been pressured to stay on, much like Lady Beaverbrook, who was endured for a seventeen-year absence for fear of affecting her largesse. This is possibly an unkind thought on my part, but in any case, I would not have continued.

The financial constraints imposed on universities by cuts in government funding are of great concern to me, especially in Nova Scotia, which has more universities per capita than any other part of Canada. These universities grew up as a result of many historical factors, and each has contributed to the fame and well being of the province, leaving an important imprint on its social, cultural and economic fabric. Universities do not drain the public purse but add considerable economic value to the body politic. It would be tragic to see them reduced or diminished further by the financial exigencies of government studies that are superficial, ill-conceived and poorly researched.

CHAPTER 14

Maritime Moguls

K.C. Irving, despite his popular image as a hard, tough business tycoon, struck me as the essence of a gentleman. When, as a young lawyer, I first met him on a matter concerning a client, he treated me with the utmost courtesy, helping me off with my coat when I arrived and listening attentively to my proposals. Afterwards he showed me how the equipment in his office could pinpoint where in the world his ships were at any given time. When I got up to leave, he again helped me with my coat and escorted me to the elevator. This was a great lesson to me—K.C. Irving treating a young punk lawyer, still wet behind the ears, with attention and courtesy—and it was an example I sought to emulate throughout my career. I don't think Irving ever lost his small-town interest in people and events.

The level of charitable giving by the Irvings and other people of means in the Maritimes has always intrigued me. The Irvings, one of the wealthiest families in the world, were for a long time notorious for a lack of leadership in giving. Although the patriarch could be accessible and cooperative, depending on the approach and the person making it, his three sons, possibly because they felt they had to prove they were as capable as the father, initially assumed a tough veneer.

During a $35-million capital campaign for Dalhousie University in the Eighties, the campaign strategists felt that Robert Stanfield would make a powerful canvasser to approach the Irvings. He came away empty-handed. Bill Hopper was the national chairman of an Acadia University campaign around the same time. Although he was chairman of Petro-Canada and a fellow member in the oil industry with the Irvings, Hopper too was turned down by K.C.'s sons—J.K., Arthur and Jack—all of whom had attended Acadia, as had their father before them.

Rev. Gregory MacKinnon, the president of St. Francis Xavier University in Antigonish, Nova Scotia, had a similar experience. He once called me, nearly in tears, en route from Saint John and asked if he could see me on his way home. When he arrived, he gave me the sad account of his reception by the Irvings, who had told him their task in life was to accumulate capital, not to dissipate it. I told Father MacKinnon that he should not be too disappointed, since the sons had not given even to the university where they had been students. To boost Father MacKinnon's spirits, I wrote him my cheque for $25,000 and sent him on his way in better humour.

After the death of Harriet Irving, K.C.'s first wife, the University of New Brunswick named its new library in her memory, hoping the family might contribute to the cost of the building. Lady Violet Aitken, the daughter-in-law of Lord Beaverbrook, was chancellor at the UNB for a decade, succeeding her late husband, Sir Max Aitken, who had followed Beaverbrook himself. She once told me that she became incensed every time she visited the campus and saw the Irving name still on the library, with no financial acknowledgement from the family. She asked the university's board on many occasions to have the name removed, but the governors did not dare to offend the Irvings and were still hoping that their patience would bear fruit.

The only institution that seems to have achieved success with the Irvings during this arid period was the Université de Moncton. I once asked its development officer how the university was able to succeed where most others had failed. "It was simple," he said. "All we did was threaten to put our oil contract out to tender, and that automatically brought in the money."

In the years since K.C.'s death, the Irving attitude towards giving has undergone a complete metamorphosis. Some attribute the change to the influence of a softer third generation of Irvings, who have nothing to prove to the patriarch. Not only have they taken the lead in actual giving, but they have also provided important leadership in many fund-raising endeavours. Several millions have recently gone to UNB, thus rewarding the perspicacious patience of the board of governors. Important medical projects and other substantial community works proudly bear the Irving name as well. Arthur Irving now serves as chancellor at Acadia, and Irving leadership bodes well for the province in many areas, if not for the Maritime region and the country as a whole.

The McCains are the only other family in New Brunswick with the financial resources to be recognized in national stature. Until the Irvings' recent change of heart, the McCains' record in giving stood in marked contrast to that of K.C.'s dynasty. The McCains have been in the forefront of charitable work at all levels, not just in money but also in leadership.

As young men, brothers Harrison and Wallace McCain both worked in the Irving empire, where it is said they obtained a good deal of their initial business training. Later, a business rivalry grew up between the Irving and McCain families, particularly in the limited areas such as trucking where they at first competed. The competition was aggravated when the Irvings stepped into the frozen-food industry in a big way. What excitement might be generated if this rivalry could now be extended into vying for challenges in community service.

Harrison used to call me occasionally for advice about some charitable matter for which he had been asked for help. Once, it was after he was approached by Galen Weston to contribute to a scholarship fund at the Pearson College of the Pacific on Vancouver Island. Harrison flew Galen Weston and me into the Stellarton area of Nova Scotia, where the three of us met with Donald and David Sobey.

The Sobeys provided an excellent lobster lunch at their late father's residence, which has since been turned into an art museum. Knowing of the bitterly competitive battle between the Sobeys and the Atlantic Super Stores for the food-dollar market, the public might have found it incongruous that Weston and the two Sobeys enjoyed a pleasant lunch together, with not a word about business. The good offshoot of it all was the agreement by the Maritimers to fund an annual scholarship for a Maritime student at Pearson College.

On another occasion Harrison called me to say he had been asked to help raise more than $2 million to fund a Pearson chair in international affairs at Oxford. Since the chair was to have the name of one of our former prime ministers, the Oxford people felt the money could be more readily raised in Canada than in England. Harrison said he didn't feel completely comfortable asking people in Canada to contribute to an English university, especially when our own universities faced massive curtailments of government funding. But I remembered that Dalhousie had once tried for similar funding for a lecture that would bear the Pearson name. The Dalhousie president, Howard Clark, confirmed that about $500,000 had been raised, but further planning for the chair had been discontinued because of other financial constraints. I asked if it might be feasible to have our Dalhousie funds contribute to the Oxford program, and to have Oxford and Dalhousie share the lecturers. Clark got in touch with Oxford and a satisfactory arrangement was consummated.

The inauguration dinner for the lectures was held a couple of years ago at the Royal York Hotel in Toronto. More than six hundred guests attended, including the vice-chancellor of Oxford, Prime Minister Jean Chrétien and members of the old Pearson cabinets who were still mobile. I was pleased to see the Dalhousie president and chancellor recognized at the head table. Conrad Black was also at the head table, and although I sat at an adjoining table less than thirty feet away, there was not a flicker of recognition from him.

One of the latest McCain contributions was the building of a new wing for the Beaverbrook Art Gallery in Fredericton, reputed to have cost in the range of $1.5 million and named in memory of Harrison's late wife, Billie. I am envious of few things in other people's lives and successes, but I regret exceedingly that my change in financial circumstances prevented me from carrying out similar endeavours to memorialize my wife's name, especially in areas where I knew she had enduring interests and concerns. This pain shall never leave me.

The recent McCain family feud over succession caused me some consternation, since I have considerable respect for both Harrison and Wallace. While many theories exist as to the cause of this conflict, I have my own opinion about its roots. Harrison's wife, Billie, was from a distinguished family. Her father, John B. McNair, was premier of New Brunswick and also its chief justice and lieutenant-governor. I doubt that the occupying of all three of these eminent posts by one person has ever been duplicated in another provincial jurisdiction. Billie, a quiet and dignified woman, was content to live in the background of her ebullient and iron-willed husband.

Wallace's wife, Margaret, is in many respects the opposite. Her mother, Margaret Norrie, was a senator and possibly the parent from whom Margaret inherited much of her drive and ambition. In addition to being very bright and personable, Margaret is also an accomplished public speaker and a most dedicated and effective chancellor ever to hold that post at Mount Allison, her alma mater. It is rumoured that she and her husband left no stone unturned in seeking her appointment as lieutenant-governor of

New Brunswick, but she brought to the office a grace, dignity and competence that had lately eluded it.

In some circles Harrison, with his dominating personality, was perceived as overshadowing Wallace both on the business stage and in the public eye. When Harrison became desperately ill a few years ago and lay close to death in a Boston hospital, the occasion was used to have Wallace appoint one of his sons to a position of prominence in the company. This could have helped to ensure the son's succession to the top spot, but Harrison countermanded the appointment when he returned to health. I suspect that Margaret's determination was in the background of Wallace's actions; in the next generation her side would not have to live in anyone else's reflected glory. In many family enterprises down through the years, dislocation has often occurred because of the jealousies of wives, rather than in the breakdown of relationships among the principals in the family business, whether brothers or other near relatives.

In his recent book *Family Ties: The Real Story of the McCain Feud*, journalist Michael Woloschuk toys only briefly with this theory as the cause of the rupture, assigning most of the blame to Harrison's imperial ego. It is my opinion that the book is biased in its portrayal of Harrison as the villain responsible for the family breakup and in its portrayal of Wallace and his side as the hapless victims. Although I have spent much more time with Harrison than with Wallace over the years, I always felt that a strong fraternal bond existed between them and that mutual concern and affection was evident and endures even to this day. Had each been left to his own bailiwicks in the business—a combination that successfully built the global food empire—and without the intrusion of other pressures and influences, the family business relationship would probably not have been shattered.

Woloschuk's book contains a paragraph I find offensive:

Sometimes Harrison would turn his imperiousness on his family. He would even berate Billie in public. "He would say things to her in front of people and embarrass her," said a former employee and friend of Harrison's. "She was isolated from the community because she never knew when he would show up and tell her to go fuck herself. I've been at a few dinner parties where things weren't going well, or something wasn't served properly, and Christ he'd take it out on her. He'd give her shit in front of maybe half a dozen people."

My wife and I were entertained on many occasions by Harrison and Billie McCain, and never did he show any disrespect towards Billie. When he lay ill in Boston, I phoned Billie, or she me, almost every evening, and no wife could have shown more care and concern. When Harrison called to tell me of Billie's tragic illness, I could sense the complete devastation in his voice.

When I asked Harrison recently if he was upset about Woloschuk's portrayal, he replied that he didn't give a damn what was written about him. What did cause him hurt and anguish were the suggestions that he was demeaning to his wife. "I loved my wife," he said, "and I love her still." This was two years after Billie's death. Recently, when passing through Florenceville, I visited the country cemetery where Billie is buried. Her grave is marked by a double tombstone with the name Harrison McCain, C.C., engraved in large letters across the top, with one side carrying the details of Billie's birth and death and the other side blank. There is little doubt as to where and with whom Harrison plans to lie for eternity.

My feeling that Margaret McCain was bitter about her husband having to live in the reflected glory of his older brother seems to be borne out by her statements in a book entitled *Women Who Gave Away Millions* by Iris Nowell, published in 1996, where she is quoted as follows:

> Behaviour that is cause for dismissal in the typical workplace is commonplace with Harrison McCain. Margaret says, "He calls every executive wife 'baby,' and at company functions he presses himself against these women and says things like, 'When is your husband going to be away?'" With incredulity widening her eyes, Margaret states, "He has tried that with me!" The executive wives are "helpless because their husbands' jobs are at risk if they do something." Margaret, however, did something.

Going to such lengths illustrates that the family rift is too far gone to be healed in this generation. It is a happy circumstance that Wallace's move into Maple Leaf Foods necessitated the family's living in Toronto and Margaret's resigning as lieutenant-governor of New Brunswick. It would have been pretty uncomfortable for the two brothers to have continued living side by side in their baronial homes in the little village of Florenceville.

Harrison and I lost our wives to the same disease, ovarian cancer, some five years apart. When Harrison called me with the news of Billie's illness, I asked for the prognosis. Two years was his reply, but Billie lived for about half that time. I was given a three-year expectation, and three years it was, almost to the day.

I attended Billie's funeral, which was held in the little Anglican church in Florenceville. The church could accommodate only a small fraction of the people, and the service was piped into adjoining premises to handle the overflow. A minute or two before the service began, Wallace and Margaret slipped quietly into the two seats that were reserved for them at the back of the church. A few moments after the service, they slipped away just as quietly. All the out-of-town people were invited to Harrison's home afterwards, with a reception the following day for local people. Wallace and Margaret did not show. It was sad to witness a business feud overtaking family solidarity, solace and comfort in a time of grief.

The McCains may be among the few people in Canada who have a private runway that can accommodate jet planes. They can fly in from any place in the world, get off their jets and walk into their homes. The McCain jets themselves are among the few corporate aircraft that carry the company name and logo proudly on the tails. Most corporate officers today try to downplay the use of company aircraft, which is considered a management extravagance, but the McCains, as a private company, have no such concerns. The plane used by Jim Pattison was parked on the runway the day of the funeral, as was the Bank of Nova Scotia plane, which brought the bank's chairman, Ced Ritchie.

One recent summer afternoon I was walking along St. Clair Avenue in Toronto and noticed a sign for Maple Leaf Foods on the front of an office building. It was after five, but I took a chance that Wallace was in his office and might be free to see me. The gamble paid off, and I was most warmly ushered into his rather spartan office. Wallace appeared lonely, and genuinely happy to see a face from down home. We talked until well after six, mostly about his plans for the new business and the composition of his new board. He avoided any reference to the family feud.

We saw each other again at a Junior Achievement award dinner held at the Toronto Metro Convention Centre, when Jim Pattison was inducted into the Canadian Business Hall of Fame. The 1,200 in attendance must have been keenly aware that Wallace and Harrison McCain, both former recipients of the award, had been carefully seated at opposite ends of the head table. After the dinner I talked in the lobby with one brother and, noticing the other going by, drew him into the conversation. The three of us chatted for a few minutes until the camera crews broke it up.

Later, on a Canada Day weekend, Harrison called to invite me to spend the holiday weekend with him at his home in St. Andrews, New Brunswick. I told him that this would be difficult because I no longer drove a car and all the people who might drive me had already made plans. But Harrison persisted and I agreed, taking what I believe was my first bus trip.

Harrison and I walked around the town, commiserated for hours, visited tourist sites and enjoyed a relaxing few days in each other's company. One night we had dinner at a restaurant with Rowlie Frazee, the former chairman of the Royal Bank, and his wife Marie, who now live permanently in St. Andrews. Rowlie told us about his first meeting with Marie's parents, who were strict Baptists.

"And what is your religion, young man?" Marie's mother had asked him.

"Anglican, ma'am," Rowlie replied.

"Hmph," snorted the mother. "That's an easy religion."

When Rowlie came on the scene, Marie had another boyfriend, a rugged fellow with a physique more strapping than Rowlie's. The former boyfriend had also gone into the Royal Bank and spent his lifetime there, retiring as an obscure manager of some small-town branch. Rowlie, meanwhile, rose to the top rung of the ladder. During spousal arguments some wives have a habit of throwing up the name of a former suitor, but during one such argument between the Frazees, in which the passions were flowing more freely than usual, Rowlie bellowed to Marie, "And where would you have been had you married your precious boyfriend, Mr. X, instead of marrying me?" Her reply: "I would have been the wife of the chairman of the Royal Bank, but where would you have been?" This is one of the greatest retorts I have ever heard and should be a delight to the ears of all wives.

CHAPTER 15

This and That, Then and Now, and Tomorrow

My experience with the bus trip to St. Andrews led me to experiment with a train trip, something I had not done since my university days. I have recently travelled to Halifax twice by train and it cost forty dollars round-trip, plus GST. A return ticket on the airline is about four hundred dollars, but with the airport twenty-five miles out of town, it costs another forty dollars by taxi, coming and going. This short-run flight costs as much as a trip overseas.

Occasionally a small independent airline has started up, offering rates at least 50 percent less than the regular airlines, with the latter quickly dropping their fares to meet the competition. When the upstart is forced out of business, the big airline immediately raises its rates again. I have often felt that the competition tribunal should prohibit the established airlines from dropping rates to ensure the death of new competition; otherwise, a new entrant trying to give the consumer a break will never stand a chance of survival.

During both trips with Via Rail the waiters in the dining car have commented on my Order of Canada pin, which I try to remember to put on when I travel. In all my years of flying on commercial airlines, no flight attendant on Air Canada or any other employee of the airline has done the same. On my last trip by train, the waiter tore up the chit for my meal. In bewilderment, I asked what that was all about. "I am so honoured to serve a member of the Order of Canada that it is my pleasure to have you as my guest," he replied. I was so flattered I left a tip that I am sure was more than ample consideration for the price of the meal. This is the only event in my life that could refute the adage that there is no such thing as a free lunch.

Through inquiries I learned that this particular waiter came from Arichat, which is on the French shore of Nova Scotia, and he has been working on the dining cars for more than thirty years.

When Brian Mulroney was prime minister, he held a luncheon in Ottawa for Mikhail Gorbachev, then the political leader of the Russian government. As an alumnus of St. Francis Xavier University, Mulroney invited Rev. Greg MacKinnon, the president of the university, to the luncheon, and he brought me. It was one of the more memorable days I have spent with Father MacKinnon.

As we went through the receiving line, we found Gorbachev standing expressionless, shaking hands mechanically without saying a word, although his interpreter stood immediately behind him. We had just passed through the line when Gorbachev was told by Mulroney that Father MacKinnon was the president of his alma mater. With that, Gorbachev asked that MacKinnon return to shake hands again. This time it was with interest and feeling, and Gorbachev even spoke several sentences in Russian, which the interpreter relayed in English as a message of congratulations. Standing alongside Father MacKinnon, I came in for a second handshake as well, although my gratuitous presence was not explained.

I have always felt an affinity with, and perhaps a fascination for, the Catholic clergy, Father MacKinnon, Rev. Clément Cormier and Father Hespergh being among the many people who have enriched my life.

Father Angus MacDonald, the longtime priest at one of the largest Catholic churches in Moncton, shared with me many of the personal emotional struggles he had faced as a priest, in the area of celibacy and in the parish. He probably felt more comfortable confiding in me than in someone of his own faith. It was after a day with Father Angus in Montreal that I returned home to the shock of my wife's diagnosis with cancer.

In my relationships with the Catholic clergy I have found them sincere, caring and dedicated in every way to the principles of their faith and to the flocks they served. It saddens me that scandals in recent years have tarnished the clergy's image through the sordid tales of what must be a very minor fraction of an otherwise committed fraternity.

I have been ecumenical in my relationships with clergy, sharing many a pleasant dialogue with Protestant ministers as well. Rev. Frank Archibald, a United Church pastor, was the dean of the Protestant clergy in our town and, after his active service in his church, moved just three houses away from us. When his wife was away, he often knocked on our door at supper time and delightfully invited himself in to share our repast, all the time insisting that my wife not go to any trouble but just let him partake of whatever fare was on the table. We came to look forward to these intermittent visits.

Many mornings Frank and I walked downtown together, I to my office, he to buy a copy of the Halifax paper, which kept him in touch with his Nova Scotia roots. One morning our discussion centred on the doubts that arose as a person progressed along the road to learning and truth. Frank did not think anyone who had not walked down that road had a right to be a minister. These doubts seem to have troubled and tormented men of the cloth from the earliest of times. Even in the twelfth century, the monk Peter Abelard wrote about the challenge: "By doubting, we come to question, and by questioning we can perceive the truth."

Frank Archibald said that we look for truth along such paths as science, mathematics and logic, and when we don't find it there, we are disillusioned. He quoted Pascal: "The heart has reasons that the mind knows not of." Such reasons, Frank said, are as much to be trusted as the conclusions of a clever argument, and moments of truth may have little to do with logic. Principles of faith need not equate to historical reality.

Mark Parent, a young Baptist minister, is one of the brightest and most intellectually acute young men that I have observed in some time. He was at a senior Baptist church in Moncton for a few years before moving to a church in the Annapolis Valley of Nova Scotia. I am particularly impressed by his knowledge of Hebrew texts, not limited to the Old Testament but extending to the deeper readings, including the Talmud, which Mark often weaves into his weekly sermons. When he left for the Valley, I asked him to mail me copies of his sermons, which he has done, and some have been impressive enough that I shared them with friends.

Not long ago I wrote Mark to say that I thought some of his sermons were at times too intellectual and above the heads of a rural congregation. A few weeks later I received a copy of a sermon in which he said that he had received a letter from "an elderly Jewish gentleman" he knew in Moncton, who suggested that his sermons might be too intellectual to be fully appreciated by rural parishioners. Mark incorporated this theme into a delightful sermon, and I complimented him on it. At the same time I said I was a bit upset to be characterized as an "elderly Jewish gentleman." To this Mark replied that he could have referred to me as an *alter kaker* (Yiddish for "old shit"), but he was sure his congregants would not have understood, and "old shit" somehow did not seem the proper term for a Baptist preacher to use in a Sunday sermon. Now that is what I call a really contemporary Baptist preacher.

My first exposure to a Baptist congregation was in 1938, when the local Highfield Baptist Church advertised an evening prayer meeting with a converted rabbi as the star attraction. Our rabbi at the time, Harry Bronstein, was a brash young man of European background but with a good command of English and lots of drive. He decided to attend the meeting and persuaded me to go along. When the converted "rabbi" finished his inspiring spiel on how he came to see the light and of the great joy this had brought him, Bronstein stood and asked him a few simple questions in Hebrew. Flustered and bewildered, the speaker had not a clue what was asked. Bronstein advised the congregation that the man was an impostor, who was taking advantage of their hospitality and generosity. Bronstein's action took a lot of courage in our small community, a courage that continued in later years when, working out of New York, he was imprisoned by the Soviet authorities for religious activities in aid of Russian Jews.

In those earlier decades it was a fairly regular occurrence for some Baptist churches to proselytize with a parade of converted Jews, but it has been a long time since I have seen the faintest trace of this practice. Indeed, during a recent Passover, Mark Parent's church was used for a seder for the few Jewish families scattered throughout the Annapolis Valley. We've come a long way.

Another luncheon I attended during the Mulroney years was one in Quebec City, at which U.S. President Ronald Reagan was the guest speaker. Much was made of Reagan's age when he was in office, one sentiment being that a man well into his seventies would not have the physical or mental resources to cope with the rigours of presidential office. In his opening remarks Reagan delivered what I consider a classic story. He said he regretted not being able to address the audience in French in the capital city of French Canada, but an old friend had once told him that he need not necessarily have command of the French language to appreciate French culture. For this extremely valuable advice, Reagan said, he would be forever grateful and indebted to his old friend Jacques Cartier. There certainly were no cobwebs on Ronald Reagan's brain that day.

At the luncheon, Jean-Paul Lemieux, one of Canada's most distinguished artists, was seated on one side of me, and I was excited at the prospect of engaging him in interesting conversation. But he was less fortunate than Reagan. Time seemed to have taken its toll on Lemieux, and my attempts at communication brought only a cursory response. Michel Cogger, who later achieved prominence in Stevie Cameron's exposé of the Mulroney years, was seated on the other side, and it was over lunch that I first learned of Cogger's close association with Mulroney during their university days.

The invitation list to the Reagan luncheon included many CEOs from across Canada, and it took hours of traffic-controller attention to clear the departures of all the corporate jets lined up at the Quebec City airport, especially when, much to the CEOs' impatience, many were delayed to clear the way for the presidential takeoff.

As a lawyer who spent several decades in the corporate world, I look on certain trends of the Nineties in business and the professions with some alarm, beginning with the rage for downsizing and restructuring.

In the race to promote the bottom line and so-called "shareholder value," each corporation has tried to outdo its competitors. In the process, hundreds of thousands of jobs have been eliminated, with an impact on the economy that has yet to be fully assessed. I can understand this bloodletting in governments, where bureaucracy has long been a bloated behemoth, a creation brought about by the very nature of government. But it is hard to believe that corporations were so badly managed in the past that they had to fall victim to this government contagion.

In the frantic drive for shareholder enhancement and the means taken to achieve it, many companies may have sacrificed their most important asset, the corporate soul. This has sabotaged the economy generally, and probably the offending corporations in the long run. It is ironic that this process has been accompanied by an escalation in management remuneration, often reaching scandalous proportions, while salaries for the lower ranks who survive decimation remain virtually stagnant. This phenomenon is abetted by the advice of outside consultants, usually arms of large accounting firms, who annually present to corporate compensation committees statistical comparisons with companies of a similar size or industry. The process feeds on itself, and will result in a continuing increment in executive earnings if some sanity is not brought to bear.

The fallout of restructuring, coming so soon after the damages inflicted by free trade, cannot help but hurt further the economic prospects for the country, already battered by the legacy of debt left by preceding governments of all stripes in the last twenty-five years or more. I was not an advocate of free trade when it was proposed, and the subsequent history has confirmed some of my grave concerns. I felt that the industrial heart of Ontario would be put at serious risk, particularly in the area of U.S. branch plants whose *raison d'être* would be eliminated with the removal of tariff barriers. These fears were supported by my exposure to Inter-City Products, on whose board I sat at the time. The company manufactured air-conditioning equipment at a long-established and highly regarded plant in Brantford, operating under the Keeprite name. It also had acquired a much larger, similar operation in Tennessee. The U.S. plant was located in the heart of the American air-conditioning market, which, because of climatic conditions, was many times the size of its Canadian counterpart, even on a per capita basis. Further, the production capacity of the American plant was such that it could probably turn out in a few weeks of operation the entire demand of the total Canadian market, not just Keeprite's. Added to this was the wage structure in Tennessee, which was much lower than the Keeprite scale and further increased the productivity spread.

As the import tariffs were reduced and finally eliminated, the fine old Keeprite plant in Brantford, in business for decades, had to close, with the loss of more than five hundred well-paid jobs. If this is the case with a Canadian-owned and -operated company, what hope is there for a subsidiary plant located in Canada by an American owner? The pain and havoc created by free trade for the industrial economy of Ontario and to a lesser extent Quebec will take years of economic restructuring to heal and correct. It can never again be the old comfortable story for Canadian industry as in the protected tariff days.

The proliferation of MBAs, and their impact on the business world, is another of my concerns. Their learning may be great in theory, but it is often of little use in the business trenches, especially in small business. I am reminded of a successful business in our area, which the founding father, a hard-working entrepreneur of ethnic background and limited education, had built into a sizable and extremely profitable enterprise. His son was an honours MBA graduate, to whom the father proudly turned over the business. Not content with the status quo, the son immediately initiated changes to conform with the theoretical modern business practices of his textbook learning. Within five years, the thriving business was no more.

Unfortunately, many such tales can be recounted across the country, raising the eternal question of whether entrepreneurial talent can really be acquired by theoretical teaching. I like to recall the story of Charles W. Eliot, the famous president of Harvard in the late nineteenth and early twentieth centuries, who was being honoured one night by a group of educators.

"Permit me to congratulate you on the miracles you have performed at the university," one of them remarked. "Since you became president, Harvard has become a virtual reservoir of knowledge."

"That is true, but I scarcely deserve the credit for that," Eliot replied. "It is simply that the freshmen bring so much knowledge in when they come, and the seniors, when they go, take so little out."

I have even less enthusiasm for the legal fraternity. The ridiculous numbers of lawyers being turned out by our overly prolific and too numerous law schools are creating irreparable damage to the profession, which even in its better days was seldom bathed in public esteem. My association with lawyers over the decades has led me to wonder why so few have the legal minds needed to properly assess and deal with the problems confronting them. A good part of a competent legal practitioner's time may now be spent trying to repair the damage caused by another lawyer's neglect, incompetence or outright stupidity.

In addition, the downturn in the economy—aggravated by the cascading proliferation of entries into the profession, with the attendant difficulty of achieving anything near an often inflated expectation of livelihood—puts the consuming public at even further risk, many times more costly than incompetence or neglect. This also tends to lead to a significant increase in frivolous actions, which further clutter up the courts and slow down the legal process.

It is no accident that the premiums for insurance covering legal errors and omissions have skyrocketed at the same time that the funds set up by bar societies to compensate clients for the acts of delinquent or dishonest lawyers have been depleted. That governments will provide funds for new law school buildings while at the same time cutting back, sometimes ruthlessly, on important social benefits is beyond comprehension.

There is another breed of lawyers, the nitpickers, who, in an earlier and less politically correct era, were sometimes referred to as "technical testicles." They drive to distraction the practical lawyers trying to get things done competently in the least time and at the least cost. To be fair, many of these technical lawyers are not motivated by greed or an attempt to pad their bills with prolonged hours, but rather by a desire to impress their client with how meticulously they are protecting the client's interests.

Then there are the litigation practitioners who feel they must ride roughshod in cross-examinations to prove to their clients that they are getting good value for their money. One of these lawyers once told me that he felt he was paid to be nasty. Ego seems to be another trademark of the profession, with many a prima donna inclined to put on a show for image and self-enhancement, even when it has no relevance to solving the problem at hand.

The biggest change in the profession is the new religion of billable hours, brought on initially by the escalating cost of office overhead and salaries, and exacerbated by downturns in the economy. The hero in a law office today is not the one who can turn out the most scholarly brief, but the lawyer who has achieved the most billable hours. Much has been lost, and many old practitioners, who have dedicated most of their careers to study, research and the pursuit of legal excellence, must be quite distressed by this present-day concept in legal practice.

If I were involved in active practice, I would be loath to have a career ruled by the demands of billable hours. "You can't make any money by settling," said one fairly seasoned lawyer with an active litigation practice. On the other hand, one of the most prominent and respectable lawyers, a senior partner in one of the largest national law firms, once told me that he prided himself on being able to keep his clients out of the courts and on settling the most important and litigious matters, which otherwise could have occupied him for years and exhausted his clients' treasuries. The recent advent of arbitration procedures should help to relieve court pressures and costs, as well as the time expended in the resolution of disputes.

Also irritating are the exorbitant fees charged by lawyers in the larger offices in the larger cities for work that could be done just as competently by small-town practitioners at a fraction of the price. When I once discussed this with a Toronto lawyer, he said that clients can only get the quality of service they pay for. At this, I asked whether a client should be obliged to pay for the extravagant art galleries that many a large city legal office has become. We should be grateful, however, that Canada has been largely immune to the outrageous jury awards that plague the American legal scene, and that we have not yet been badly affected by the U.S. contagion of class actions.

Lest I be considered too harsh in describing the warts on the legal system, I will add that the profession, in its loftiest ideals through the ages, has displayed many characteristics that have placed it in the forefront of the protection of individual rights and freedoms. It has justly earned its designation as the senior profession.

In my addresses to graduating law classes, I tried to inspire the graduates by telling them they were entering a noble profession. And I left them with a principle to govern their professional lives: "Excellence prospers; mediocrity perishes." I have respect for a first-class mechanic or garbage collector who does his work to perfection. I have little respect for a second-class professional who demeans his vocation and harms a client in the process.

I am also too old, cranky and impatient to accept with good grace some of the gadgets of modern communication. The hellish invention of voice mail, which comes with large law firms, requires many frustrating minutes spent listening to recordings and punching numbers before a live person is reached who can provide help—if you're lucky. When I have to make such calls, I steel myself for the ordeal I am sure to encounter. I prefer dealing with a human.

The computer culture, another concern, has been a boon to the accumulation, storing and dissemination of endless amounts of information, a great deal of it useless, but I fear it may rob young people of their capacity to think, analyse and create. Fax machines, too, while a modern blessing, can also be a curse. In the old days, a letter received could be contemplated for a day or two, which allowed time for a considered reply. Today, the fax sender usually requires an immediate response.

During my years in practice I came into contact with numerous real estate agents, and here again my impressions are not overly complimentary. In their zeal to garner their all-important and often extravagant commissions, they seem to have little difficulty in being indifferent to the truth.

Reporters are another group whose prolific numbers I find offensive, particularly when I see them thrusting microphones in the face of some politician or celebrity, as if it could ever be possible to record something of consequence in such circumstances. It's a waste of manpower that could be much more usefully employed.

If I have left the medical profession intact, it is not because it is unblemished, although many dedicated doctors earn every cent they are paid. The medicare system in Canada may be criticized, but it is still a jewel compared with conditions in the United States, where unbridled commercialism and greed and a jungle of disorganized and unharmonized medical plans have brought the medical system almost to a collapse.

An elderly couple I know were on a vacation in the Orlando area of Florida when the woman's legs swelled up and she was barely able to walk. Her husband took her to the local hospital, where she was diagnosed as having heart failure that required immediate bypass surgery if she was to survive. This, of course, was after an inquiry ascertained that the woman carried Blue Cross medical coverage for out-of-country stays. The surgeon advised that the procedure would cost U.S.$120,000, which had to be paid up front. The distraught husband was prepared to mortgage everything, including his soul. But a call home to Blue Cross brought the suggestion that his wife be flown back to Canada in a medically equipped plane.

The Florida surgeon said the patient could not survive the trip, and if she did, she would be subjected to medical expertise in Canada that was inferior to that in the U.S. Refusing to be frightened or intimidated, the couple accepted the Blue Cross offer and were home in about three hours. And in the woman's hometown hospital, after the usual tests, no problems were found with her heart. She was given diuretic pills, which reduced the swelling in her legs in a couple of days, and she walked out as hale and hearty as ever. The bill for the two or three days in the Florida hospital came to more than U.S.$10,000. The moral of the story is never to get sick in the United States, where the damage to your bank account can only be exceeded, at times, by the damage to your health.

This chaos in the present-day American medical structure is different from my own experience long ago. In 1939 my mother had a growth on her throat, which was diagnosed locally as malignant. Our local medical expertise then was primitive, and the prognosis suggested my mother get her affairs in order as quickly as possible. Her sisters in Philadelphia insisted that she go there for an operation, and in May of that year I accompanied her to that city by train. We visited a general practitioner, who called the office of a surgeon, Dr. I.S. Ravdin, to arrange for the consultation and operation. I was present when the general practitioner made the call and overheard him refer to "limited finances."

Ravdin was the chief of surgery at the hospital of the University of Pennsylvania and one of the most eminent surgeons in the country. The surgery was successful, and to our great relief the tumour was diagnosed as tubercular and not malignant. The bill was two hundred dollars, although I suspect most of the surgery was done by Ravdin's assistant, Dr. Jonathan Rhodes, who himself went on to achieve prominence in medicine. Years later I was pleased to read that when Dwight Eisenhower, as president of the United States, required cardiac surgery, Dr. Ravdin was chosen to perform the operation.

That trip was my first out of Canada. After my mother's successful discharge, we celebrated by going to the 1939 World's Fair in New York. Billy Rose's aquacade with Esther Williams left quite an impression, but more interesting to me was a huge poster of a train engine that appeared to be heading straight for us viewers, with bold lettering boasting *Canadian Pacific—The Greatest Transportation System in the World*. That boast has long dissipated.

Cars have never been one of my weaknesses, and I have never been seduced into seeing them as a status symbol. The old cars of the Twenties and Thirties had much more character and individuality than the modern versions, which adhere to more or less standard patterns. My father owned a Hudson in the Twenties, and Hudson models were also favoured by the rumrunners during Prohibition. While I rarely drive today, I still maintain an old Chrysler Imperial and Cadillac Seville, both from the Seventies.

I have had more than a cursory interest in aircraft, and although I never aspired to piloting, I have enjoyed the convenience of five or six private aircraft, from prop jobs to turbo props and jets. Today, I seldom find the need to fly.

Reflections

I was in an airport terminal when I overheard a conversation in which one woman said to another, "There is poor Mr. Cohen, who lost both his wife and his business at the same time."

I appreciated the stab of human feeling and understanding in that comment. Many people have expressed sympathy to me in recent years over my great loss, but invariably they are referring to my financial dislocation, this perhaps reflecting the vulgarity of today's values. They don't understand that the business loss was a minor tragedy compared with the loss of my wife.

It has been said that while human history has been obsessed by success, it is equally fascinated by tales of failure, although not just any failure. To be more than a footnote, failure must be on a mega-scale: the Reichmanns in commerce, the Edsel in industry, the Conservative party in politics after Brian Mulroney. These failures will probably endure in our annals for some time.

It has also been said that defeat breeds disdain, and an absolutely crushing, humiliating defeat breeds scorn. I pray that my own fall from corporate grace will never be considered of such epochal proportions, but it has completely altered my declining years from the course I had planned. And it has left me with deep wounds of concern and embarrassment that will never heal.

The fallout from the business debacle quickly manifested itself in other aspects of my life, apart from the extreme discomfort of no longer being able to take a leading part in charitable endeavours, of having to say no for the first time to the innumerable causes I had always proudly supported. It is not easy to learn to say no late in life.

For years, my counsel was actively sought from many quarters. I was often flattered to have other lawyers ask for my advice, not only on legal problems but also on personal, financial and estate matters. Even more gratifying was hearing from members of the judiciary about investment or estate matters and, on the odd occasion, about a legal judgment. In my glory days I dealt with twenty or thirty people a day in business or legal consultations. An equal number of people called me, and I never left my office until all the phone calls were answered. This was often at the expense of my wife and family, and in retrospect it was an unfair choice of priorities. My daily business mail was also voluminous, arriving stacked up and requiring more than an hour each day for opening, sorting and cursory perusal, with additional time for responses.

When the corporate collapse became known, it was as if a Churchillian "iron curtain" descended on my life almost overnight. Days, sometimes weeks, may go by now without a phone call or a visit in person, and the meagre mail that arrives intermittently includes little more than a bill or a request for a donation. It is almost as if I had died and gone to my reward.

Where my polite suggestions to a client or a friend on business matters were once treated almost as gospel, today even the communications that I initiate, rare but earnest, many times go unheeded. I often feel that my business reversals might make my advice more pertinent in some respects, particularly in the context of the old investment axiom that extols the virtues of diversification and emphasizes the dangers and pitfalls of putting all your eggs in one basket. As Bernard Baruch said in his autobiography, "I have told of my failings and mistakes, if only because I have found that failure is a far better teacher than success."

In contemporary culture, respect, prestige, power and influence are closely allied to financial resources, and the depreciation of the latter quickly diminishes or eliminates the former. Before the fall, charitable organizations often approached me to be the honoured guest at high-priced fund-raising dinners that would recognize me as a "national treasure," with tributes from leaders in the political, commercial and cultural life of the country. I always scrupulously avoided such tribute dinners, but today any hint of such approaches has evaporated anyway, leaving me to feel less like a national treasure than a national disaster—or, as it is sometimes put in the world of sports, as if I had gone from "hero to zero" overnight.

The vicissitudes of ignoble fortune, the lack of demand for what time and talents I have left to me, and the disabilities that naturally come with age have led to a style of living that now almost resents any intrusion. And it opens the mind to contemplation of the philosophy and meaning of life. Here again, I have read and reread the words of George Wilson, my old professor at Dalhousie University. In his last writings, he explained why his choice for a life of scholarship was history.

> If there is any meaning and purpose in human existence, it must be revealed to him who studies the long record of man's journey through the ages. Many men, in many ages had sought a meaning in the human story. To them, I turned [to see] if they could show me a path through the wilderness. They had striking things to say and threw light in many a dark place, but none gave a satisfactory answer.
>
> The greater our knowledge, the more profound our ignorance. In a very real sense we know nothing. Our wisest answers are but questions still.

The final page of Professor Wilson's last work is especially poignant.

> What a man does in life is of little importance; what a man achieves in life is of little importance; what is important is what he has become as he travelled from the cradle to the grave. Was the centre of his existence always within himself, seeking power or wealth or pleasure, believing that success was measured by the judgment of the world? Or did he realize his own insignificance, how worthless were the prizes that the world had to offer . . . And that it was only as he forgot himself, as he lost himself in the worship of knowledge, of truth and of beauty, as he felt the sadness of the world and was filled with sympathy for all those that suffer, that he found himself and entered the kingdom of the wise . . . To me there can be no other salvation . . .
>
> Wisdom is the ultimate goal. The wise man is a saint who has added wisdom to his saintliness. Reward was not his motive. He is as he is because he cannot be otherwise. From the slime he has mounted far. If God exists, with God he dwells. Here is his home.

I get much inspiration and even comfort from these words written by Professor Wilson when his death was imminent. At the same time I have rejected out of hand his sad conclusion, expressed in the title, that life is *All for Nothing.* I have rejected, as well, the pessimistic conclusions of other great minds and thinkers, such as Thomas Hobbes, who wrote in *The Leviathan* that the "life of man [is] solitary, poor, nasty, brutish and short." If life is all as he paints it, then we should welcome the fact it is short. On the other hand, I have often felt that there could be merit in Aldous Huxley's conjecture that our Earth could well be the hell of another world.

In all of this I have gone back to my early love of Latin and to the *Aeneid*. Virgil, in his powerful prose, writes of the many misfortunes suffered by Aeneas in the struggle to found the city from which eventually sprang the Latin fathers and the walls of glorious Rome. In contemplating all of these hardships, he draws comfort from the words *"Haec olim meminisse iuvabit"*—"all this, too, it will one day please you to remember."

Regrettably, there are too few days left for me to draw such sustenance. But, like many other older people, I do try to obtain solace and comfort from memories.

But when I close my eyes and get lost in reverie, I can still conjure up visions of my old town, when the blacksmith shops kept their hearths blazing, and grimy smithies pounded on the hot iron shoes, with sparks flying. I can still remember the days when traffic stopped for a funeral cortege and men doffed their hats and stood respectfully at attention until the procession went by, usually not even knowing the person for whom the bell tolled. It was a quieter, more relaxed and less hurried time, with a dignity and civility that I miss today.

In these moments of reflection, I recall some of the verses of Alfred Lord Tennyson's vision of nature's evening. When I first read these words in my youth, they did not have too great an impact on me, but now as I approach four score years, they have special significance:

Old age hath yet his honour and his toil;
Death closes all: but something ere the end,
Some work of noble note, may yet be done,
Not unbecoming men that strove with Gods.

And then again:-

We are not now that strength which in old days
Moved earth and heaven; that which we are, we are;
One equal temper of heroic hearts,
Made weak by time and fate, but strong in will
To strive, to seek, to find, and not to yield.

Index